Port of New York

ALBERT P. RYDER

VAN WYCK BROOKS

CARL SANDBURG

MARSDEN HARTLEY

WILLIAM CARLOS WILLIAMS

MARGARET NAUMBURG

KENNETH HAYES MILLER

Essays on Fourteen American Moderns

ROGER H. SESSIONS

JOHN MARIN

ARTHUR G. DOVE

SHERWOOD ANDERSON

GEORGIA O'KEEFFE

RANDOLPH BOURNE

ALFRED STIEGLITZ

Port of New York

by Paul Rosenfeld

With an Introductory Essay by Sherman Paul

UNIVERSITY OF ILLINOIS PRESS, URBANA, 1961

Contents

Paul Rosenfeld

by Sherman Paul

The Class of 1912 at Yale wasn't unusual. Of its 298 graduating members, 57 expected to go into law, 54 into business, 20 into medicine, 10 into banking and brokerage. There was a conquering confidence: "Symington will enter Wall Street." According to a poll, the most valuable courses had been "Social Conditions" and "Elementary Economics," with "Tennyson and Browning" not far behind. Kipling was the favorite prose writer, Tennyson the favorite poet, and "Crossing the Bar" the favorite poem; *Ivanhoe* was the favorite novel. A majority of the class favored William H. Taft as the presidential candidate in the coming election.

One of its members who was still undecided about his vocation and whose tastes, one suspects, were not entirely represented by the class polls was Paul Leopold Rosenfeld. He does not appear in the lists of "most to be admired," "best athlete," "best natured," "most brilliant," "most original," "most optimistic" — not even "best dressed," for Yale had succeeded in getting others into Brooks Brothers suits. At the bottom of the list of "most scholarly," his name appears, his scholarly bent having been recognized by seven of his classmates if not by those who award Phi Beta Kappa honors. The face in the photograph in the *History of the Class of 1912* is a bit Prussianly severe; perhaps the moustache and high collar account for it. But there is no familiar nickname in the personal history printed beneath; and we learn that

Port of New York

he had always roomed alone and that he had been an editor
of "The Lit.," the least popular college publication according
to the polls, its six votes undoubtedly cast by the six members
of its board.

Military school had prepared him for Yale, but it had not
prepared him to be a conqueror in what he later called —
taking the phrase from Henry Adams — a "coal-power civilization." His father, Julius Rosenfeld, had been a small manu-
facturer; his mother, Sara Liebmann (Clara in the class
history), was an accomplished pianist. Until her death in
1900, when Paul was ten, the family lived the well-to-do
brownstone existence of upper West Side Manhattan that also
characterized the cultivated middle class German-Jewish
families that produced Alfred Stieglitz and Waldo Frank.
The father had literary, the mother musical taste; and the
manner of their life, to judge from Rosenfeld's story, "The
Dark Brown Room," and his novel, *The Boy in the Sun,*
would have put him at ease in the drawing rooms of bourgeois
Vienna or Berlin. They summered on the New Jersey coast,
typical of those families that later disturbed Henry James
and that led John Jay Chapman to cry out: "Judea —
Israel — the Lost Tribes — lost no more! found — very much
found, increased — multiplied — as the sands of the sea —
upon the sands of the sea — in the city of the sea — Atlantic
City. . . ." The mother's death destroyed the family. The
children were cared for by their maternal grandmother. The
father, whom the son spoke of in the class history as "retired"
but who died before Paul entered Yale (according to his
friend Jerome Mellquist), disintegrated under his sorrow.

Paul Rosenfeld

Riverview Military Academy at Poughkeepsie, where Rosenfeld was sent in 1903 presumably to improve his posture but actually because "choicer institutions," as he admitted, would not accept him, did not make a soldier of him. His memories of the place are empty of military occasions. "On its parade-ground," he relates, "I discovered the advantage of piano lessons. Correctly to execute the maneuvers when the command was 'Squads right!' or 'Squads left!' I found I had merely to imagine myself at the keyboard. Promptly I knew which of my hands was left, which right. It made me a trifle slow, but never fatally so. Finally I attained a sergeant's rank." He always remembered the low highlands and the Hudson, for he later took Sunday excursions there; and he remembered a Mr. Charles H. Hickok who ran a music store and who, pretty much at his own expense as it turned out, twice brought the Boston Symphony Orchestra to Poughkeepsie. At the Academy he took piano lessons, first from a "lady teaching by the noiseless method," the "pathetic, bosomy" Miss Virginia Gorse who began the first lesson with, "I'm glad to see you have rounded finger-nails. People with flat finger-nails, you know, are always deceitful"; later from a pale young man named Arthur Moore Williamson. If Mr. Hickok remained in his memory as an exemplar of the selfless devotion that makes culture possible, Arthur Williamson figured there as an exemplar of the talent that cultural wastes like Poughkeepsie (all the world's Poughkeepsie, he said) failed to nourish. No humor is intended when Rosenfeld describes this spectacled, infinitely sensitive, suffering young music master, who at five was rapturous over

Port of New York

a Mason and Hamlin piano, who developed heart disease at
fifteen and suffered from gastric disturbances, and who
fainted when calling on a young lady to whom he intended to
propose. For in his unpretentious way, Williamson opened
the door to the world of music which by 1920 Rosenfeld had
made his own. Cadets may contrive strategems in order to go
home, but certainly not, as Rosenfeld did, to escape to New
York for a concert. His debt to Williamson is recorded in
the dedication of his first book, *Musical Portraits* (1920).

Rosenfeld left few recollections, musical or otherwise, of
his years at Yale. In his sophomore year he read George
Moore and Arthur Symons, and Moore, he later acknowledged, influenced his feeling (already partially developed by
his reading in George Meredith, Morris, Pater, and the early
Yeats) for a "high," sensuous style. He heard Horatio Parker,
professor of music, play the organ in Woolsey Hall, but
Parker's *Mona*, an opera which Rosenfeld heard in 1912 and
ever afterward defended as the best American opera, was
never associated with his college years. He has nothing to say
about his work on "The Lit." or about his initiation into
journalism on a New Haven newspaper. Journalism, however, seems to have been the career he had in mind, for he
entered the Columbia University School of Journalism in the
fall of 1912, and following his graduation in 1913 began to
report for the New York newspapers. Six months of journalism were apparently enough and probably brought about the
"revelation" we are told occurred on 42nd Street, where
Rosenfeld decided that, having a private income of five thou-

Paul Rosenfeld

sand dollars a year,[1] he could follow his own calling. The calling was still uncertain, but it led immediately to Europe; and there, in London, in May 1914, he discovered in Bechstein Hall what Randolph Bourne was also discovering in Europe — his own generation and its "modern desire" to reach beyond the material to more spiritual satisfactions.

The experience of music was Rosenfeld's passport to this new world. He heard his way into things, and music undoubtedly kept his sensibility fluid and responsive. Such courses as "Social Conditions" and "Elementary Economics" did not enable him to see the social manifestations that Bourne saw so well and reported so carefully. Concert halls filled his horizon, not the rallies of socialists and suffragettes, the lecture rooms of Oxford and the Sorbonne, or the new architecture and planned communities to be seen on the Continent. He would grow in social awareness, but this awareness always sprang from his knowledge of the travail of artists whose heroic mission, he believed, was to explore and to shape contemporary experience. The signposts of his awareness of the experience of his generation are the concerts he heard; the Armory Show of 1913 did not jolt his eye in the way that the music of Stravinsky and Schönberg (which he later described in cubist terms) jolted his ear. He came to painting and literature by way of music, and his account of his own discovery of modernism in "Grand Transformation Scene — 1907-1915" is a story of concerts.

---

[1] Lewis Mumford believes his annual income was nearer ten thousand dollars.

Port of New York

The first concert goes back to the Riverview days when he
had slipped away to New York and had heard the *Pathétique*
symphony. As in most everything he wrote, such backward
steps prepare for the leap into modernism; it dates an epoch,
and Rosenfeld's truthfulness about his response, that "awareness passed into ecstasy," dates a sensibility that would learn
increasingly to pass from ecstasy into awareness. The second
concert in London shocked the young listener because, although he had already left Tschaikowsky behind, he still felt
that music with the power to exalt and satisfy had ended with
César Franck and that recitals of new music promised him
nothing. Perhaps his account of his tastes benefited in the
retelling by his mature criticism, for he had already worn out
his enthusiasms for Wagner, Debussy, Mahler, and Loeffler.
As for American music, it was idealistic, a "pale wash," represented by the "gentlemen of Boston," the Chadwicks and
Converses. What one got in the concert hall was "Victor
Herbert emerging from the wings with an invisible shillalah
to conduct his Rhapsody of favorite Irish airs." Such music
left him among the "flat buildings on upper Broadway" with
their electric signs and automobile displays feeling that he was
in a world "without bloom, without mystery; dusty, smart
and empty." Even the music of the Europeans, of Strauss,
Reger, and Mahler, disclosed "the banality of a world post-
humous to the wet, singing one"; and until that night in
Bechstein Hall, with the cheap seats crowded with intent
young people ("it was my generation — and alert, and out in
life as gardens were"), with Scriabin, hitherto unknown to
Rosenfeld, at the piano, there had been no one to tell him

Paul Rosenfeld

that "not lyric impulse but the rhetoric of romanticism, the passion for passions — and New York, were dead."

The nineteen-year-old boy in the black velvet jacket and slippers who played his "atonal ectoplasmic compositions" one winter afternoon in 1915 in the playhouse on 57th Street completed the transformation. After this concert by Leo Ornstein ("It was all new, this music. . . ."), there was for Rosenfeld a "singular bloom on 57th St. . . . So strong, so promissory, New York had never lain." This music registered what Rosenfeld had believed to be lost: "The direct sounds of souls in contact with present existence: infinitely delicate and serious representations of the complex and nervous patterns of experience rising out of the relationship between the organism and the modern environment; encouragements to the accurate expression of every living sensation, perception, emotion." One imagines Stieglitz's photograph of the single slender tree rising from the wet city pavement when Rosenfeld expresses his sudden sense of "the perennial fecundity and youthfulness of life" and his realization that the new world he had discovered in this music would be "less dream-laden, more realistic with material than the romantic had been" and more "democratically affirmative of the natural variety of attitudes and impulses."

The years from 1914 to 1916 when the new music seemed to Rosenfeld to be saying, "YOUR TURN, AMERICA!" were devoted to literary apprenticeship. He worked at a novel, and though he never succeeded as a novelist, he remained a *writer* who approached critical writing, as few have done, as

Port of New York

a creative art.[2] In retrospect and in the dedication of *Port of New York* he gave the credit for his awakening to Leo Ornstein, but his critical work and the program it served must be credited to the mediation of the ebullient Waldo Frank. Frank had been sent to Yale rather than to Heidelberg because his father wanted him to be an "American"; he had taken his degree, even an M.A., had gone into journalism and shortly afterward had packed his bag for Paris. There he found that he was not "needed"; he returned home where he "belonged," led an itinerant existence in what he later called "the American jungle," and began his career as novelist and critic, fully aware that in matters of expression "the present generation of Americans [were] more profoundly pioneers . . . more original adventurers than Columbus." Rosenfeld probably met Frank at one of Claire Raphael's musical evenings when Frank played the cello in an amateur trio; and it was through Frank that he came to know Alfred Stieglitz, Van Wyck Brooks, and Randolph Bourne, each in his way a center of artistic or creative enterprise, and all devoted to the cultural possibilities of American life.

Frank was one of the initiators of *The Seven Arts,* a short-lived but seminal little magazine which rallied the adherents of contemporary art with its declaration of policy, "AN EXPRESSION OF ARTISTS FOR THE COMMUNITY." Its editorial proclamation expressed the common faith of a group of critics

---

[2] It is characteristic of his generation of men of letters that his style more often than his judgments was criticized. Criticism was a personal art, and though Rosenfeld valued impersonality he never relinquished the testimony of his personal contact with the object.

Paul Rosenfeld

who, unlike the lost generation that shared the '20's with them, never quite forsook the generous hopes for America that had stirred them in their youth. "It is our faith . . . that we are living in the first days of a renascent period," the proclamation began, "a time which means for America the coming of that national self-consciousness which is the beginning of greatness. In all such epochs the arts cease to be private matters; they become not only the expression of the national life but a means to its enhancement." *The Seven Arts* was to be the channel for the flow of these new tendencies, especially of the conviction that the aesthetic is inextricably a part of the social; and the very existence of the magazine was to create a community of artists — a school such as Henry Adams wished to found. Even though it died within a year, the spirit that animated it and the artists it had united found outlet in mazagines like *The Dial, The Freeman,* and *The New Republic;* in *The American Caravan,* an annual volume of new writing; and in *Twice A Year,* a book-length magazine devoted to the arts and to civil liberties which began in 1938 and offered a place to those still living and memorials to those, like Bourne, Stieglitz, and Rosenfeld, who had died.

Rosenfeld began to write on music and literature for *The New Republic* in 1916, but it was Frank, the associate editor of *The Seven Arts,* who brought him into the community of artists whom Rosenfeld was soon to champion. He made it possible for Rosenfeld to appear in the first number, that of November, 1916, with articles on the American composer and on "291." "291 Fifth Avenue" was the first gallery and workroom of Alfred Stieglitz, who might fairly be said to have provided the example and tended the soil from which such literary ventures as *The Seven Arts* grew. For years he had singlehandedly fought for both European and American modern art. In 1903 he had founded *Camera Work,* a sumptuous quarterly, indeed a folio-sized gallery, in which he presented the history of photographic art, the work of contemporary photographers such as Paul Strand and Edward Steichen, and reproductions of the drawings, paintings, and sculpture of Rodin, Cézanne, Picasso, Picabia, Matisse, Brancusi, Marin — artists whom he had already exhibited for the first time in America at "291." Patron, teacher, crusader, Stieglitz sponsored Alfred Maurer, John Marin, and Marsden Hartley in 1909, Arthur Dove in 1910, and Georgia O'Keeffe in 1916; later on when he opened The Intimate Gallery in 1925, he added Charles Demuth to the group of painters for whom he had established the gallery; and annually, first in The Intimate Gallery, then in An American Place, he showed their work.

As an art critic Rosenfeld was almost exclusively the interpreter of the painters in Stieglitz's group. He was fiercely loyal to Stieglitz, filially bound to him. He emulated him by becoming a discoverer, patron, and receptive critic of new talents; and the courage and faith with which he espoused the cause of art were comparable to Stieglitz's, drawn from the belief in the value of art that both profoundly shared: "the bridge to consciousness of self, to life, and through that, to new life and creation again." He took his aesthetics from Stieglitz, the work of Brooks, Frank, and especially Bourne,

Paul Rosenfeld

providing the cultural framework for the findings of his sensibility. More than anyone else, he was the liaison between *The Seven Arts* and "291."

The war broke the momentum of the movement. Indirectly it led to the closing of "291," and it closed out *The Seven Arts* when its backer and some of its editors could not agree with Bourne that the intellectual must choose between "the war — or American promise." It took Rosenfeld to Camp Humphreys, Virginia, and it hastened the death of Bourne, who died in Rosenfeld's apartment in 1918. It chastened many a democratic faith; it brought in its wake those illiberal, reactionary undercurrents that Bourne had fought and that made a mockery of normalcy. For some, like Rosenfeld who remained loyal to Bourne's vision of America, it toughened the faith by revealing the strength of the opposition. If it seemed to be free and hospitable, the age of normalcy was nevertheless a cold war within America for those intellectuals who had taken to heart the lesson of Bourne's death. Critics thought of "Daisy," but did not marry her; and even the "Daisy" Edmund Wilson temporarily possessed was a *jeune fille* of his own sentimental boyhood.

Bourne, Brooks, and Frank were more influential in the early years of the movement than was Rosenfeld. Or perhaps one should say that they had a public stature that the self-effacing Rosenfeld never acquired. They were primarily culture-critics; he was a literary, art, and above all, music critic interested in culture. They did not know or master the arts as he did or leave behind so large and solid a body of criticism. Brooks was the acknowledged leader, having clarified the cultural scene in *America's Coming-of-Age* (1915) and in *Letters and Leadership* (1918). Bourne, as Rosenfeld said, was "the great bearer of moral authority while America was at war," a more political, forward-looking, and resolute "bannerman of values" than Brooks; had he lived, Bourne probably would have been the sovereign intellectual spokesman of his generation and Brooks and Frank would not have fought, as they did, a subtle battle for leadership. Not only was Frank recognized as a significant experimental novelist; *Our America,* a study of American culture compounded of Brooks' leading ideas and his own mysticism, was acclaimed in 1919, and his collected critical essays, *Salvos* (1924), and his *New Yorker* portraits of famous contemporaries gathered together in *Time-Exposures* (1926) made him a prominent critical figure in the '20's. His militancy and the avant-garde nature of his fiction were probably more acceptable to the younger writers (an issue of *S4N* and a book were devoted to him) than Brooks' querulousness and indifference to contemporary art. Bourne had been doubtful of the way in which Brooks intended to treat Twain, and none of Brooks' friends, having deferred judgment during his years on *The Freeman,* felt that he had redeemed himself with *The Pilgrimage of Henry James* (1925). That book, as Brooks himself admitted, broke his career and his mental health.

The '20's brought Rosenfeld forward. In that decade he published a novel and seven volumes of criticism. *Musical Portraits, Musical Chronicle, Modern Tendencies in Music,* and *An Hour With American Music* were concerned entirely with music; *Men Seen* treated modern European and Ameri-

Paul Rosenfeld

can literature, *By Way of Art* the arts at large, and *Port of New York* those Americans who in spirit or in fact were related to "291" or *The Seven Arts* and whose work dispelled the Brooksian gloom about creative America. These books, his private solicitude for innumerable artists, and the editorial labor of gathering and publishing the work of new writers in *The American Caravan* (which he began with Lewis Mumford and Alfred Kreymborg in 1927), represent the largest single effort on behalf of contemporary art of any American critic. Edmund Wilson, always a shrewd observer of his colleagues in criticism, recalls that Rosenfeld "at that time enjoyed a prestige of the same kind as Mencken's and Brooks', though it was not so widely felt as the former's." Not so widely felt, but deeply felt: if *Paul Rosenfeld: Voyager in the Arts,* the testimonial volume which followed his death, is any indication, then, with the possible exception of Stieglitz, Rosenfeld was the most warmly regarded critic of his generation.

Not only his work but his personality, with which the work is so alive, explains this gratitude. Gentleness perhaps describes his total quality, a genial (in the Emersonian sense) responsiveness which permitted him, without grasping, to reach out to people in the same large way that he reached out to art-objects and to the environment. Lewis Mumford speaks of his "lyrical wisdom," that profound wisdom of experience emotionally mastered. This wisdom took him to the creative springs of art and taught him that "good equals the communication of life" and that "the personality with a living object [never] goes into itself." Sin, he believed, was the withholding of love; the most intense emotion was tenderness.

By temperament Rosenfeld was a romantic. His values, however, must be placed between the evils of romantic yearning for the past and Flaubert's horror at man's everlasting filth and ferocity. He is a romantic in his belief in the primacy of the heart; for, though he is classic in his desire to see the external world clearly, he knew that the intellect could not fully capture the rhythms of life. Neither a transcendentalist nor a naturalist, he was the kind of humanist who takes life for his scripture. In his own experience he had had the doubt of all things earthly and the intuitions of some things heavenly of which Melville had spoken, and from his own suffering and awareness of the reality of death he had won a tragic sense of life and liberated his joy in living.[3] "To live," he said, "is to touch others with the antithesis at the heart of the world, with sorrow as well as joy."

His response to art and life was therefore something more than aesthetic. He judged both art and life by the possibility of "life completely used, exercised to the fulness of its capacity for tragedy and for delight, and deprived by death of nothing of worth." Though he appreciated the pioneer aesthetic achievements of Joyce and Eliot, he rejected the "comédie intellectuelle" of the one and the "fantasy of The Waste Land" of the other; and it was not that he overlooked the actual waste lands, but rather that he believed them to be relative conditions. Even now — he found in the case of D. H. Lawrence — "someone is always finding his age pro-

---

[3] See "The Hospital," *Men Seen.*

Paul Rosenfeld

pitious to his form of artistry [,] the world and someone's idea
are always managing to harmonize." To Lawrence, Rosenfeld accorded the highest praise. For Lawrence had not suc-
cumbed to the "parasite" of mind; he had had "new,
increased and more complex capacities for feeling," and had
therefore beaten out the rhythm of his age and helped men
live more truly. Rosenfeld's measure of art was individual
and social health: "We cannot be sincere and not crave
fullest living."

Such attitudes were not prescriptive, yet had a seriousness
that artists at least responded to. They were embodied in his
person and exuberantly expressed in his own rich art of living.
What he wrote in admiration of Guillaume Apollinaire applied to him: "Possessed of a voracious appetite for many
kinds of experience, a swift sensibility and an inextinguishable
intellectual curiosity, he communicated his joys and games
and sensations not less through the forms of ordinary existence
than those of literature." The Apollinaire of "metro'd electric
Paris" was everything that the cosmopolitan and cultivated
Rosenfeld wished to be in New York — a "vivid and distinguished person," a "cavalier of life." No auto-intoxicated
D'Annunzio searching for some grandiose situation, posture,
or movement to fill his emotional emptiness or using art to
compensate for "inward incapacity," Apollinaire "had the
gift of procuring for himself aristocratic pleasures among the
ordinary house-walls and in the ordinary paths of urban
life."[4] He was one of those people, as Henry James might

---

[4] Edmund Wilson noted Rosenfeld's "capacity for presenting even
the most abortive incidents in the life of human intelligence as events
in a significant, exciting and highly picturesque adventure."

have said, on whom nothing is lost. He nourished his art with every motion of the boulevards, with convivial talk, and with the pleasures of good food which he often prepared himself — as did Rosenfeld. And beneath his bonhomie was a strongly developed communal feeling and a combativeness in behalf of ideas that made him the champion of the cubists much in the same way that similar traits made Rosenfeld the champion of the artists of his time. The portrait that Rosenfeld drew can stand for his own, for its surest lines are those that delineate his "sensuous alertness," that show his awareness of the fact that he was "deliberately used by those interested in the advancement of their own affairs," and that his willingness to serve the general cause had cost him his own complete self-expression.

Everyone acknowledged Rosenfeld's cultivation, and no one more than Sherwood Anderson. Anderson, whom *The Seven Arts* and *The Dial* had lifted to fame, had come to believe, as he said in a letter, that he was the product of the "same thing Brooks talks so much about in his *Mark Twain*." Having been raised in a "different atmosphere than most of your fellows," he felt that he never really deserved the praise of a "truly fine aristocrat" like Rosenfeld who had done him the honor of leading him through Europe. Alyse Gregory, managing editor of *The Dial,* noted Rosenfeld's fine manners and remarked that he "followed the Latin rather than the Anglo-Saxon tradition and made of human intercourse an art." And Edmund Wilson, perhaps with a tinge of envy, said that more than any other American writer Rosenfeld had "the real freedom of the Continent," the gift of living

Paul Rosenfeld

"in touch with the great artistic life of the world." In the curious way in which his father's generation had marked the Jew (Justice Holmes, for example, called Harold Laski "the Jew"), Wilson attributed Rosenfeld's gift to the concurrence within him of American, European, and Jewish backgrounds. But whatever the reasons, and Wilson's have their share of truth, Rosenfeld did absorb European culture in an unself-conscious way and more wholly than did early apostles of culture like Lowell and Norton and later apostles like Eliot and Pound. This may account in part for the fact that he did not feel the need to adopt in criticism the magisterial tone. It accounts, certainly, for the reverence with which Wilson treated Rosenfeld in his brilliant imaginary dialogue between the older critic, who represented the living and human values of tradition, and Matthew Josephson, expatriate editor of *Secession,* who represented the explosive cultural nihilism of the younger generation.

Looking back in the '40's over his career, Rosenfeld observed that the present state of culture in America at best "possesses a memory with a span of possibly ten years." It is a telling observation about the large work and small expectation of the intellectual in our society — a society still Jeffersonian in its belief in the sovereignty of the present generation — and it was true enough in Rosenfeld's case. Rosenfeld lost his place, but not as Edmund Wilson wanted to believe as early as 1925 when, perhaps with the possibilities of his own *Axel's Castle* in view, he wrote that Rosenfeld had broken down our provincial prejudices and inhibitions against

Port of New York

artistic expression and had permanently bridged the gulf between Europe and America, and that therefore the need for
his services was over. Rather, he lost his place, as Wilson
recognized when Rosenfeld was dead and possibly from his
own later experience, because the climate of each succeeding
decade was different. Rosenfeld knew that it was "an era of
sudden developments"; generations were "littered every four
or five years. . . ." And therefore Rosenfeld knew that work
such as his was never done. Goethe expressed his acceptance
of the thankless and unremitting job of criticism: "We acquire little thanks from people when we try to elevate their
inner necessities, to give them a great conception of themselves, to bring to consciousness in them the magnificence of
a true, gracious way of being. I say this not to humiliate my
friends. I merely say that thus they are, and that we ought
not to be astonished that everything remains as it does."

Many things but mainly the discontinuity of the cultural
conditions of the '30's and '40's brought about Rosenfeld's
decline. The public indifference and the burning-out — so
Wilson generalized on the depressing story of the American
intellectual — seemed to go together, and many of Rosenfeld's friends noted his loss of confidence. But the only book
he published after the '20's, *Discoveries of a Music Critic*,
was his ripest work. It should have made clear to those who
had doubted (was the dedication to Wilson ironic?) the
depth of his awareness of social, historical, and intellectual
forces and his skill in relating them to art. He had already
rejected, in the case of D'Annunzio, an art subservient to
preconceptions and political formulas, and once more took

Paul Rosenfeld

his stand in "The Authors and Politics." He had no mercy for the exhorter in art, not even for a friend like James Oppenheim, poet and editor of *The Seven Arts;* and where the artist was an "advertiser" like Gershwin or a propagandist like Shostakovich, he had abdicated for Rosenfeld the essential individual integrity of aesthetic vision. In an essay on "The Nazis and *Die Meistersinger,*" he defined the uses and abuses of nationalistic art and reaffirmed his belief that "art is one of the great potential agents among a democratic people." But these views did not endear him to the majority of artists and editors who in the '30's had moved politically to either the left or the right and had accepted the security of doctrine.

Other changes, such as T. S. Eliot's ascendancy in elite critical circles and the commercialization of what had been an independent press, reduced the outlets for his highly personal, emotionally evocative prose. Even *The New Yorker* refused to print the articles it had asked him to write and Knopf turned down his proposed book on *The Seven Arts* group. And these rejections were doubly severe because the crash of '29 had destroyed his financial security and forced him to play the game of supply and demand for which he was not equipped.

Personal difficulties — the crucial years after forty which he said were "devilish" — compounded the difficulties of survival. Fully aware that irresolution gets down to the "nucleus of sex," he tried unsuccessfully to resolve in an autobiographical novel, *Concert in Rome,* what he could not resolve in life. But this failure was not due, as some suspected because of his political stand, to his unwillingness to forsake bourgeois comforts, though it may have been due to his unwillingness, in reduced circumstances, to ask another to forsake them. He refused not so much to embrace life as to offer his life without all of its former resources. Diabetes, the war, the book on literary genres that he began after rigorously re-educating himself — all these things taxed the limited strength with which he maintained his quiet cheerfulness and dignity. Judged, however, by his desire to live boldly and dangerously "in the fashion of the artist" and by the critical necessity of remaining at the "battle-line," he was not the kind of failure he believed Brooks to be. Often lowered to menial and per-functory reviewing, he was still able to speak out for the courageous publishing of *New Directions* and for new talents like Henry Miller.

The photograph of Rosenfeld taken in these years by Stieg-litz catches the limpid sorrowful eyes and the full heavy in-clined head; the severity, if ever it were that, of the college photograph is gone. No conqueror of an age, only its sensitive recorder whose "activity of spirit [was] an infallible sign of health," Rosenfeld died in circumstances of "indecent un-ceremoniousness" (a phrase from *Port of New York,* written two decades before) that only make more ghastly the terrible anonymity of American life. Stieglitz died on July 13, 1946; eight days later, having already sent a memorial article on his beloved mentor to *The Commonweal,* Rosenfeld had a fatal heart attack while attending the neighborhood Loew's Sheridan motion picture theatre at Seventh Avenue and Twelfth Street. The cold and careless obituary in the New

Paul Rosenfeld

York *Herald Tribune* reported that the movies were *The Green Years* and *Night Editor*. Toward the end, it mentioned that Edmund Wilson had said of Rosenfeld that "he gave himself away to the artists of his period." Essentially that was just what Rosenfeld had written of the lonely Stieglitz.

II

Appreciative, aesthetic, impressionistic, romantic — these are some of the terms that have been used to define the criticism of Paul Rosenfeld. From the standpoint of current critical "authority" they are all invidious terms. We establish our own rigor by means of them and with them we cauterize portions of our sensibility and exclude values we do not wish to accommodate. Our criticism is but another mirror of our response to life: intellectual, discriminating, precise, it is curiously impersonal, dry, beggarly. Turning in on itself, it manifests the dehumanization of the other arts. Although it is concerned with defending the ways in which art uniquely realizes the fulness and complexity of experience, in practice it anatomizes the work and only infrequently summons a personal sense of those values it cherishes most. Criticism has become a discipline and, like the discipline of science, its individual practice (or art) has been constrained by the common program it serves. For at least three decades we have been afraid to show our passion in criticism or to push on to the moral of our aesthetic experience. For many in our time it is perhaps enough that art is thus made safe and the values it enshrines secure. We have come closer to Dr. Johnson's desire for a criticism with the certainty and stability of science; we have quoted but neither fully understood nor practised what Henry James said of criticism, that "to criticize is to appreciate, to appropriate, to take intellectual possession, to establish in fine a relation with the thing criticized and make it one's own."

Rosenfeld used criticism in the large Jamesian way. James judged both critic and novelist by the same standard; for criticism, he said, "springs from the liveliest experience" and offers an opportunity, like fiction, for the active mind and the free play of intelligence. Everywhere in James the bedrock is sensibility — vital intelligence. The critic therefore is judged by his "indefatigible suppleness," by his capacity to remain open to impressions, by the quality of his feeling for life. He is "to lend himself, to project himself and steep himself, to feel and feel till he understands, and to understand so well that he can say. . . ." Where the novelist gives us the "sense of life," the critic gives us the "sense of art." But if, as in Rosenfeld's case, the critic is a novelist (with Jamesian proclivity), then perhaps his criticism gives in a less realized form than that of fiction a sense of life as well. For the impulse of all his writing, Rosenfeld wrote, was in response to "the latency pressing, directly upon me and my time."

This is not to say that Rosenfeld is the paragon of critics, but only that such qualities as he brought to criticism give his work a permanent value. To place him, as many still do, with James Gibbons Huneker helps to distinguish his virtues rather than to maximize his faults. Both of course had gusto and an unremitting devotion to the life of art; "bohemian" describes both of them only if we remember that it also

Paul Rosenfeld

describes the Rudolphs of *La Bohème* and the Thoreaus of this world. Both approached art temperamentally and emotionally and both wrote lush and lapidary prose in order to convey their vivid impressions and to excite response. They were impressionists then, for isn't bejewelled prose a hallmark? And friend and foe alike found fault with Rosenfeld's prose.

Some tripped over the infelicities of his Frenchified and Germanicized English. Many felt the prose unnecessarily rich. Malcolm Cowley even says that Rosenfeld's "obstinacy" in clinging to this "style" after the literary fashions had changed accounts for his decline. The style, however, was never a manner or fashion; it changed with the critical occasion. There are times at the beginning, middle, and end of his career when Rosenfeld writes as lucidly as Edmund Wilson. The style was in fact a means of exact emotional notation. Joseph Warren Beach perceptively observed that it was "complicated, intensified, knotted up, tangled up, speeded up"; that the lapses which brought Huneker to mind were not characteristic; that it registered the world of the skyscraper — a fit prose, certainly, for one who shared the new world of Ornstein and Marin. The prose also tended to be richest when Rosenfeld was most wholly engaged. Its ebb and flow is one measure of his vitality. It is incomparably full and fine in *Port of New York,* probably because this book is most profoundly and generously *his* book, warmly alive with his men and his ideas and the hope of the future. Most important, the prose did not exist for itself; there is none of Huneker's exhibitionism in it. It serves the object and the experience of the object, always to the end of translating the experience of new, inaccessible media — Stravinsky's music, O'Keeffe's painting, Anderson's prose — into the more familiar verbal one. If this is paraphrase, then it is paraphrase by way of sensibility and not, as it is so often in others, by way of intellect alone. The simplest test of this method, which might be called objective impressionism, is to look at pictures or listen to music with Rosenfeld in hand. "I have never seen a picture of Marsden Hartley," Beach wrote, "but I shall recognize without a label the first one I come upon." The critic who can help us to such recognitions (more than identification is involved) has himself taken possession. He understands so well that he can say.

With such criticism of Rosenfeld as that by B. H. Haggin and Thomas Craven we need do nothing but note it. In a radio address, Haggin said: ". . . Mr. Rosenfeld has been engaged all these years in over-estimating the second- and third-rate pioneers of our own time, and this, I think, in order to raise himself in the estimation of others. Ordinarily one does not speak of motives; and I am not questioning the honesty of his intentions when I speak of a pose, in the sense of a determination to appear comprehending and sensitive to everything new, which is evident in the very manner, the mannered manner, of his writing, and in the pretense of discerning in a piece of music what is not there." Thomas Craven said as much indirectly when he wrote that he could only see clouds in Stieglitz's cloud studies.

The most serious criticism of Rosenfeld is that of Edmund Wilson. With the freedom that characterized the fraternity

Paul Rosenfeld

of men of letters in the '20's, he addressed the author as well as the book. The heart of Wilson's criticism is that Rosenfeld "gives us loosely imaged rhapsodies when what we are demanding is ideas." The "orchestral style" does not perform the "closer and severer function of analysis and exposition." Rosenfeld, therefore, is not a critic of the "philosophic sort." When Wilson is generous, Rosenfeld is a "romantic commentator on [the arts] who is also a commentator on life"; "he is sensitive, intelligent, well-educated and incorruptibly serious. . . ." When he is niggardly, Rosenfeld is said to be "unreflectively appreciative"; "receiving in his soul the seed of a work by some such writer as Sherwood Anderson, himself one of the tenderer plants, he will cause it to shoot up and exfloreate into an enormous and rather rank 'Mystic Cabbage-Rose.'" Wilson is embarrassed most, apparently, by the evidence of Rosenfeld's emotion. The virtue he wants in Rosenfeld is his own: the ability to follow "intellectual tides," to fully appreciate the social, political, philosophical, and scientific currents of the day.

Some of this criticism was well taken at the time, but most of it is curiously off-center and ambivalent. Though Wilson represents Rosenfeld in "The Poet's Return" as one who understands the value of tradition and standards of excellence, he says elsewhere that Rosenfeld has no political, moral, and aesthetic ideals; and because he covets Rosenfeld's cultivation, he enjoys having Matthew Josephson say, "I tell you that culture as you understand it is no longer of any value . . . the subway and the shower themselves are more magnificent poems than anything by Schubert or Goethe."[5] In matters of art and life Rosenfeld of course had aristocratic tastes; every fine sensibility is aristocratic. This does not, as some would have us believe, gainsay the democratic faith. Democracy is more than a "popular" manifestation and, as the democratic Rosenfeld knew, was not irreconcilable with every human excellence. The best was its proper goal. But the tenor of Josephson's speeches is that Rosenfeld is not in touch with popular culture; he doesn't consider jazz, for example, or the writer of "advertising copy" who forges our literature. Yet Rosenfeld wrote on jazz and scored its sentimental evasions with an edge as sharp as F. R. Leavis' in his attack on the "literature" of advertising. Rosenfeld was not unsettled by the dichotomy between highbrow and lowbrow, a dichotomy presumably of taste but actually of class, which established the need of proving one's democratic allegiance by a show of lowbrow preferences. One has only to read *I Thought of Daisy* to realize that Wilson, though writing extensively about popular culture, personally never really liked it.

Except for a fine memorial article, all of Wilson's criticism of Rosenfeld was written in 1924-1926. The books under review were *Musical Chronicle* (1923) and *Men Seen* (1925), both admittedly miscellaneous collections. *Port of New York* (1924) was not explicitly mentioned in the review of *Men*

---

[5] 1924. In 1956, Wilson wrote: "For myself . . . I have not the least doubt that I have derived a good deal more benefit of the civilizing as well as of the inspirational kind from the admirable American bathroom than I have from the cathedrals of Europe."

Paul Rosenfeld

Seen or in the memorial article. Even more curious is the fact that Wilson's essential judgments never altered; for his friend John Peale Bishop had shown in his brilliant review of *Men Seen,* and Rosenfeld's later books and essays demonstrated, that Rosenfeld had political, moral, and aesthetic ideals. Every critic of course has such ideals and it is the business of a critic of critics, as Bishop knew, to locate them. Wilson was perhaps objecting that in Rosenfeld's work these ideals were not sufficiently intellectualized. Or it may be that they amounted to profoundly emotional commitments which he did not share. His misgivings over Rosenfeld's reluctance to ally himself with the Communists in the '30's seem to be a clue to Wilson's earlier response. (In his own uncertainties, as his *Imaginary Dialogues* and *I Thought of Daisy* show, he has felt the need to formulate not his ideals so much as his positions.) Rosenfeld's ideals are clear enough and conviction certifies them. Broadly humanistic, they cohere in his concern for the artist who must be free in his art so that he may bring men to fuller consciousness and a more abundant life.

The artist is Rosenfeld's representative man or stock-personality, and the adventure of art the most rewarding way of life. "Artist" of course must be liberally construed. The nineteenth-century's special interest in art and culture is freighted in the word. Educators like Margaret Naumburg and "intellectuals" like Brooks and Bourne are artists. Anyone qualifies who has thrown off the traces of the bourgeois — even the "new" professor Bourne described — if he takes the adventure of art seriously. For the adventure of art, like Thoreau's uncommitted life and Whitman's life on the open road, is in fact what Bourne meant by the experimental life; it discovers new worlds because it leaves behind the preconceptions that make the world old. It is a serious matter and not a game because the stake is life. Leisure class parasites of culture and literary dandies are its greatest betrayers. "Peacocks" like D'Annunzio and Ezra Pound play the rôle of artist; they use art for costume and gesture. They share the faults of those self-pitying artists who follow art without genuine conviction and who are overborne by the modern malady of fear. Eliot and Wallace Stevens are their representatives, for they made of Laforgue's Pierrot "the spiritual type of all correct young men in mourning. . . ." The artist for Rosenfeld is a composite of Emerson's American Scholar and Whitman's poet. He is especially defined by his lack of nostalgia for the past and by his willingness to "relinquish his old modes of apprehension, be born in harmony with the new order, affirm it, venture forth with it on its voyage into the unknown, cleave to it for good or ill." He is committed to the living present, the node of past and future. The inevitable sorrows and defeats of his adventure overcome neither his love nor his hope. All of his duty is comprised in the need to beat out "the rhythms of his age." He stands for what man might be when he casts out fear and works in freedom. And if we find him grandiose it is because we now mean something less by "autonomous" than Rosenfeld did.

The social dislocations of the industrial revolution forced the displaced intellectual to consider the artist a redeemer.

Paul Rosenfeld

Brooks' diagnosis of the split in American society between the highbrow and the lowbrow and his faith in the leadership of the artist are special instances of the general cultural problem of the nineteenth century. "It is the poet alone," Rosenfeld wrote in presenting Brooks' views, "who can make society take the shape which can satisfy the human soul. It is the poet alone who can end the schism in American men; can turn American life toward personal ends, and develop out of an anarchical competitive horde a community of men who give and enrich themselves in giving." With or without the poet this version of the good society (recently called a fantasy of cultural brotherhood) has behind it a century of American progressive thought; it is the core of the progressive vision. But such views often compelled the artist, whose art alone had not brought immediate social change, to seek political power. The artist was not only the putative shaper of society, he was its product, and before he could shape truly the society from which he sprang had itself to be changed. Here was an old dilemma: Herder's organic thought, which stands behind Brooks', at once empowered and victimized the artist. Emerson, Whitman, John Jay Chapman — every intellectual — had faced it; for it was the old burden of the American Scholar who must perforce do as well as say, cultivate the soil as well as his art.

Rosenfeld recognized the dilemma, but he did not follow Brooks who fashioned it into a rationale for failure. Rosenfeld was closer to Bourne than to Brooks. More political than Brooks, Bourne nevertheless expected less in the way of "leadership" from the artist. He expected the artist — and all those in socially useful occupations like architecture, education, medicine, and letters — to revolutionize by individual example, by the commitment and life-style of his work. The fundamental problem of the experimental life was psychological; Rosenfeld did not project, as Brooks did, the psychological onto the social and read into a "hostile" environment the cause of the artist's failure. The artist failed because of personal weakness. Rosenfeld, for example, said that Mahler failed not because he was a Jew in Vienna but because "he was a weak man." "He permitted his environment to ruin him." Strauss was spoiled by inner weakness, Liszt by cynicism. An age was never hostile, though it might be "exhausted." That was why the Gilded Age was not "prolific of expressive individuals"; its "determined musicians, men like Paine and Lowell Mason," he said, "were forceless; weak personalities." Of course every society connived with weakness, but even in the most meager, third-rate civilization stalwart artists like Sherwood Anderson (and even the less stalwart like Twain) had been able to achieve greatness.

Personal weakness, moreover, was often seen in the artist who betrayed his gifts and the ultimate social usefulness of art by turning irresponsibly to politics. Rosenfeld remembered the folly of the intellectuals in World War I, and when he wrote "The Authors and Politics" in the '30's, he spoke out with the old conviction of Bourne. The authors accepted the "prophetic rôle," they turned to politics; but they had allowed themselves to be swept "underneath a partisan flag and into the arms of a dogma. . . ." Rosenfeld did not eschew politics. He feared preconceptions — whether they

Paul Rosenfeld

were the neoclassicism of contemporary aesthetics, a Puritan morality of sex and success, or a political line. And in politics he feared most the authors' "readiness for corporative political action," for this readiness soon dissipated the "responsibility toward, or consciousness of, the particular interests entrusted to the artist's care and advocacy."

The fervor of a minority of one sounds in Rosenfeld's defense of these interests:

It has never been . . . the function of the artist to espouse the cause of "the world" and to defend its special interests. These special interests have everlastingly been those of power and of booty. . . . His concern is not with possessions, but with the uses of things, indeed with a particular use of them . . . how material is had and held, and in what spirit. What he naturally champions is something the world is not interested in: the use and administration of material possessions in sympathy with "vision."

Vision of what? Vision of "life" itself, the mysterious forces which lie in and about and beneath and behind things, the "something" forever beautifully expressing itself in them; the "divine" known to man in his moments of spontaneity, and felt by him through free contact with other individuals and objects. For the artist is himself formed by things to receive his greatest gratifications not through having, or holding, but through feeling life, . . . the basic forces of the universe. They themselves, these forces, are perpetually declaring themselves to him through people and their lives, and through inanimate material itself: inspiring him with awe, or wonder; and inspiring him with the desire to represent them. For, wonderful or ghastly, godlike or cruel, they *are;* above all, vision of them brings the visionary

into touch not only with the immediate instruments of his revelation, but with other men, and the whole world. . . . And if
the artist seeks, through manipulation of material to bring to
light that which he has felt in his moment of vision, it is largely
for the sake of fully understanding that which has been revealed
to himself and making all men see and recognize the truth: but
most of all, to move people toward him in the spirit in which he
himself has been moved toward them.

For the most part, the artist's struggle aims at, and ends with,
the representation and the social acceptance of the thing which
he has "seen." But, as we have said above, he will actively
champion from time to time the general administration of material possessions in sympathy with and in the interests of vision
itself. That is, he will become the impassioned advocate of
things produced out of feeling: things having the quality of
life and awakening feeling and bringing men into touch with its
divine source and object. . . .

Those who deplored Rosenfeld's refusal to join the Com-
munist ranks overlooked the most telling point in his confession of faith. He saw (as Chapman had seen in the early
days of socialism) that the ideal of "rich corporate existence
and spiritual growth" had not in fact been furthered by the
change in political allegiance. This ideal of social wealth had
always been dear to intellectuals caught up in the American
game of salvation by individual acquisition; and yet, following closely the political activity of the '30's, Rosenfeld noted
the lack of any "quarrel with the whole blindly wasteful
tendency of American life. . . ." At the rallies he did not
hear of the desire for "the right to the good and the sincere
job" or of "the social necessity of a living use of materials."

Paul Rosenfeld

Instead, behind the revolutionary talk he heard the old demand for bourgeois comforts. The "revolution" was simply distributive; its end was not a change in the quality of life but "cars, silk stockings and radio sets for all."

History may force us to grant the justice of Rosenfeld's observations, but somehow, in our own preoccupation with things, we find quixotic the partisan of a better life. Rosenfeld might have taken comfort from Thoreau, not only because the '30's taught him a bitter lesson in simplicity but because his stand was never popular. He now feared that the artist's cause had been lost from the beginning and that a society seeking spiritual ends was "incapable of realization in the world." America, he wrote, was not "the first land to believe that, made economically secure and comfortable, life will automatically grow blessed." He did not spare himself hard truths. Perhaps it was the world's misfortune to be destined to belong to "the stupid." But if it were, it was still the "artist's business to tell it so." It was the artist's business to fight for life against death. The waste land and martyrdom were not the only alternatives.

Rosenfeld placed the artist in the world but beyond the politics of possessions. For the artist was fundamentally an anarchist. His intuitions revealed the ever-changing order in things. To this order he was faithful when he shaped material "in accordance with its own nature and the idea to which it conforms. . . ." For in this way his work was "expressive," carrying us, as Rosenfeld said of great music, "out of ourselves and beyond ourselves, into impersonal regions, into the stream of things; permitting us to feel the conditions under which objects exist, the forces playing upon human life." The nature of vision committed the artist to an open world, and in this sense the environment proved "hostile" only when the artist himself refused to embrace it. "What we call a favorable environment, and what we call creative ability," he explained, "are actually two aspects of a single force, basically or at one with itself, and productive in its two-part play. Of these parts, one is the 'not-I,' the other the 'I'; but essentially they are lovers. . . ."

This aesthetic might be considered transcendental. It proposes that art mediate the inner and outer worlds. To that extent its symbolic embodiments are "correspondences"; Stieglitz's "Equivalents" are the supreme example. But unlike the Emersonian aesthetic, it has no Over-Soul in which to moor the symbol. In repudiating Zola's naturalism, the generation of artists from whom Rosenfeld took his aesthetic did not return to the Emersonian notion that the "inner" was the "above." They no longer believed that the world was an emanation of the ego. The truth of things is revealed in fidelity to both inner and outer worlds. They believed, however, in the centrality of the self and in the discoveries of feeling; if faithfully responded to, the external world would reveal the inner truth of life. Thus the artist was to seek the "expressivity of the objective world" and therewith fashion the "subjective form." Art, Rosenfeld insisted, must get us somewhere new and true, and that somewhere was a new world of feeling. And he listened intently for these new and true "rhythms" because he believed that they disclosed the bases of new social relationships and order.

Paul Rosenfeld

Only by spontaneously and openly responding to the world can the artist capture the rhythms of his time. Without preconceptions he must woo the "not-I." His love affair with the world is an exploration of reality to the end of adjusting men to the world and to other men. "Ready-made elysiums" therefore do not comfort him. The "pink world of received ideas and sentiments" that Rosenfeld found in the work of Gershwin and other popular artists weakened the "lure of the actual. . . ." Such work removed men from contact with reality. It offered easy security, not freeedom for living; it was not mature. But judged by this aesthetic, even the work of serious American artists was faulty.

The cultural critics of Rosenfeld's generation investigated the causes of this creative immaturity. Rosenfeld himself did not undertake this work; he took his cultural bearings from Brooks' *America's Coming-of-Age,* Frank's *Our America,* William Carlos Williams' *In The American Grain,* and D. H. Lawrence's *Studies in Classic American Literature.* We now know the inadequacy of these studies, especially those of Brooks and Frank which are neither good history nor good literary criticism. These critics did not read enough or well. They were in fact psychologists rather than historians, and their account of America is more rewarding as psychology than it is as history. They offered their generation the kind of relevant cultural description that we now find useful in the work of sociologists like David Riesman. They used the past, though they were led by Brooks to believe it insufficiently "usable" for a vital American tradition — Brooks acknowledged that "once you have a point of view all history will back you up. . . ." The work of Brooks and Frank, therefore, fits the aesthetic or individual problem better than the political or institutional ones. But considered as cultural "myth," it reaches deeply into the American experience. We are moved by its embodiment in Hart Crane's *The Bridge* and Fitzgerald's *The Great Gatsby,* and in Rosenfeld's *Port of New York.*

Rosenfeld most brilliantly applied the "myth" in his criticism of contemporary art, and because he assimilated its various elements he provides perhaps the best introduction to it. The first strand of the "myth" might be called the utopian dream of America. Columbus had gone to sea to discover the good place, the "divine land." But America had "interposed"; it was not the "Earthly Paradise." Mankind however did not renounce the "dream," and the voyage of yearning — "the divine delusion" — continued on the American continent. This dream left its mark on the national character: the American was restless and maladjusted, enamored of the distant and the future; the present world, the present moment had no wonder for him. In the pejorative word of the time, the American was a "pioneer."

To call the American a pioneer is to bring forward another element of the "myth." We might, with Richard Hofstadter who analyzed its relation to populist thought, call it "soft agrarianism," or with Lawrence who had more in mind than a *mystique* of farming, the "spirit of place." The common point, however, is the need for roots and the love of the soil. "Pioneersmen," Rosenfeld explained, "are not earth-builders,

Paul Rosenfeld

not people who take root and love the earth that nourishes them, and have a sense of responsibility to the men who are to come after them. . . ." The pioneer scratches the earth and moves on; he is an unrelated and solitary despoiler. Even worse when one recalls Rosenfeld's aesthetics, he withholds love: "something that is in the human power to give had never come and opened [his] pores to the light and the green and the wind." He does not feel as the people of older countries do, that the earth is an organism like himself and that it has to be "cared for." He has not learned from the Indian (whose corn dance Rosenfeld saw in Santa Fé in 1926) that "if he put himself in harmony with nature, nature would put herself in harmony with him." Americans, then, did not have "the land love, ground love" Anderson appreciated in Dove's paintings; they were not like Thoreau, "deeply earth-submissive."

The dream and the restlessness left the "testimony of disinherited things" of which Brooks spoke so eloquently: things "old without majesty, old without mellowness, old without pathos, just shabby and bloodless and worn out." America was an impoverished civilization. "The trip from the old to the new world upon which we are all in spite of ourselves embarked," Rosenfeld said, "has gotten most of us not to a city spreading 'its dark life upon the earth of a new world, rooted there, sensitive to its richest beauty. . . .' " The green breast of the new world had succored something else; we had come "no further than a low smoky shore looking rather like the Bayonne littoral from the Staten Island ferryboat on a sunless winter's day: a slatey weed garden of wharves, gas-

Port of New York

tuns, church spires, chimneys, habitations set against ghostly blueless hills." There was nothing in this landscape to warrant Whitman's confidence that the life disembarked here would be a good one. "We have been standing at the rail," Rosenfeld said of his generation, "uncertain whether the shore before us is indeed solid earth upon which one can walk and nourish oneself. . . ."

Disenchantment with an America without a conception of the nonacquisitive, creative life is at the bottom of the historical explanation that followed from this sunless view. (One need only read the letters of Bourne, Hart Crane, or Anderson to sympathize with it.) From the beginning the American had been self-seeking; that might explain why in the closing paragraphs of *The Great Gatsby* Fitzgerald had written that America "pandered in whispers. . . ." Protestantism had emphasized individual salvation; it had not been conducive to communal life; and its fear of "earthiness" had made men "avert their love from the soil and the things that nourished their bodily life." The devil in the garden was in fact not so much the historical Puritan as it was the contemporary puritanism with which he was confused. But the historical Puritan (if Tawney was right) had done enough harm: his secularized faith was capitalism, his gospel "success," his modern avatars the lowbrow business man of practical grasp and the highbrow professor of genteel spirituality. Pioneer, Puritan, Professor still lorded it over America.

While Brooks told his generation what this triumvirate had done and what they were doing or not doing for American expression, Rosenfeld undertook in terms of their formative

Paul Rosenfeld

influence to explain the shortcomings of contemporary artists. He pointed out, for example, the "sexual fear" disclosed by the undeveloped foregrounds of Ryder's paintings. "Ryder," he wrote, "could not bring his whole man into entire contact with the object. The upper, spiritual regions of the body were singing flesh to him. The lower he could not fit into his scheme of beauty." Hartley, too, had "not been able to lose himself in his 'object' "; though he employs sexual forms, the mournfulness of his canvases suggests withholding, an unfortunate result of the Yankee alienation from the soil.[6] In the case of Kenneth Hayes Miller, an excellent painter of the nude, Rosenfeld perceived "the not entirely successful struggle with the blood." Why Miller should paint his feeling for flesh "more swimmingly through the smooth and stubby protuberances of the landscape than through the body itself," that, Rosenfeld remarked, "is known to God alone, who alone can sound the mysteries of the Yankee soul." In any event, this struggle with the "blood" could not be overcome in a generation.

Alienation — lack of relationship to thing, flesh, soil — this is the deepest source of incapacity, of truncated life and incomplete expression. "From a lack of touch," Williams wrote, "lack of belief." The relationship of the artist to his object, Rosenfeld found, was "typical of the American in his general contacts." Behind the weaknesses of Ryder, Hartley, and Miller was "the attitude taken by the whole of society to the

---

[6] Rosenfeld forecast in 1924 that the wandering Hartley would have to return to Maine, the place of his deepest feelings. Hartley returned in the 1930's.

soil that nourishes it. . . ." We are reminded also by Rosenfeld's "struggle with the blood" of Lawrence's blood-emotion
— the emotional consciousness or consciousness unmediated
by concept and abstraction that makes for flowing, immediate
contact. This emotion embraces equally the flesh and the
soil; indeed the relationship to the soil for which Rosenfeld
speaks is something sexual, something compounded of passionate desire, yielding, and tender care. The romantic feeling
for nature, he later wrote in an essay on "Mozart the Romantic," is feminine; in "The Land Awaits," America is
"She," still very much Pocahontas awaiting the husbandman
— the artist — who will touch her stirring body lovingly.

Finally, the nationalism fostered by these cosmopolitan
critics was only another way of calling attention to the need
for such vital relationships — relationships other than those of
the cash-nexus. Patriotism was absent in this nationalism.
And this nationalism, which Bourne called trans-national, was
not limited to those of certified Anglo-Saxon stock. America,
Rosenfeld claimed, is "the native soil of anyone who *feels* it
to be his." That is why these particular critics and artists
were able, when even the hundred percenters failed, to redis-
cover America.

Signs of vital relationship or organic connection became the
evidence of the creative readiness of American life. Sandburg,
whose sentimentalism disturbed Rosenfeld, was valuable because he helps us "feel roots beneath us in the soil . . . feel
the tie ineluctably come to be between us and this new world
earth." The poet feels "the woman power in the soil," and
knows Pocahontas' body, "lovely as a poplar, sweet as a red

Paul Rosenfeld

haw. . . ." He at least does not have to return to Europe "to feel his rootfastness"; he has approached and helps us approach a forbidding environment; he has whetted our desire for New York and Chicago, not for Paris. Dove's work, a "sort of 'Leaves of Grass' through pigment," communicates a "direct sensuous feeling of the earth." Marin, too, is fruit-bearing because he is rooted in America, and perhaps with Thoreau's essay on wild apples in mind, Rosenfeld says of him: "Marin is fast in American life like a tough and fibrous apple tree lodged and rooted in good ground."

With this acceptance of the soil (an acceptance large enough to include the possibilities of the industrial machine on its surface and all the past plowed into its depths) there was new response to the body. If Hartley had not gone far enough in referring the universe to the body, others had, among them Anderson, O'Keeffe, Dove, Williams, and Stieglitz. Anderson, who never really appreciated the title "phallic Chekov," reminded "an age that it is in the nucleus of sex that all the lights and confusions have their center, and that to the nucleus of sex they all return. . . ." He plumbed the American loneliness and the truth of human relationships. Georgia O'Keeffe was *woman* painting, Dove *man*. And Williams, able to relate the "white thighs of the sky" and "the round and perfect thighs/of the Police Sergeant's wife/ perfect still after many babies," was, with Stieglitz, himself unrivaled in catching the vitality and spirit of sex, a surety that life might grow hopefully beyond the Bayonne littoral.

This "myth" of "the soil, the unconscious, the community" answers a very real problem. It arises from the need in our culture for intimacy, communion, and fulfillment. The stranger in Anderson's story, "Tandy," speaks its very essence: "I am a lover and have not found my thing to love." This "myth" may look backward, as so much thought since the industrial revolution has, to a more golden day; but it also looks forward to a "new generous way of life. . . ." One may cavil with its simplicities, with the melodramatic shape it takes, and with its reading of the malady of an entire civilization in terms of the artist and his difficulties of expression. And yet, after all, it is only another version of the constant vision of realized personality and being that one finds in Emerson, Thoreau, and Whitman; in Chapman and others who felt that commercialism had destroyed significant social life. If the artist has become the stock-personality, it is because he represents for us the highest measure of consciousness and the most life-furthering activity. "The land has no need intenser than the need of men who see justly," Rosenfeld believed, "men who go the artist's personal, passionate, disinterested way." For only when men willingly turn the self outward to the object is art and civilization possible: "Giving alone builds cultures and cities for men."

III

Port of New York is Paul Rosenfeld's best book. *Men Seen* has a wider range — twenty-four poets, novelists, and critics from eight literatures; *An Hour With American Music* perhaps because of brevity hews the exposition to a sharper line; *Discoveries of a Music Critic* is more mature. But composed in the fullest confidence of his powers, *Port of New*

Paul Rosenfeld

York is a *book,* almost perfectly organized, thematically developed and controlled to the last word. It is not a collection of essays, a miscellany like *Men Seen.* Where *Men Seen* expressed Rosenfeld's "happy realization that the world is filled with individual, separate destinies" and that this pluralism was equally right for the imagination and for democracy, *Port of New York* expressed his sense of the desirableness of communal ends. It was, he said, a "picture of a number of individualities moving through several gateways toward a common point." The common point, as we have seen, was the discovery in expression of the "new" America. This mighty theme Rosenfeld was capable of handling notably. He had the gifts of understanding various media and of sympathizing with personalities as different as Sandburg and Hartley; he was a portraitist in the Jamesian tradition and a critic who unfolded his criteria within the book with the mastery of an artist. The substantial achievement of *Port of New York* was itself an assurance of the creative vitality it affirmed. ·

The personae of this drama of cultural awakening (these critics were fond of metaphors of dawn and day) are all treated with large sympathy. In *Port of New York,* moreover, the sympathy never softens the critical judgment as it does in *Men Seen,* where minor talents and friends (like Jean Toomer, to whom he dedicated *An Hour With American Music*) are placed among the host of great modern writers. There may be a lapse in the case of Roger Sessions, the only composer in the book, who at the time had demonstrated his gifts in a single composition; and he may have been included,

Port of New York

as the chronicle-writing of this essay suggests, because he re-
called the kind of excitement Rosenfeld had once felt in
listening to Ornstein. Ornstein of course had figured in
Musical Portraits, but by 1924 he was on his way to obscurity,
remembered in the dedication by the sadly aware but ever-
generous Rosenfeld. Of the writers connected with *The Seven
Arts* and "291," those he could not fully or heartily endorse
were relegated to the less exacting *Men Seen:* Kreymborg,
Oppenheim, Frank. Frank, the most serious omission when
one considers his stature at the time, was probably neglected
because Brooks provided the essential cultural themes — and
without Frank's special pleading to the Jew; but we know
that in 1921 Rosenfeld had justifiably but severely criticized
Frank's novels and that this had ruptured their friendship.
Margaret Naumburg, Frank's wife, was included, in her own
right and not by way of reparation. Others, like Lewis
Mumford and Hart Crane, whom we would now place in
such a book, had not yet arrived.

Where Wagner had served to summon the nineteenth century as the background for *Musical Portraits,* Albert Pinkham
Ryder, a painter inspired in several canvases by Wagnerian
themes, served to summon the dark American past as the
background for *Port of New York.* He did not express with
Wagner the material triumph of the age, he expressed its
terrible homesickness. In his haunted moonlit pictures we
are still at sea, Flying Dutchmen or Christopher Columbuses
without compass and chart, driven on by the "romantic
inhuman lure" so characteristic of American idealism. We

1

Paul Rosenfeld

see beauty only at night in these Poe-like paintings; we cannot accept the sun-lit world; the moon betrays us and life emptily glides by. We are restless and without will, victims of what Brooks, not yet Freudian enough to call sublimation, called the malady of the ideal: "the sickness of those who are captive to some shadowy unsubstantial ideal order and, while possessing little faith in the ideal which holds them, are nevertheless prevented by it from slaking their thirst for experience in the real substance of the world." Ryder, the most original and deeply expressive American artist of the nineteenth century, records and thereby ends our wandering; he brings us to the shore of "the inhabited solid earth." Rootless and solitary, fearful of sudden experience and sexuality, unskilled in his medium and only partially expressive, he provides in the negative those themes whose positive aspects Rosenfeld will use to strike up for a new world.

Brooks follows because he supplies the compass and the chart, and also, one suspects, because his significant work is done. Rosenfeld devoted the longest essay to Brooks. He thought him the most important critic since Whitman, a much-needed model of the cosmopolitan man of letters committed to America. But he felt that Brooks was personally incompletely integrated, that his personal irresolution had loosened his grasp of American reality, and that (as *The Pilgrimage of Henry James* soon proved) he would have to clarify his own life before he could see America clearly. Rosenfeld gratefully acknowledged the debt his generation owed Brooks: "With him came the philosophical and intellectual basis of the movement, the analytical scheme of the past." His criticism itself had relieved the cultural situation. And yet, tried by his own belief in the leadership of the man of letters, he was beginning to show signs of failure. After *Letters and Leadership* his prose began to decline; Rosenfeld noted that personally he had less vigor and vivacity. *The Ordeal of Mark Twain* revealed a "strabismic vision," and its "perverse thesis" accused Brooks of "shooting with loaded dice." Intent on finding victimization everywhere, Brooks had lost faith in the heroism of the artist; by preaching and by indulging passivity, he had himself become a hostile environment. Rosenfeld's greatest fear was that in "playing safe with life" Brooks had renounced the bold and dangerous life-style of the artist, for this would have been the earnest of his commitment. As it was, he had retreated from the "critical battle-line" and had turned away from the contemporary writers who needed him most. The young man who had once adventured on life now sat unmindfully behind a closed door. Unsparing criticism, but so prophetic! And Rosenfeld had the right to judge because he followed the credo of the early Brooks more closely than did Brooks himself. By implication Rosenfeld thus defined his own positive critical stance and work. The remainder of *Port of New York* made it good.

In turning West to Sandburg, Rosenfeld hailed a half-formed poet who at least took chances with life. Here he struck earth. Some of the fog enshrouding the Flying Dutchman is dispelled: "We drift aimlessly in the currents of air that circle the globe; strain away to some otherwhere. But for Sandburg the magnetic pole of life has situated itself in

Paul Rosenfeld

mid-America." We are no longer homeless. Hartley, with his New England delicacy and refinement, complements the raw Westerner. Both, however, are only partially successful: Sandburg is sentimental and Hartley uses his brilliant technique to shield himself from the bitter emotional assaults of life. Rosenfeld develops the theme of "soil" with Sandburg; with Hartley he advances his aesthetics; and in William Carlos Williams, who follows and concludes the first movement of the book, he portrays a successful artist. Williams gives himself completely to the American environment and the medium of his art. Superior to Eliot in his "mature capacity for insight," Williams is able to face the evils of life and the harshness of America. Because of his work, Rosenfeld feels at last that the land is "habitable." The journey from the old to the new world "has led us somewhere. . . ."

The second movement of the book deals with teachers who devote themselves to the necessary education in realities. Margaret Naumburg, director of the Walden School, represents the kind of social vocation Bourne had called for; she is the artist-as-educator, the Bronson Alcott of the group, who works in the living medium of the child. Her experimental school is comparable to Stieglitz's gallery: it opens into life and is dedicated to the development by expression of the full personality. "The human being is poisonous," Rosenfeld says, "in proportion to the amount of his unfulfilment." The "organic" education of the Walden School, which mediated the extremes of old-fashioned authoritarianism and Dewey progressivism, proposed to reduce the poisons by liberating the child. Opposed to the routines, repressions, and values of the

Port of New York

bourgeois world, trans-national in character, this school is a new society: the possible American society in which the artist-man would fulfill his inner needs for expression (individuality) and for fellowship (communal life).

Another teacher with a realistic spirit is Kenneth Hayes Miller of the Art Students' League. A minor but honest painter, he is important because he does not indulge in the "illicit revery" and pre-Raphaelite evasions of prominent artists like Arthur B. Davies. His work rids us of "the burden of fraudulent idealism which lies heavy on each American back." Finally, Sessions, a New Englander of ancient Puritan stock, typifies the young man whose promise the new education might release. Trained by Horatio Parker at Yale and commissioned by Smith College to compose the score of the "daring" commencement play, Andreyev's *The Black Maskers,* Sessions represents in his preparation and the occasion of his work, a native creative insurgence within the enclosure of the American college.

Major figures and eminent creators comprise the final movement. Themes are recapitulated in terms of strength and success. John Marin, for example; is an ancient mariner wholly unlike Ryder. Rooted in Maine and New York, American in every fibre, courageously and completely true to himself and his medium, he is for Rosenfeld the prototypal artist. With Stieglitz, who climaxes the movement, he stands on the peak of assured achievement, one of the greatest painters and discoverers of our time. Dove, Anderson, O'Keeffe — all indebted to Stieglitz — express in their realized art the favorable results of root-taking and sexual libera-

Paul Rosenfeld

tion. In addition, Anderson's career, his struggle to become a writer in an acquisitive society, makes him the heroic artist whose victory over the environment refutes Brooks' thesis. Bourne, too, is an exemplary individual, the "artist-fighter," who formulated as no one else did "the creative will of American men." He is placed here, next to Stieglitz, because both are spiritual guides to a trans-national democracy. Bourne of course countervails Brooks. He dedicates us anew to the unfinished task of American culture.

Had *Port of New York* been an historical narrative, the portrait of Stieglitz would have begun rather than ended it. Stieglitz ends it perhaps for the very reason Anderson wrote:

Old man — perpetually young — we salute you.
Young man — who will not grow old — we salute you.

He ends it, where Ryder began it, because in his art he transformed the moonlit landscape of the soul into the daylight modern world. He was the master of light. He created a new traditionless art. He conclusively demonstrated the aesthetic uses of the camera, making a "machine" serve the spirit. With the camera he "cast the artist's net wider into the material world than any man before him. . . ." He captured the inner meaning of every manifestation of life — soil, grass, water, tree, sky, cloud, animal, woman, house, skyscraper, airplane, city. His brave individual life was steadily affirmative. And the history of his work at "291" summarized the entire movement only to elicit once more the desire for the creative group and to stir again for similar ends a combativeness for ideas. For Stieglitz was the outstanding example of

Port of New York

the initiator: he showed how groups answering to the living needs of men begin in the interstices of institutions.

Rosenfeld's world is the world of Stieglitz's pictures. In the "Epilogue," we stand with the immigrants of Stieglitz's "The Steerage"; we watch the shuttle of ferryboats and trans-Atlantic liners. We come to port at last. Europe no longer pulls us back. There is an almost unaccountably subtle change in the spirit of place. "Through words, lights, colors, the new world has been reached at last." The good sun shines on America;[7] in its light the "smug safe bourgeois values" are gone. The mature life of work, growth, and love is possible now. The root has found welcome soil. In the dazzling brilliance of this picture, in Rosenfeld's overwhelming lyrical affirmation, we may momentarily forget that every generation, even those thankful for this tilth, must put to sea. Should we remember, we may take courage from the adventure of one generation willing to hazard for the gift of life.

[7] Emerson: "The sun shines to-day also." (*Nature,* 1836)

Port of New York

ALBERT P. RYDER

From a Photograph by Alice Boughton

CARL SANDBURG

From a Photograph by Dana Desboro

MARSDEN HARTLEY

From a Photograph by Alfred Stieglitz

JOHN MARIN

From a Photograph by Alfred Stieglitz

ARTHUR G. DOVE

From a Photograph by Alfred Stieglitz

SHERWOOD ANDERSON

From a Photograph by Alfred Stieglitz

ALFRED STIEGLITZ

From a Photograph by Paul Strand

GEORGIA O'KEEFFE

From a Photograph by Alfred Stieglitz

Foreword

Port of New York has composed itself. I did not deliberately set out to write a book about the movement
of life in America. Nothing more formal than separate
essays about certain American moderns was planned. But
shortly after some of the articles were written and published in *The Bookman, The Dial,* and *Vanity Fair,* to
whose editors I here make acknowledgment for the per-
mission they have given me to reprint material already
printed by them, there commenced settling upon me the
project of assembling the papers written and those I had
still to write, in the shape of a book. For no sooner did
I begin making headway in expressing what it was these
poets and critics, novelists and educators, painters and
photographers had given me indeed, than I commenced
discovering that the feelings excited by their works were
closely related, so closely as to constitute variations of a
single feeling. These creators, independently, through
different mediums, and in different manners, had nevertheless all of them given me the sensation one has when,
at the close of a prolonged journey by boat, the water-
gate comes by, and one steps forth and stands with solid
under foot. For the first time, among these modern men
and women, I found myself in an America where it was
good to be.

1

Foreword

It was a group, so it appeared, which I had set about describing. These individual men and women, in different regions over the land, were kindred. Their various actions had a single tendency. It was as though a single identity were creating through several forms. And, imaginary or real, this group has determined the constitution of my book of journey's end and land's beginning. If artists to the precise number of fourteen are treated of in *Port of New York*, it is not because I have had any desire to assert that the number of important workers in America is limited, after the fashion of the number of certain celebrated "points," to double seven. The book makes not the slightest pretense of singling out all the artists in America. It does not even pretend to declare who is who among the living and the "great." There exists, for our benefit, much not merely of promise, but of solid achievement, which does not figure in it at all. If, then, there are fourteen portraits in this book, it is for one reason only: the reason that during the last eight or seven years, the works of fourteen men and women at different times gave me the happy sense of a new spirit dawning in American life, and awakened a sense of wealth, of confidence, and of power which was not there before.

P. R.

Albert P. Ryder

THE Ryders hang dark on the museum walls; pools of very dusk in gilt borders; cold glamorous patterns pitched so low that for a while they resist the eye, and open with extreme reluctancy their dreamy spells. The rigid, heavily enameled surfaces have the color of night when the moon is small and chill and hard; of ancient tapestries sewn with threads of tarnished metal; of sere leaves in November and the smoke-blue of winter woodlands. Disks of saddest silver burn icily amid profound and undulant blacks. Blacks glide smoothly, silently, like streams in the dark; pierced by brightness only in pinpricks, and limited by areas of citron or of gray nearly as low in key as they themselves. Dullest gold of nightcloud edge is subtly and mystically harmonized with sable, or with the aureate brown of embossed leathers. The utmost reaches in vibrance in the gorgeous, fissured rectangles are rose-violets of the ultimate agony of day in the west, and rims of light pale as the greening skies of the afterglow.

Areas of these paintings do not lie in life. The canvases become convex with form only at the center of the picture. Almost never do they commence to swell from the lower border. The base of the Ryder is generally an evasion. Often it remains a space undefined in darkness. Sometimes, as in *The Forest of Arden*, or the small purplish marine in the Brooklyn Museum, it is set with puny human figures. Nevertheless, it stands an evasion. The figurines are stiff, extraneous, insignificant, damaging to the elfin music of the tones and lights. The canvases remain curiously void, embryonic, until the foregrounds are transcended, and the middle and the upper reaches arrive in all their somber glamour.

But, where the Ryders live, they breathe forth a mysterious life, a treasure of forms and spots and shapes more tender, more exquisitely original than anything which before them, or during their time, flowed from the brush of an American. Painting had been done in the new world since colonial days, since tavern-sign decorators had been lured to portray with their sour technique, sharp-faced Puritan dames as shepherdesses of Versailles or in the "character" of "sultanas." Three generations of sober craftsmen before Ryder had learned from Romney and Constable, from Munich and Barbizon. Contemporaneous with Ryder were a number of exquisite brushmen, Fuller, Martin, Twachtman, who gave pigment a sensitive life. Not any of them scattered Rembrandtesque jewelry comparable to that which shines from his dusky cloths. A breathless delicacy rendered these quivering capricious rims and mysterious tones, a delicacy as intense as that when all life becomes tremulous palping finger-tip. The tender conjunctions of shapes, the strange subtle

Albert P. Ryder

promontories and capes of pigment are elusive as colors and sounds and lights in a dream. Shapes as fantastic as the fleeting rack in the heavens, as skeins of blown silk, appear. Forms breathe out like opened faint-hued flowers with corollas of softest crimson, or like the creaming evanescent foam about a flying sloop. Forms stand dark and sinister like sudden shark's teeth; stand wise and wrinkled and old as the trunks of ancient willows; unfurl with slow calm sublunary gesture.

The Ryders are the first deep expression of American life in the medium of paint; irrelevant as they may seem to asphalted Fifth Avenue which extends white beyond the walls on which they stand, and to the day which spreads so garish and brisk in every direction. Their tender mysterious tones and sensitive forms, their shades of sundown and midnight, harmonies of argent and indigo, speak what we as Americans have lived in the society of the red, white, and blue. By the sides of these poems, in the still, soft-lighted galleries where they are set, there hang many paintings pretending to the "physiognomy characteristic and western": tugs pushing valiantly fistily up the Hudson, mountain walls of Lake George; *Alpenglühen* on the Presidential Range in New Hampshire; pictures of the Good Gray Poet, the coastland of Maine, and sweet girl graduates in classic draperies. Before these, we do not stop and feel with thrill "America." If we feel them related to the new world at all, it is chiefly for their purely negative qualities; for the meat

5

and the spirit of life which they want. They leave life where it was, a-rest on dry familiar sands. But the Ryders start a sudden music; bring a sense of something in life from which all of us stem. A surging tumultuous space has been cleared about; roving, heaving waters swell beneath us. We have been set afloat and left to grope our way, without compass and chart, and by the lights in the breast alone, across the oceanic tide to the unknown other shore.

We have been given a feeling of the universe; a feeling of cloud confines and frosty starlands focused indeed from the breast of a sea, from the deck of a certain wandering caravel. The Ryders make us sail with Columbus on his final voyage; not any of the four trips made by him for the crown of Castile; but the fifth, the trip which commenced only when he had died, and the new world lay open to Europeans. After the death of the Genoese, Johannes V. Jensen tells us, there began spreading among sea-folk the legend of a phantom ship and a phantom captain driven over the Atlantic on a termless voyage; a phantom bark erroneously connected with the name of a Holland sea-captain; erroneously, for the reason that the ghostly master of the ghostly vessel was not Vanderdecken, but Christopher Columbus himself, discoverer of America, bound in vain search of the land which he had wished to find when first he sailed from Palos. Passage to India had never been the major objective of the admiral. There had been another. It is probable passage

Albert P. Ryder

to India had never been more than the rationalization of the purpose of an irrational desire. It was in search of the Earthly Paradise that Columbus had fared out into the ocean. The wind that had blown him forward was man's immemorial dream of a divine land somewhere upon the globe, a golden-aired, apple-laden place where life was effortless sovereign beauty, slow perfect gesture and breath drawn in everlasting unchanging fulfilment. If the eyes of the Genoese had peered through mists and into horizon gray, it was for sight of the promontories of the ineffable land for which all mankind yearned. Columbus had imagined the sacred mountain somewhere in the region where the Guiana shorelands lie, and when at sea he felt the soft tropic waters of the Orinoco, he knew he was nearing the estuary of one of the streams that descend the blessed slopes.

But America had interposed. America had made an end of the divine delusion. There was no Earthly Paradise. The earth was everywhere what it was in the Old World, no Hesperidean garden of luscious fruits and dreamy skies and endless summer afternoon, but a realm submitted to suffering and age and death, where men had to labor in the sweat of their brows. It was then the Flying Dutchman set sail, damned to pursue, his vessel freighted with the desire of human kind, a termless voyage across the sea of the heart. If the consciousness in men had had to resign the dream, unconsciousness had not let go of it. The goal was gone. The yearning continued. The distances were strangely musical. The modern malady, the pathos of farness, was upon the world. Till at last some sailors saw, without, through a mist, sailing against the wind, the cursèd caravel with its black spars and high poop; marked its ghastly admiral and its heaven-mocked crew of men.

The voyage persisted nowhere more wildly than among the settlers of the American continent. Restlessness, maladjustment, had brought most of them out of Europe. Restlessness, maladjustment, remained in their blood. Pioneersmen formed a large portion of the colonists; pioneersmen, who are not earthbuilders, not people who take root and love the earth that nourishes them, and have the sense of responsibility to the men who are to come after them, but people who scratch the earth a little, then move on again, and again, unrelated, solitary, blown by some relentless wind. But even in men who were not forever pushing on from new border to new border, did the wandering mood obtain. It held people who sought to take root, to make a home and a community. Something of them was always in a prairie-schooner, always refusing an allegiance to their small space of ground. Generation transmitted the restlessness to generation till it became a national characteristic. It is always the distant that is musical for the American. Like the Mélisande of Maeterlinck, his psyche looks always into the "otherwheres." The present world, the present moment, has no wonder. The sun, which thrusts towards him a con-

Albert P. Ryder

vexed, full-blown world, and presses immediate and large the colors of things, annihilates his imagination quite. Only the night, that blunts the spearheads; removes and makes indistinct the pitching buildings; and renders the world strange and dun and dimensionless, brings beauty up in him. Or, it is the past, the future, Europe and Asia, the "wild" West and the "opium-tainted" East full of impossible brown charms. No American is happy in a room, happy over a tiny hill, happy over what little he has, content to sit and watch three trees growing in the yard before his house. The demon always whispers that color is to be found far off, away, in the distance, in some one else's house, in some one else's bankvault. There has always to be frenetic movement: stupendous shooting skyscrapers, motor-racings, families on wheels, lightning change, rebuilding, tearing down, putting up, refurnishing, moving, blasting, enlarging, spreading, bursting. Every one lives beyond his means. The wishing stone is forever warm with rubbing. The fancy is perpetually overworked with perfections that are certain to arrive of themselves with the sun of the day after the day after to-morrow. Life glides emptily by; the demoniac moon draws the accursed craft.

And Albert P. Ryder was not merely a man who painted *The Flying Dutchman;* gave again and again the sail bellying into the fathomless heaven and the tragic ghost peering over the rail of the phantom bark on icy sterile oceans. He was himself the Flying Dutchman. No things called him their own. No place of trees and meadows held him to them, bade him rest with them and share their fate; no house or home, woman or children. His life in New York was lonely steering under the compulsion of some lodestar balefully gleaming afar. It was unutterable solitude, lone wandering, unending homelessness. Ryder was a tramp in body all his days. New Englander, American, inheritor of pioneer blood, he was what the portrait by Kenneth Hayes Miller shows him: a man of the massive corporeal forms, the great bones and sinews of the fathers of the races which have learned to do a titanic labor; helpless nevertheless in the world of men. He was a bearded king in Ultima Thule; a magnificent old derelict. He was a man who could not take root. Held to the common daylight by thinnest bonds alone, it became autumn and evening very quickly in him. During the last years of his life, the painter was merely the specter of himself, impotent to produce his music of night and fall. He sat, owl-like in his dusty-paned lodging underneath the Sixth Avenue elevator tracks; unable to complete a work; unable to set anything definitely outside himself; unable to come to decisions. He scraped pigment off, put it back again, painted out a silver rain, painted in a stiff scarlet-coated figurine; delivered a painting to patrons and dealers, then rushed back to demand it of them; kept it another three years, painting in a cloud-form, scraping pigment off. It was as though nature had indulged him awhile against some law

Albert P. Ryder

of gravity; then brought it into force again and pulled him down into a void.

Every work set forth by him sings doom of vain search and solitary faring. Conscious and unconscious in his art breathe flight underneath the indifferent, sorcerer's moon; life that could not take the present moment and fulfil itself therein, never could fling itself loose and relaxed onto the sod of the instant, but yearned always away into blue and remote and impalpable distances; and in the arms of the beloved was restless and unappeased, and only in solitude and in deprivation felt in full flowering the bush of desire. The Flying Dutchman was always in Ryder's mind. He painted him under many forms; as *Death on the Racetrack*, the skeleton horseman with scythe flitting round the ·deserted course into the immeasurable autumnal distance; as *Jonah*, cast into the ravening black sea, calling in vain for help in the very jaws of the monster upon the faint legendary god shining afar. He painted him as *Macbeth* to whom voices from out the night presage inevitable guilt and unfathomable evil; as *Siegfried*, whom the merwomen in the river and the leaves warn of impending doom. Like fanfares, the sense of the romantic inhuman lure, of the proud stark aloofness, comes through the many somber and argent masses. In a thousand glimmers and undulances, the canvases give the unearthly compulsion of the wanderer's ineluctable objective; speak the song of the soul pressed forth again from the harbor and the city, a-plunge once more through

11

Port of New York

its own remote and icy element. The ineffably glamorous, unseen world swims near in the gentle regions, the
age-old oaks catching in their ivy-laden boughs slow-drift-
ing clouds, the harmonies of palest rose and cobweb gray.
It lies behind the mists flying through the azure night-
sky, lies behind the old windmill in the citron-colored
moonshine.

It comes as nocturne, heavy with the condition of light
under which it made itself manifest to Ryder's eyes. He
must have been a blinded man in the noon. The street
in the work-hours must have been to him merely a
noisome cavern underneath an elevated roadbed; a
jumble of hideous unbearable piles, a stamping ground
of agitated clowns; curbs littered with packing-cases and
lined with yawning drays; air rent with the clatter of
commerce and the shrilling of human throats calling,
cursing, beraying the universe. Only as the roughness
of hue faded from the walls of the city, only as the sky
grew soft over the Jersey bluffs, and the world became
a few lines and areas of soft color, and the moon shone
watery and potent over New York, did the plastic hour
arrive. For the evening and the night, with their stillness, their vagueness of outline, their lack of dimensions;
the moonlight, with its unreal day, delicate parody of the
world of the sun and the reason, were like the place which
his mind rejected but his bosom felt. The walls rising
ghostly and gray, the evening standing high over the
rooflines, set him once more in a world of honey-sweet

Albert P. Ryder

coloring, tenderer than the winds of a spring night in the deserted city streets, apple-scented, golden-lit, where the mountains stand soft and protective like huge mothers; and sent him musical with sentiment of a fate.

Unconscious self as well as conscious brought the seafarer. He is present in Ryder's art as basic form no less than as manifest content. The paintings have his secret passivity and stillness; groundplan of the soul that cannot become earthfast, and has to express itself in outer restlessness and motion. The hushfulness of the Ryders, their low vibrance, their freedom from intense and robust clashfulness, from contrapuntal movement, set them apart, give them a voice for dreamful moods. Color in the modern sense, as interplaying form, they have scarcely any. At best, they have tone, merely. There is something almost mysteriously still in them; they are a little like waiting women, their hands in their laps. The formal defects too of these moony canvases are characteristic of the state of life which brought them form. Something of fear of sudden experience, of constraint, speaks out of the state of the pigment. There is no fluency, no lightness, or mercuriality in it. It lies curiously cramped and unrelaxed, in little waves and ridges of enamel. Very Ctesiphons and Ecbatanas of brush strokes, cities underneath whose streets lie the walls of five or six buried cities, offer themselves to the eye within the frame of each Ryder. Disciples pretend the buried Ctesiphons are underpainting. They are too pious. Despite his poethood,

13

the man never learned to handle his medium fluently.
Fissures appeared in the surfaces even before the works
quit his room for the dealer's shop or the home of the
rare patron. Ryder used to wave a heated poker close to
the cracks; he had some theory to the effect that the red-
hot iron would heal them. But the fissures remained;
and multiply.

Sexual fear in particular speaks from the forms. It
was the sexual expression of the mechanism of resistance
to the present moment that kept the foregrounds comparatively empty, and gave interest preponderantly to the
middle and upper reaches of the canvases. If to the conscious mind of an artist his canvas is a rectangle of stuff
prepared for pigment; to the unconscious, it is the trunk
of a woman. The regions of the rectangle have a cor-
respondence to the regions of the flesh. The means of
communication is the application of paint; but the application of paint becomes to the unconscious a form of embrace. The canvas is brought to life through a marriage:
the full speech of body to body and soul to soul. The
works of Rubens and of Renoir, men born without fear
of life, fully fused in body and ghost; the works of
Cézanne, of Greco, of Rembrandt at his best, are convex
from the very base of the canvas, commence swelling with
form of large amount in the foreground. Forms tangle
and increase and develop, launch themselves from the
edge of the frame into the middle and backgrounds of
the paintings. The foreground may be a preluding. It

launches the picture nevertheless. In these men, the animal nature was fully spiritualized; the genitals contributed to the dream of beauty; and the portion of the canvas which corresponds most directly to the abdominal centers had no terror for them. They were under no compulsion to flee the complete surrender to the present moment. But Ryder could not bring his whole man into entire contact with the object. The upper, spiritual regions of the body were singing flesh to him. The lower he could not fit into his scheme of beauty. He was under the necessity of keeping a distance between the object of his interest and himself. The complete union, the complete seizure of the present moment, he did not wish to achieve. Hence, the dead areas in the surfaces he painted.

But the art of Ryder brings the voyage to a close. Others had stood with him upon his deck, and not seen the truth he saw. For Ryder was what the others about him in the close of the nineteenth and the commencement of the twentieth century were not, a poet. He worked from feeling. Life at length had brought forth in the west a painter able to work from what he perceived upon his eyelids when his eyes were shut. There was in him a sort of coördination of personality which the other painters, even the sturdiest among them, Homer, Martin, Fuller, wanted quite, or possessed in merely negligible degree. So strong was it that it permeated his very clothes, and made the coat and vest, the shirt and scarf he wore, the hat he bore around in his hand, curiously personal and expressive. And while the others, weak in imagination, remained dependent always on the material facts which started their vision, and once deprived of the view of them were at completest loss, Ryder's imagination operated, and let him work from the image in his brain. He could see with closed eyes what it was the night clouds which he studied wandering over roads and through streets, the greenwood, and the wistful New England hills made to occur in his blood. Hence, it was what lay between the objective world and himself which was deposited in opaque color by his brush. The mystic hues of sundown combined harmoniously with his own personality. The racks of mist chasing wildly through the illimitable icy seas of heaven moved at the dictation of his own spiritual rhythms. The white horse alone in the dim stall, the ashen-hued nymphs at the wood's edge gave again the beat of his nerves, the tingle of his blood. A state of inner being came to stand, rich and sumptuous and dreamy, among the other things.

In us, too, in the moment of perception, the Ryders create a sum. The realm of feeling into which they initiate us brings to a close a long cycle of wandering. We know these wild romantic sweeps, these cold and dreamy lights. Out of a picture-frame there comes an intimate address to the American in us; there comes something full of what lies between us and American life. Feelings hitherto heavy and confused in us are suddenly lifted out of us and off of us and placed outside us massively; and to

Albert P. Ryder

be an American and to have shared in the painful western adventure becomes a wonderful thing. In that moment a baleful spell, the Dutchman's baleful wandering spell, begins to snap, and black spars to settle into the sea. We may not know it; but the long prelude to the new world is over; the curtain is about to be rung up. With the painter of night we stand upon one of those faint lines where one world comes to an end, and another, newer, thrusts mysterious coasts up on the horizon. To-day, perhaps, still the oceanic waste, and flight under the inhuman, sorcerer's moon. To-morrow, the inhabited solid earth and the faces of men. It is we that have been moved.

Van Wyck Brooks

I

In the years flanking immediately the beginning of the great war, there commenced in America a stirring of long-shut eyelids. During that period, a vision began defining itself upon the retina of a critic second in pregnancy for the nation to scarcely another seen since Whitman died. In casting his glance out over the transcontinental span of the land, over all that had hitherto seemed to him no more than a bewildering jumble of gaudy and melancholy life, Van Wyck Brooks perceived the many opaque, irreconcilable facts suddenly possessed of transparency. Beneath the vast film of dreary, unformed objects and hordes of individuals out of many races and many conditions, there was patent the outline of a unit. Through the elephantine stretches of landscape, amid all the muddy grays, there ran a streak of definitely local color; and the unfused masses of inhabitants revealed somewhere in the states of their minds a common patch left by a common experience.

There had been no time for many years, it seems, during which Van Wyck Brooks had not been straining to read the face of the United States. A profound instinct appears to have impelled him to search it since ever he had become a reflective being, making him in a dim fashion aware that through the successful perception salvation was to be found. But a brief while after he had been graduated from Harvard; and whilst the majority of his classmates, like the majority of the classmates of all the world a year or two after commencement, was still dumbly feeling about in law schools and in brokerage offices for occupations even mildly interesting, as well as remunerative, he published *The Wine of the Puritans*, a dialogue on the subject of American civilization. And it is not difficult for us to recognize in this booklet of 1908, sadly tangled skein of silks although it is, the temper of the mind which, a few years older, was to give itself in all brightness in *America's Coming-of-Age*. As in the senior-year photograph of the author with which, from time to time, *Vanity Fair* regales our view, features of a slightly virginal jack-rabbit cast manage somehow to adumbrate the distinguished head of the future stiff little colonel of literature. Brooks, even at uncoördinated twenty-three, was already the type of the new sort of American man-of-letters. A scholar, cosmopolitan in point of view, read extensively in several European literatures, he was not at all averted from the American scene. He was familiar with Dresden, with Paris and London, not as tourists, but as residents, are; and still, he was perfectly aware that his fate and that of the rest of the people of the terrible, sprawling republic were in-

Van Wyck Brooks

extricably involved. He suffered from the third-rateness, the sogginess, the impotence of American civilization. The thousand meannesses upon fields and shores, upon hills and river-banks; the thousand scraggly industrial towns, the heavy, pompous and shabby dwellings, the decaying New England villages, billboard grins and railway gashes and soiled harbor furniture, depressed him to earth. The spectacle of the youth of a land concentrating its mind entirely in the carburetors of motor cars; the vision of a population traveling about Sunday afternoons in automobiles, and swallowing the scenery through their open mouths, seemed to him a collapse of very life. Nevertheless he was prepared to demand of recalcitrant America, upon her proper soil, the redemption of the formal pledges she had made him and the rest of her offspring.

Indeed, the paragraphs of *The Wine of the Puritans*, each of which appears to be setting out to traverse the universe by a different route, and to be doing everything but joining in a procession, contain in vague and embryonic form a number of the ideas developed unforgettably in Brooks' later writing, and destined, it seems, to occupy him persistently all his days. The dialogue marks the shadowiness, the pale other-worldliness, of classical American literature. The author stands an instant before Mark Twain and other American humorists, and hears amid the laughter the strident bitterness and ugliness. He is about to see that the new world has been

21

Port of New York

broken between the protagonists "Highbrow" and "Lowbrow," those publics of theory and of action infertile with one another. For Brooks was conversant with the cultural history of Europe. He knew for what it was that Lessing and Herder, Ruskin and Arnold, Brandes and Taine, each in his day and land, had battled; knew that they had fought every one for the purpose of making their compatriots recognize that all that man undertakes to produce, whether by action, by word, or in any other medium, ought to spring from a union of all of his faculties; and that productions springing from isolated faculties are, almost uniformly, worthless. Because of their effort, something of what had been seen from many a Patmos had permeated the societies of which these critics formed part; and something of what was playing in the common life had permeated into the cabinets of lonely thinkers and artists, and suffused with vital breath their work.

But in the new world, he knew, all intellectual culture floats a head severed of its body. The ideas produced by man during his career, carried through seven days of Atlantic damp, lose their virtue like tea exposed to the salt air. Received with a show of sincerity, they remain unapplied. If, as Brooks was later to phrase it, "in the American mind Nietzsche and A. C. Benson, the lion and the lamb, lie down quite peacefully together, chewing the cud of culture," it is merely for the reason that the American perceives in no writer the constructor

Van Wyck Brooks

of a platform of practical existence, and in every one merely a spinner of charming arabesques. And yet, though Brooks might be extremely discontented with the rôle assigned by American civilization to the life of ideas, no one else, certainly not the guardians of the great words which have reverberated through humanity on its march, appeared to be conscious of the transmogrification. His colleagues, professors and critics, saw no sea-change. Or, if they did, they accepted indifferently the situation, and continued feeding out the virtueless substance entrusted to them as though it were the very living herb.

If they did not, these perceptions, in the dawn of the career, become members of a single image; if no rhythm arose from the deep within Brooks and floated them on a single element, it was probably for the reason that in those years he was himself not as yet sufficiently integrated and balanced to express himself in an organism at once trunk and branch and flowering shoot. The three little works that succeeded his first, *The Malady of the Ideal*, *John Addington Symonds*, and *The World of H. G. Wells*, reveal the delicate temperament of Brooks in manful struggle against the academic limitation. He was indeed, in these books, making an effort to overcome his limitation by viewing himself objectively. If he was engaged in writing of Symonds and Amiel and "Obermann," he was also, in these types of half-poets, wistful and disinherited of the world, examining instances of spiritual maldevelopments kin to the maldevelopment which had claimed so many illustrious victims among the American artists. *The Malady of the Ideal*, the title bestowed by him on the booklet composed of the delicate essays on Amiel and Senancourt and Maurice de Guérin, was indeed the name of the wicked distemper which had wasted the minds of innumerable members of the American *intelligenzia*, and which might have been felt by the author dragging upon his own. It is the sickness of those who are captive to some shadowy unsubstantial ideal order and, while possessing little faith in the ideal which holds them, are nevertheless prevented by it from slaking their thirst for experience in the real substance of the world. But if these works show Brooks striving to transcend his limitation by objectifying it, they also show the solution still as yet a little beyond his power. An exquisite style smooths these writings; a singularly mature mind plays here; but the author shrinks from fastening a vital grip on the bowels of his subjects. He remains well outside Symonds. We never get a sense of the pulse of that feverish and unhappy life. Only a furtive page or two denotes that Brooks was even aware of the dreadful nervous disease which victimized Symonds; which filled his days with black and made it easier for him, in the phrase of Arthur Symons, "to write the history of the Renaissance than to write the history of his own soul." Even in the book on Wells, wherein Brooks, striking away from the careers of shy, strangely passive men, treats of a writer whom he admires precisely because he has

Van Wyck Brooks

bridged theory and action, we get no picturesque sense of
the battling personality whose expressions " 'the ideas of
H. G. Wells' " are. The strutting background of Ed-
wardian England against which these ideas were thrown,
is vaguely pictured only. Nor do we get a judgment on
Wells' novel-form. We are, on the contrary, given the
queer treat of seeing a writer who has been above all other
things a propagandist, handled in the manner and form of
a chill and orthodox thesis.

Only then, and after Brooks had completed this study,
had things moved sufficiently to permit him his integrated
vision of America. Perhaps, in some region of practical
living, he had shortly made a great whole-hearted choice.
Out of many divergent roads, he had singled out one in
the determination to follow it, and had commenced the
march. In being brought whole-heartedly into the state
of movement toward an ideal goal, a rich nature had been
pointed. Unto the apt scholarly pupil of the academic
culture-critics, young Renan to these new Jesuits, there
was joined a robust, humorous, stocky lowbrow. So Van
Wyck Brooks penetrated American life. There was clarity on his own life; there was clarity out on the continent
stretched before him. Those fellow-Americans, hitherto
so strange and remote and unknowable to him, were coming close. Ideas received from an hundred sources; from
Emerson, from Whitman, from Walter Lippmann, were
forming themselves in a new wedge. In all things, in
all people, he saw active to some degree the principle

which through three centuries of American existence had divided the world of ideas and the world of practice; the principle which more than any other had determined the headless, undistinguished thing known as civilization in the United States. Significantly, he called his picture *America's Coming-of-Age*.

II

The sense which dawned on Van Wyck Brooks in that hour of emergence was the sense that something had been almost universally refused things in America. In crass and dreary villages, in singed mountainsides and bleak milltowns, there was but a single voice; and that voice was shot with the pain and the pallor of starvation. Amid a profusion of natural wealth, immense fecund stretches of forested territory, river-avenues and rich-wombed mountain-chains and powerful warming suns, there was a gray poverty, like the poverty of some girl of round and mature form to whom an adult mind has not come. This rushing, iron stream ran hounded between its deformed banks. Men had hacked into the face of this noble purple-shining line of cliffs. Streets of brick and wooden houses were like offspring bastardized and disinherited and cast out from the paternal home. What had been bestowed upon every dingle and knoll of the English countryside, what made every poplar-guarded farm-enclosure of France roll fat as the sides of its nour-

ished munching kine, had been almost uniformly withheld this side the Atlantic. Here, everywhere, one heard
the testimony of disinherited things. It was to be heard
in the fag-ends of great cross-town thoroughfares, "ten-
tacles that lie there sluggish and prone in the dust, overtaken by a sort of palsy." The "crazy, weather-beaten
houses among the unkempt acres, the weed-choked gardens, and insect-ridden fruit-trees" of rural Long Island
repeated the burden. Out on the prairies, "in the con-
coction of corrugated iron and clapboards thrown together
beside a Western railway to fulfil some fierce evanescent
impulse of pioneering enterprise," it echoed a thousandth
time. "Old American things are old as nothing else anywhere in the world is old; old without majesty, old
without mellowness, old without pathos, just shabby and
bloodless and worn out." And from the folk which toiled
and hurried and died among these sad things, there came
the selfsame speech. To these loud, automobiling, vic-
trola-playing, successful people, farmers and townsfolk
alike, bankers and miners all, something that is in the
human power to give had never come and opened their
pores to the light and the green and the wind. A sort of
dense, sallow prisoning integument had formed upon their
flesh. They, too, had never known "a day of good growing weather."

The warmth of the human hand had been withheld.
Men had not used the soil as lovers use. Men in working
the soil had not thought of the future generations. Men

in touching materials had not touched them out of the secret need of coming to other men, of speaking and pouring forth something of which their heart was full, of uttering an everlasting "waas hael!" to the great living substance of life. Rathermore, they had come to the land with the purpose of getting out of it what they could for themselves. They had touched soil and trees and waters without thought of anything in the universe save themselves and the infinitesimal fraction of the race immediately sprung from their own loins. The imperial profusion was there to be used in any fashion in the business of getting immediate returns from it. It was to be raped, to be treated as a footstool, as a wretched slave; to be sacked as a captured city is sacked by freebooters. Or if it was to be held and given to, it was to be fenced off like a private domain, and made to utter to heaven the power and the eminence of its possessor. And what men had done to the soil they had, of course, done each other. Every one was there to be worked and milked by every one else of his substance. Life had one single purpose: that of giving as little and getting as much as one could.

There may have been need, in the first centuries of colonization, for fierce self-seeking. The individual had literally to fight his way to survive. The continent had to be claimed for habitation; swamps and wildernesses had to be turned arable. That day passed soon. Unfortunately, in the hour when material life was sure, when death through famine or at the hands of the red man was no longer to be feared, and culture and community should have taken possession of the new-swept house, the giving instinct was unable to erect itself. For there was no power in the new world to check the wild development of the purely acquisitive instinct roused in the settlers. In Europe, there had always been a King, in his person the symbol of both the material powers and the "free, non-acquisitive, creative conception of life." He was the father, the incarnate conception of life lived for the sake of a community, for the sake of the dead and of those to come as well as for the sake of the living. He was the overlord; and the land came from God through him to the tiller, and was to be handed back through him to God again. Whilst he was there, trade might indeed flourish. But trade would never dare set itself up as the end of life, as in America it finally did, the monstrous thing; and through the mouths of certain of the inspired prophets of Wall Street pretend it was philanthropy disguised; and, at Commencement time, stand up in its white piqué vest before a crowd of young boys ready to be sent into the world and have its puppets confer upon it, as savior of society, the highest academic honors. Whilst the King was there, art, ideas, religion, were the expression of life no less than trade and war. And where he was weak or dispossessed, there were still enough relics of a generous giving past to show the man, Ruskin or Morris or Péguy, what it was to give of himself. From cathedral spires and out of the forests of symphonies, from poems danced and poems spoken, from song and sonnet, harmonies of color and systems of thought, voices cried out incessantly the sweetness of giving; of giving, not for the sake of self-righteousness, but for the sake of increasing the capacity for giving; of taking, not for the sake of begetting stuffs, but for the sake of letting others learn to live.

Not only was the gracious model of a King, a court, an aristocracy wanting life in America. Not only was there no Gothic art to lift the heart out beyond itself; no nourished countryside to play gentle nurse to the trembling human soul and heal its wounds and urge it forth again to fresh attacks. There *was* present evangelical Protestantism. And that helped far more than it hindered the erection of the process of the accumulation of goods into the goal of individual existence. For evangelical Protestantism placed accent on personal lone salvation. It made men prone to forget that it was through the common life, that they lived; and that it was what lay between man and man, and not within each severally, that mattered most. It made men solitaries and egoists for their souls' good. "The white wooden houses (of New England), the farms, the patches of wood, the self-contained villages, each with its town-meeting, the politician, the minister, the lawyer, the merchant, were, in fact, very much what Emerson called his own sentences, 'infinitely repellent particles.' "

Besides, with its fear of earthiness, evangelical Protestantism made men to disregard and avert their love from the soil and the things that nourished their bodily life. It made them seek to live, not with the earth, but above it, away from it. It called them persistently to transcen-dental spheres. So Puritanism readily became, in a more profane century, the puritan's will to material power. The man averted from the giving life, the man trained to seek his soul's salvation alone without his fellows, and prevented from reveling in the abundance of earth, only too easily sought his body's salvation in battle joined against the rest of the world, and in total contempt and disregard of the rights of men and things to their exist-ences. What remained in such men of the old tribal good-will and community of spirit was lost when they cut off from their England, their Holland and Saxony. Even the Englishman's manner of giving, his sportsman-ship, could not maintain itself in such undisinterested minds. And no new fellowship could find in them a fertile ground. The arrival of settlers of less closely related blood made a community less a possibility, and the union of America, the fraternity of the republic, more shadowy still.

So business, which, when conceived merely as a social process, supplies the materials upon which evolved human life of course must base itself, became, since here it was uncontrolled by human values, incompatible with the per-sonal end of life: the fulfilment of personality. For it is the desire which finds far greater satisfaction in making the gift than in getting any material return that is the impulse which drives the individual to ever higher integrations of all his faculties, intellectual and volitional; and this desire is not the motor of business. Alone the life of expression, the disinterested existence conducted in faithfulness to the feelings, conjoins the faculties of action and of theory, and makes flower upon the human body a mind true and meet to its character. Giving alone builds cultures and cities for men. It takes the man of action outside himself and gives him vistas of the life of ideas. It takes the man of theory and shows him the empirical fact and makes his barren schemes turn into practical ideas.

Hence, under the regiment of business and of its apostles in pulpit and chair, there had appeared in America two types of a simplicity which Europe, for all her own split between the faculties of theory and action, does not know. There appeared the two types, the one exclusively theoretical, the other exclusively practical, the "Highbrow" and the "Lowbrow." The one is "a superior person whose virtue is admitted but felt to be an inept unpalatable virtue." The other is "a good fellow one readily takes to, but with a certain scorn for him and his works." This latter is the typical business man, "in practical affairs charged with an almost stupefying cynicism, energy, and capacity" (the words are quoted by Brooks from a letter of George Cabot Lodge's) "in every other respect a sentimental idiot possessing neither the interest, the capacity, nor the desire for even the most elementary processes of independent thought." He is Nietzsche's "slave." The former, meanwhile, is the typical university professor, cherishing ideals "precisely because they are ineffectual, because they are ineptly and mournfully beautiful, because they make one cynical, because they make life progressively uninteresting, because practically and in effect, they are illusions and frauds and infinitely charming lies." The one type, the man of action, "dedicates himself to the service of a private end which knows nothing of theory, which is most cynically contemptuous of ideals, flatulent or other," the other, the preponderantly intellectual, can become professor of economics in a college, and there "dedicate himself to the service of a type of economic theory that bears no relation to this wicked world at all, leaving all the good people who are managing the economic practice of society . . . to talk nonsense in the wilderness."

Between them, these two incomplete types had ridden and muddled American life. Two apparent opposites, they are indeed secretly in league to preserve in power their parent, the acquisitive instinct; secretly playing into each other's hands to prevent the arrival of the serene man of the world, combination and annihilation of them both. For Highbrow, in persisting in his ways, and refusing to enter the arena of action, has permitted Lowbrow to lord and lowbrow it there to his august pleasure. And the supremest instance of the curious subterranean alliance was the classical American literature of the nineteenth century. In Europe, a mighty literature of revolt against the tyranny of the industrial age and its bankers had sprung up. Tolstoy, Carlyle, Ruskin, Morris, had thundered against the meanly acquisitive life. Where literature was not directly polemical, literature nevertheless denounced the lies of society. But in America it had retired discreetly from the field into its tower of ivory. Or, rathermore, it had remained ignorant of practical life. "Two things," Schiller had taught, "are necessary for the poet and artist. He must rise above literal reality, and he must, nevertheless, remain within the sensuous. Where both these exigencies are fulfilled equally, there is esthetic art. But in an unfavorable and shapeless nature and society he (the artist) too readily abandons the sensuous along with the real and becomes idealistic, and, if his understanding is feeble, fantastic even; or, when he wishes, and is obliged by his nature to remain in the sensuous, he obstinately clings to the real and becomes realistic in the narrower sense of the word and even servile and vulgar if he wholly lacks imagination. In both cases he is not esthetic." Something of the sort happened to the American writers and deprived them, marvelously original as many of them were, of the principle of life. Into the second inesthetic category there went the journalists and the magazine people; into the first, the purer talents who have made our belles-lettres. Brooks said: "Their serious knowledge, their high accomplishment, their refined taste, were suspended in air, so to speak, deprived alike of the creative spark that lifts men above themselves and of the animal underproppings that maintain their contact with rude reality." They were limited unconsciously "to a sort of idealism whose essence lay in the very fact that it could have no connection with the practical conduct of life." Out of this all too unworldly refinement, there sprang the style of Emerson, "that strange, fine ventriloquism, that attenuated voice coming from a great distance, which so often strikes one as a continual falsetto. If it is extremely irritating,—if it is filled with assertions that fairly insist upon being contradicted, it is because so often Emerson is abstract at the wrong times and concrete at the wrong times, because he has so little natural sense of the relation between the abstract and the concrete." Out of it, there came the fiction of Poe, that "Byron without scope of action and without purging emotions," "perhaps of all writers who have lived the least connected with human experience. In his pages—crimes occur which do not reverberate in the human conscience, there is laughter which has no sound, there is weeping without tears, there is beauty without love, there is love without children, trees grow which bear no fruit, flowers which have no fragrance—it is a silent world, cold, blasted, moonstruck, sterile, a devil's heath." There came the talent of Hawthorne "like a phosphorescent pool; you touch it, you move your hand there, and a thousand subdued elusive lights dance through it, but before you can fix your eye upon one it has retreated through the clear water, the still depths that in effect are impenetrable. He models in mist as the Greeks model in marble; his beings take shape in the imagination with a sunlit perfection, but only for a moment; they melt and pass; the air is filled with a phantasmagorical movement of shapes, grouping themselves, putting on corporeality as a garment and at the same time dissolving into the nebulous background. If, like the greatest poets, he sees life as a fable, he feels it rather as a phantom than as a man. . . . Could anything be more exquisite? Could anything more entirely fail to connect with reality in a practical Yankee world?"

Here, then, in the very temple of the ideal, veiled business had its sovran shrine. Emerson and Rockefeller, Longfellow and Morgan, were all really the same man. The poets had "crooned to sleep the insatiable appetites of the soul." The business-men had seduced it into perverse ways. Life in America, deprived of leadership, prevented from taking the direction necessary to its health, had turned ugly, ugly in people, ugly in things. And Van Wyck Brooks, standing in its frothing center, could well be haunted by the thought that, whilst his fellow countrymen were congratulating themselves upon the inevitable grandiose destiny of their nation, the North American republic might indeed be proving itself one of the great globe's greatest failures.

Van Wyck Brooks

Yet American art had to show the consequences of one life, at the very least, lived in obedience to the promptings of the completed man. One poet, at the very least, had given himself disinterestedly to all things during the best of his years, and in that largesse of a great heart commenced for the country a middle tradition, "a tradition which effectively combines theory and action, a tradition which is just as fundamentally American as either flag-waving or money-grabbing." That poet was Walt Whitman. It was the genius of Whitman that he did not range himself in the idealist limbo with Emerson, Hawthorne, and Poe, and remained strictly within the sensuous while rising above literal reality. "Having all the ideas of New England, being himself saturated with Emersonianism, he came up on the other side with everything New England did not possess; quantities of rude emotion and a faculty of gathering human experience almost as great as that of the hero of the Odyssey. . . . Everything which had been separate, self-sufficient, incoördinate—action, theory, idealism, business—he cast into a crucible; and they emerged, harmonious and molten, in a fresh democratic ideal based upon the whole personality." With Whitman, then, for the first time, a great organic personality appears for American culture. A way of life is opened proper to the American, as Francis' or Nietzsche's or Dostoievsky's

37

were proper to their own fellows. With Whitman, indeed, it is the new world that really commences. Everything, objects held high and held base, appear laved and shining in new wonder. Whitman accepted more than his own body and its gross and delicate organs when he discarded the terms body and soul and called them one. In that sudden perception of all the elements of life, he embraced a world entire in his love; called nothing common or unclean, everything lovable; took away from everything the values man had placed upon them, or, rathermore, gave value to everything, and gave all a new start. It was indeed "salut au monde" that was called out through the cosmos. It was hail to every man, every woman, every prison, every sickness, every dunghill, every grave. Everything was again become a simple element of life, from which the American was to make a new combination for his new culture. Since form signified selection, Whitman discarded form; his form was a sort of vast fluidity, like nature herself, for he wanted to be nature. He wanted to be the base upon which the democratic character might rear itself in the shape of its proper spirit. He cleared the forest; he assembled the building-stones; and he called upon the future to erect the mighty pile.

Unfortunately, this middle, liberal, democratic tradition with its ideal of the self-development of different and even conflicting personalities had never cut its path through American nature. In a sense, the old Whitman

Van Wyck Brooks

himself had been renegade to the Whitman of the active prime of his life. "As he grew older," Brooks insists, "the sensuality of his nature led him astray in a vast satisfaction with material facts, before which he purred like a cat by a warm fire." His own disciples, in the way of all disciples, were too happy sunning themselves in this greatness to take the trouble to understand the veritable tendency of this life and carry it out into the world in the form of ideas. The social ideal posited by Gerald Stanley Lee, a convinced Whitmanite, is the very opposite of the personal, democratic, warm ideal of his master. His *Inspired Millionaires* is indeed a very "Apotheosis of the Lowbrow." It instances once again the highbrow's habitual making of the bed to "Krieg, Haendel, und Piraterei." Indeed, the entire epoch after the Civil War, instead of moving with Whitman, moved back from him. Then, if ever, the impersonal end of life dominated the scene. It was the full noon of the "Captain" of industry and his Achates, the muckraker. Pragmatism, the one force in American thought since the Spanish War, certainly did not bequeath men a deeper feeling and reverence for life, and render them humane and generous. Pragmatism had assumed the right to formulate the aims of life and the values by which those are to be tested. And this end, as formulated by John Dewey, was "social efficiency"! It had sought to establish as an ideal something which is not an ideal at all, but merely "a means toward the realization of human values." Its masterpiece

39

of character had been the sort of Walter Lippmann young man; fresh from the universities, a-burning with no greater desire than that Congress pass certain labor legislation before he die; and quite prepared to walk, in the name of a philosophy of adjustment, in any way taken by the crowd, whether it be the way of education or that of war. And Brooks demanded: "Has not the purpose, has not even the scope of social efficiency ever been determined by individuals who from time to time repudiate the social organism altogether and, rising themselves to a fresh level, drag mankind after them? Life proceeds not by burnishing up the existent ideals, but by the discovery of new and more vital ones, thanks to the imagination, which reaches out into the unknown whither the intelligence is able to follow only by a long second. Does not pragmatism therefore turn the natural order of things inside out when it accepts the intelligence instead of the imagination as the value-creating entity? It does, virtually if not absolutely, and in so doing crowds out and replaces the essential factor from which all dynamic creativity springs. It becomes, in a word, the dog in the manger of our creative life.—It makes its bed where the winged horse of poetry ought to lie."

At last, the light given Brooks fell upon a vacant spot amid the chaos of machines, buildings, men. Like Whitman before him, he saw upon what it was that this inert, jumbled, headless life waited. The need of American life was the poet. Men wanted above all the leadership of the man who could wake up in them the sense of the human needs and move them by means of it out of their old inhuman bad ways of living. "To be sure," he knew, "it is for the State to weed out the incentive to private gain," and strike from without at the mad acquisitive instinct. But socialization of the tools of industry alone could not transform society. The image of the business man had to be rejected from within. Only "a complicated scheme of ideal objectives, upheld by society at large," might force Young America to "submerge its liberties in its loyalties, and unite in the task of building up a civilization." And none but a poet could find those ideals germane to this people, and set all men moving out toward each other, out toward life, out toward the beloved community. For none other than the poet is the rhythm-beater of human life. It is he creates the outline of objects which magically compel the human will. A poet's phrase, a picture of a hero, of a superman, of a saint, will suddenly hang above men like a red star in the sky, and men's lives will find direction mysteriously, and move almost unconsciously toward a single ideal point. Virgil pictures a legendary man, in the grace of piety and candor, full of premonitions of the imperial grandeur of his colony; and decades after his death, a line of emperors, each more like the pious Æneas than even his predecessor, creates the age of Trajan and the Antonines and gives the world one of its high great breathing-times. An unhappy exile from a murderous Italian city writes in a sort

of vulgar tongue, almost a *patois*, a poem full of hatred
of Italians and love of Italy. And, hundreds of years
after his death, despite the Empire and Spain, Austria,
the Papacy, and the house of Bourbon, men who can
scarcely understand one another, and have almost never
recognized their commonalty save in the tercets of Dante,
are ripe for Cavour and Victor Emmanuel and ready to
take each other by the hand. It is the poet alone who can
bring all the faculties of life moving together and pro-
cure for life that all-pervasive style that is the condition
of civilization. It is the poet alone who can make society
take the shape which can satisfy the human soul. It is
the poet alone who can end the schism in American men;
can turn American life toward personal ends, and develop
out of an anarchical competitive horde a community of
men who give and enrich themselves in giving.

But if the poet was the one to produce a revolution in
American life, almost a revolution in life would have to
produce the poet. Anything resembling the operation
Brooks demanded would, under present conditions, be incomparably difficult of performance. It would resemble
most the business of "standing on clouds and attempting
to gain purchase for a lever." The man would be obliged,
before it would be possible for him to create, to create the
very will to his art. His first work would of needs be
the titanic work, himself. Still, Brooks saw upon the gray
continent signs indicating that the deed of the poet might
not remain impossible of performance during the next

century of American life. Life itself was slowly veer-
ing. The impersonal end of life was losing its com-
pulsive might through the situation in which the business
world found itself. The morn of fierce pioneer enterprise
was past. Long since, the nation had touched its geo-
graphical confines; it was in the process of touching its
economic. The career of a million dollars, therefore, no
longer offered golden fruit to every mouth. Besides,
many lips were rejecting it of instinct. The horde of
vague, fumbling, restless young intellects about him on
many sides was testimony enough. And perhaps, like
Hofmannsthal, some evening as his commuter train passed
another crowded with people, men and women, each seized
in great, outspread, soiled, butterfly-like newspapers,
Brooks fancied that these readers of vile literature were
in truth unconsciously, somnambulantly, searching for
their great modern poet. A call might start him. A call
might create the sense of need, and influence the answer.
In this faith, Brooks turned to the high solemn business
of summoning to leadership the man of letters.

IV

The young man who now came forward carrying the
two slender books, *America's Coming-of-Age* and *Letters
and Leadership*, which represented his discoveries, had
done a critic's work more important than any done by an
American of his time; perhaps as important as any per-

formed by an American since the foundation of the country. It was not primarily his defense of the calling of literature, the overt point of his work, that made him a place immediately beside that of the author of *Collect*. It is not the consciously undertaken erection of values. What assigns to Van Wyck Brooks to-day a sort of premiership among living American critics is the circumstance that, in the process of painting the picture of the situation which renders imperative the appearance of the poet, and in the act of attempting to create a conscience of the necessity of literature in order that it, in turn, might force invention, he drew for America the outline of its past; and gave it something of the sense which life requires so that it can advance. To every individual, maturity, the power of giving, comes in part through his ability to judge objectively his forebears. Dispassionate sight of one's ancestry inevitably accompanies dawning self-sufficiency and the power of self-fulfilment. The individual is able to see the truth about his descent. The moment of knowledge rejects authority and marries him to his own individuality. The undeveloped, directionless state of American society had caused it to romanticize its past in the manner in which impotent persons romanticize their parents. Being incapable of inward motion, it either yearned helplessly backward to the conditions of its own infancy or yearned helplessly forward to other conditions; and its emotions created two equally distorted and contradictory pictures of the facts.

Van Wyck Brooks

Brooks, therefore, by enabling it to perform with something of ease the act of judgment upon and reconciliation with its very past, has given American society an opportunity of moving to maturer planes. Like the prudent farmer, he places a little pole by the side of the budding lima, giving it the opportunity to grow strong, if grow at all it can. What he has written of Highbrow and Lowbrow is nothing else than critical history. If he has not made a detailed picture of events, he has nevertheless permitted us to glimpse the inner lives of those who assisted in making the events. He has pointed to and laid bare the motive underlying the incomplete husbandry, the incomplete poetry of America; and in so doing he has made it possible for every living American to feel his way back again into the past of the land that nourishes him. The motive, the impersonal ground-swell, persists in every human being American born. It persists in the descendants of the settlers of the nineteenth century as well as in the descendants of those of the seventeenth. Nay, it persists in the immigrant of ten years since. It is the condition of desire of those who quit an old community and do not succeed in taking other hands and establishing a new. For an entire population, therefore, Brooks has begun the creation of an "usable past." There is no one now who cannot feel in himself the men, farmers, house-builders, railroad-lawyers, sea-captains, merchants, who lived upon this ground before himself. But an hour since, they were more remote and inexplicable to him than were the peasants of France, the knights of Germany. Now, they can come very near, be as plain as the men in overalls down on the street. They are, he can see, very like this person known a few years ago or like himself when he went to public school. They are himself only ten, twenty, an hundred years earlier born; himself as he might have been had not the time-spirit given his clay the little original twist given that of all his generation.

As yet, it is too early to foretell the ultimate range of influence destined the ideas of Van Wyck Brooks. But if it be legitimate to draw inferences from the life given by them during the first five years of publicity, then we may expect for them indeed a bright career. The two volumes in which they are exposed have had a quite appreciable influence on the new American literature and been carried by it further into the common consciousness. One dawning poet, Sherwood Anderson, coming in numbers of *The Seven Arts* upon the essays which were later revised and published as the book, *Letters and Leadership*, found deep, as yet scarcely articulated beliefs of his own about American life corroborated in them; felt himself sped upon his course as an artist by the critic. But it was upon an entire group of fellow-critics that they descended with the releasing might of the truth; and kindled in these brains responses which have augmented the initial accomplishment of Brooks with work of similar tendency and scarcely smaller importance. Much of Randolph

Van Wyck Brooks

Bourne's ironic rejection of the pragmatists, many of the apocalyptical plunges of *Our America,* much of the appreciation of American art done by other critics, are movements made through the door opened by Brooks when he organized for American literature the ancient and honorable manner of criticism popularly associated with the name of Taine, who had it of Winckelmann and Herder, who had it of Montesquieu. To be sure, the critics of the *Seven Arts* group, long before they encountered his mind, had been re-oriented by the new Freudian psychology to the social and subconscious background of art. Beside the general enthusiasm, the sense of the common existence, the desire for communion in American culture, which existed throughout the membership of the young group, there existed a common awareness of the unity of the phenomena of the pioneersman and of the American art of the past and transcendentalism and pragmatism. Moreover, before the publication of *America's Coming-of-Age,* critics in the country other than the *Seven Arts* men had been perfectly aware that every original work of art is to a great degree the evolutionary product of social conditions, deriving many of its characteristics from climate, national character, national manners, politics, and religion, and that in attempting to apply to American works the method of criticism which de Gourmont has declared the sole practicable, "le renouvellement des motifs," it was their privilege to examine these factors and other subconscious ones. But no critic before Brooks

47

had had the depth of insight into the nature of American life and of human life in general, the erudition, the sense of the function of art, and the knowledge of psychological theory necessary to one attempting this method. Hence it was left him to show how the relief of existing forces, from want of which American letters had gone so lame, might be created by the practice of this manner of criticism.

Therefore, a profound corroboration came to the members of the nascent *Seven Arts* group after a hint had led them to a new book called *America's Coming-of-Age*. And when, finally, Brooks himself with his simple Harvard blandness, his smile like a pleased savage's, his cockscomb of hair, his abrupt pumping handshake and his watchchain depending from the lapel of his miraculously precise and well-pressed coat, walked into the office of the infant magazine and joined in the conversation, he brought in the guise of his solid knowledge of the American background, his long-refined ideas, his piercing insight into the national temper, some of the fattest kernels poured for the common good into that busily grinding mill. With him came the philosophical and intellectual basis of the movement, the analytical scheme of the past. True, upon the base laid down by Brooks, the others have builded in many instances more boldly than he himself has done. There was even in these years an occasional evasiveness in his writing, keen, pointed, and sparkling though, almost invariably, it was. Francis Hackett has seen fit to dignify this trait with the name of Greek chastity. One wonders whether it does not resemble something a trifle more prim and shrinking than was the antique *ascêsis*. Ideas seem to come to the man in magical plentifulness. Out of a welter of apparently insignificant facts, he manages inevitably to extract one supremely to his purpose. But, from time to time, something incapacitates him for the act of warm, throbbing, immense capture. In attempting to systematize his thinking, one is oftentimes forced to indicate basic relations which we see implied, but not really discovered. Bourne, Frank, and others in several instances pushed further than Brooks in the very veins divined and marked out for exploration by him. And still they owe to him the immeasurable debt owed by all men to the intrepid pioneer.

v

The two small volumes with which Brooks opened his career contain to this very day the major portion of his achievement. In most of what he has written since, life does not course with like vigor, nor America move with like vivacity. Some work of high quality he has been doing. The introduction to the edition of Randolph Bourne's essays, called *The History of a Literary Radical,* despite a complete absence of any remark of the significance of Bourne's unflagging opposition to the war morale, certainly as great a proof of the purity of his instinct as any given by him during his short life, remains well-nigh the warmest, tenderest, most distinguished piece of writing Brooks has done. *The Ordeal of Mark Twain*, in spite of the strabismic vision at the base of it, contains pictures and comments deprived of which American history would be very much thinner. From time to time a keen and happy post-mortem of some exploded American reputation appears in *The Freeman* beneath the caption under which for the last two years Brooks has been publishing articles weekly. Capital execution also has been done upon the hordes of Philistia led by Professor Sherman, Max Eastman, and attended by the shade of Hamilton Wright Mabie. The *James* promises much.

And Brooks remains one of the important figures in present American civilization. There is scarcely a writer in whom finer, steelier materials lie waiting assemblage. The man has in him a noblesse, a distinction, a largeness of spirit, that comes over one with all the refreshment of the deep blue after muggy skies, of hill-stream water after scalding noon. For many men there must ring a moment of faith in American life when first this spirit speaks to them. An exquisite literary gift is present in the man always; one feels the delicacy of Hawthorne and Howells sprung anew.

But if he is present among us, it is in temporarily diminished figure. He is present in the world of books as the electric current sometimes is present in the light-bulbs of the day-coaches on the New York, New Haven, and Hartford Railroad. Every one who has had occasion to do any

Van Wyck Brooks

traveling by night on the line between New York and Boston has had the experience of seating himself in a brightly lit coach, only to find a few minutes later that the illumination has suddenly grown feeble. Within the bulbs the wires are still aglow; one can see the other passengers and the aisle. But the page one had been reading has grown gray, and deciphering the letters has become strainful to the eye. Juice has been withdrawn. So it stands with the importance of Brooks. The courage of the artist is not as active. The importance of every living worker flows ever to some degree from out the potentiality of development felt in him. And for the moment one does not feel in him as great a potentiality as one did a few years since, even though one looks forward with quick interest to the series of studies of American authors, Henry James, Hawthorne, Melville, Henry Adams, which he is like to produce. For there is no doubt that for the last few years he has, like Sandburg, too, been running with diminished candle-power. One has to do no more than examine his prosemanship to be sure of it. His writing is no longer as full of delicious sharp little etchings of the American scene as it was. It is no longer full of apposite images of authors drawn from real contact with their work. Brooks does not seem to be in touch with his subject as he was when he wrote the acute and sparkling little essays on Poe, on Lowell, on Longfellow, and the rest of "Our Poets." Elegant his style remains. He retains a capacity for light formulation and nimbleness of statement that is almost French. But, while the writing of *America's Coming-of-Age* is like a blue wire a-glitter with buzzing igniting electricity, that of *Letters and Leadership*, although still hard and elegant, wants the dance, the irrepressible joviality, the continual transmutation of prose into a sort of gay music, which the former has. *The Ordeal of Mark Twain* is gray cold wire which at times rasps. With what glee would we not exchange the slight exasperation, querulousness, and stiffness of some of the last pieces for the sport of the old pert sprite pricking up his pointed ears!

It seems that Brooks is playing safe with life. No doubt events not at all under his control have been unfriendly to him. The death of Randolph Bourne, for one thing alone, has deprived him of a powerful stimulus. The little soldier of liberty was the best of foils for the somewhat diffident scholar. If Bourne got from Brooks the ideal companionship he craved so much, he also gave in return some of his own ebullient revolutionary spirit. But it is questionable whether this or other misfortunes would have been as influential as they have been, were there not in Brooks himself some desire to relapse into passivity, which has taken advantage of the difficult situation to put itself through. It is to some such inward state that we must ascribe the not very invigorating work performed by him these latter years. Inward motion was the state which made his mind creative. Out of the performance of some great whole-hearted choice among the

Van Wyck Brooks

ways of life, there had come the shining, vivid writer of *America's Coming-of-Age*. Through that movement had come to Brooks the magical power of giving life to others and bringing them, too, into motion.

The step taken was a commencement. Brooks had come out from behind the skirts of the public. The vision of the poverty of the country constituted a break with the mass of people whose manner of life affirmed that poverty. He had opposed to the folkways the standard of the humanistic life. It was needful that he continue to affirm that standard by making it visible in his own spiritual manner, by living boldly, dangerously, in the fashion of the artist, by giving himself to life as men in America had never dared give themselves. But it seems that for some reason he has shrunk from continuing the challenge. For some reason he has wanted the world to stand still, to eternalize the moment in which he had himself come of age, and make it valid for the remainder of his life.

The a-prioristic theories which he has lately been seeking to make his subject-matter substantiate recall the representations formed by those who are seeking to avoid making a choice and are therefore divided against themselves. It is regular with folk who are seeking to evade the necessity of some preference that they tend to project the blame for their own confusion onto forces completely external to their own egos, and at the same time tend to acquit themselves of the necessity of effort by representing themselves the possessors of some sort of virtue which entitles them to having everything done for them. Now, since the time of the writing of *The Ordeal of Mark Twain*, Brooks has no longer been affirming that America has been getting the sort of artists expressive of her condition. On the contrary, he has fallen into a fantastic dualism of an hostile environment and a victimized "creative impulse." Lohengrin, he avers, inevitably falls victim to Telramund. Just how it happens that the impulse, which we call creative because it *can*, in America comes to inevitable defeat,—that, Brooks does not try to explain. He wishes to believe that America produces men who, if they had issued into a different world, would have become Swifts and Rabelaises, but who, since they are born in America, become not brothers to the great satirists, but fall into comparative failure. And since he wishes to believe this thing, he is no longer content to let his subject-matter speak for itself, as once he was, and to establish his theory on the base of the empirical fact. No, rathermore, he comes to his subject-matter with the intention of making it prove his theory and justify his unconscious wish.

The violent substantiation of this a-prioristic theory to which he forced his material, spoils the book on Clemens, brilliant as much of the analysis is. It is, after all, not the business of the critic to force the facts to justify him in his beliefs. His beliefs may be perfectly rational; nevertheless, it remains his business to permit the evidence to speak for itself, as much as he can make it, and then adjust

Van Wyck Brooks

his theory to the result obtained by analysis. But Brooks has not let the facts speak. For he has made certain assumptions of fact that are fairly illegitimate. He has assumed that the man Samuel Clemens was a failure because he ought to have been something other than what he was; that under different circumstances he might have been a satirist of the grandeur of the authors of Gulliver and Pantagruel. Now, Brooks may possibly be right. But in our present state of ignorance of what constitutes the environment and what the individual; of what the new-born child brings into the world along with him, and of what he actually finds there, the matter remains shadowy and far too doubtful to be adjudicable. Besides, Brooks furnishes no real proof that something in the guise of his mother, his environment, his wife, the Reverend Twitchell, and William Dean Howells did indeed prevent Clemens from achieving his destiny and made a "failure" of what could have been a world-figure. The experiences which Brooks has considered decisively ruinous to the great things Twain might, or should, or would have been, are not at all experiences exquisitely peculiar to Samuel Clemens or to men who fail. There have been few boys whose mothers have not, unfortunately, attempted to do to them the stupidly repressive things Mrs. Clemens the elder did to the boy Sam. There have been many artists who have lived for a while in atmospheres as raw and as destructive as that of Twain's mining camp days; there is little in Brooks' description of that life

which distinguishes it much from the *milieu* found in the
average barracks or in army cantonments. Nor is there
evidence at hand to disprove the fact that Anne Hatha-
way, Christiane Vulpius, and Madame Hanska were
very different in mind from Mrs. Clemens the younger.
Shakespeare and Rabelais both had opportunity to deal
with Reverend Twitchells; had they not, the one could
not have drawn a Dogberry, the other consigned with so
much glee certain "pilgrims" to be eaten by Gargantua in
a salad. No; what remains curious is the fact that
Clemens should have permitted these people and situa-
tions to mould him as they did. There really lies the
problem. But recognition of this as the problem would
have made it impossible for Brooks to represent the career
of the man as a stream ruinously diverted by forces out
of his control. And so he never squarely faced it.

This is not the only side on which Brooks, in his eagerness to make the facts substantiate his perverse thesis, re-
fuses to see the object as it really is. Throughout the
book we find him, like the district attorney eager to con-
vince of crime, stressing only the evidence favorable to
the prosecution. He is not fair to Twain. To prove
him a defeated man, he scarcely allows that the man
wrote any splendid stuff. It is his failures that are dwelt
upon. With almost cruel joy Brooks notes every indication of suffering and humiliation and despair in the
mental life of his subject. He seems at times to be beating the man for his weaknesses, even though ostensibly

Van Wyck Brooks

he has declared him the victim of an unfavorable environment. It might seem Twain had done him a personal wrong, and he were taking his revenge. But by Huck Finn he passes rapidly and never laughs a laugh over the fun, or notes the moments when Clemens wrote in something approximating the grand manner. For had he permitted himself to do so, while demonstrating the third-rateness of the civilization in which these things were achieved, there could have been no talk of defeat. Twain would have seemed thrice the marvel.

There is another fact which leads us, like this last, to the conclusion that Brooks is no longer in intuitive relationship with things. And that is that he has not put in his appearance on the critical battle-line where he has been sorely wanted. He has not joined in the business which he himself often declared almost primarily the critic's. In his arraignment of the "humanists" and other critics of the middle generation in *Letters and Leadership*, he asserted some of "the predicament of the younger generation in America" to be "due to the fact that interest, in short mere friendly interest, for severe interest we cannot expect, is the last boon these writers (More, Babbitt, Spingarn, Sherman, etc.) yield it. Since the days when Socrates sat in the market-place and played the midwife to so many inarticulate minds, it has been the joyous prerogative of criticism to be on the spot when thoughts are being born. . . . In America of to-day an immense amount of creative energy has at last conclusively turned itself

57

toward the field of the arts. If it does not in many instances come rightly and fully to a head, if it fails very often to eventuate in thoughts in themselves vitally important, does it not all the more behoove criticism to condense the vapors that confuse this creative energy and to spring loyally to the support of groping minds that bear the mark of sincerity and promise?" But in all the three years of his editorial office on *The Freeman*, is it more than a very few times that we have seen Brooks himself, now that he, too, and the rest of the *Seven Arts* crowd have become of the middle generation, "springing loyally to the support of groping minds that bear the mark of sincerity and promise"? He has his weekly "Reviewer's Note-book" column; it would enable him to see to it at least that the "groping minds which bear the mark of sincerity and promise" get the criticism they so sorely require. For of criticism there is a need in this country which increases with every year. The greater portion of what passes for such is the mutual scratching of the backs of novelists and poets and the log-rolling of colyumists for publishing houses.

To be sure, Brooks has defended in his column the "creative impulse." He has trounced Sherman and Eastman for manœuvering to shatter the younger writers' trust in their feelings. He has pointed out oftentimes in what manner so many of the American authors of the late nineteenth century met shipwreck. Many of his papers contain very just ideas bearing in on the literary history

Van Wyck Brooks

of America. But very few of the new talents have benefited directly by Brooks' criticism—have gotten his attention personally. The new writers who have awakened
his interest have been chiefly English and Scotch reviewers
and Brazilian novelists. Even when, as in the article
contributed to *Civilization in the United States,* he dis-
cusses *The Literary Life,* there is nothing in the article
which is really to-day, nothing which envisages the conditions under which the men are working at this hour.
He is writing, for all his apparent modernity, his use of
psychoanalytical terminology, of the world of fifty years
ago, under the impression that that is the world of to-day;
even then, not seeing it quite straight, either. As in the
book on Clemens, he is shooting with loaded dice. So,
in his perpetual absenteeship, he calls to mind, from time
to time, the image of a planter who does something to pro-
tect his seeds from the birds which would gobble them
up; but when the plants commence to sprout and the
garden requires constant weeding and hoeing and watering, spends his entire time expounding with great blandness just what were the causes of the failure of last year's
crop and seems to perceive in the far horizon clouds,
mines of invaluable wisdom.

Through the recent failure to see as clearly as he
used, therefore, it has come to pass that Brooks temporarily constitutes toward us something which at many
moments resembles nothing quite as closely as the unfriendly environment which he has felt opposing him and

every other creative American. He exhibits the very want of sympathy for art and the artistic life of which he accuses society. In his effort to lay blame on some one or other for the non-appearance of great commanding, poetical figures, he comes near denying the heroic element which lies at the base of all creative power, and which constitutes its worshipfulness. In drawing an exaggerated picture of the obstacles which surround the aggressive, militant life in America; in externalizing numerous problems which are truly internal, he is really offering plenary indulgence to everything in the living which would collapse into passivity and non-resistance. He is unjust to the memory of many artists. For he belittles their figures by dwelling far more on what they have failed to do than on what they have accomplished. It is Whitman's later invalidism and his absurdities that we find most often pictured by Brooks till we are nigh forgetting, listening to him, that Whitman was the greatest singer produced by the modern world. It is more the fact that Henry Adams published anonymously his novels, and less the fact that he wrote them and wrote his autobiography and his other books, that is stressed. So, too, the later evaporation of Melville's talent; and not *Moby Dick*. Masters, Frost, and Robinson are cited to prove that "in the West as in the East, the individual as a spiritual unit invariably suffers defeat"; but of the miracle that in such a land and such a civilization anything as good as the writings of these men should have come to pass, no

Van Wyck Brooks

mention is made. With all his apparent enthusiasm for the artist, he does not appear vitally interested in art when it appears. He leaves the younglings to the mercies of their own numbers.

It is in vain that he seeks to influence American life by crying from time to time, in tones which recall the white-banded nonconformist minister exhorting his congregation of sinners, "Writers of America, ask yourselves whether the hour has not come to put away childish things and walk the stage as poets do!" It is in vain that he stands before America admonishing her like a modern Hamlet his guilty mother; accusing her of having been privy to the murder of the creative impulse, and of having espoused the assassin; comparing the two to the advantage of the former, "a station like the herald Mercury," etc.; and at last warning her, "Go not to mine uncle's bed!" It is in vain that he breaks into decorous jeremiads: "Weeds and wild flowers! Weeds without fragrance and wild flowers that cannot stand the heat of the day!" The development of artists is not achieved through exhortation. Like the giving of life, is it not done through preaching. The career of the artist is made easier in America by every one in America who is an artist, by every one who with ever greater fidelity sees life as it truly is. Where that seeing is not present, all preachment deteriorates imperceptibly into an insidious communication of the old inherited poison.

Port of New York

As we look on Brooks, we, too, perceive a dualism. We perceive two images, each trying to superimpose itself upon the other, and neither decisively succeeding. The one is the image of a young man stepping out of a gaunt, dour house into a luminous dawn. Like Herder, like Ruskin and Arnold, out of the houses in which herded the barbarous unshapen members of their races, this youth steps out of the dry, the coarse, the wooden-nutmeg world of genteel America. He carries in his spirit the traits of his folk made delicate and firm and fine. For he is the child these people have been carrying among them many, many years; and he is merely fulfilling the civilized impulse half-asleep those many years in their veins as he strides from among them out into the world of which they are afeared. And as he advances, irradiated by faith in this new generous way of life he is going, he turns a last time and calls them to go with him along the new, sweet path he is treading.

The other is the image of a young man, a little older. But the aristocratic head is set upon a body inchoate and unleavened with sedentariness. There is a monumental, an almost uncontrollable wish to sit, in this body. In this picture, too, there is a house. The windows of this house are closed. Upon certain ones the shutters are shut; in others, the shades are drawn. It is a prim, pretty, but strangely introverted dwelling, turned in on itself away

Van Wyck Brooks

from the street. And the young man is not coming out through the door. The door is shut; behind it, inside, he sits most of the time. Life drives up one morning in the shape of a lovely visitor and lifts the knocker and sends her merry summons. The young man seems to hear; and yet he does not rise to let the lovely caller in. Or, worse still, he does not hear the knock.

Of these two images, one must eventually come the more to resemble the career of Van Wyck Brooks. It is yet too soon to fall to guessing into which of the two patterns his mind will definitely settle. Both remain distinct possibilities; and *James* may show the winner. This much is sure, the one destined to absorb the other will be widely seen. The man has brought a great freshening, and he is already a small classic. And yet, the dominance of the sitting position would mean defeat. It would be a great defeat for all America. The land has no need intenser than the need of men who see justly, men who go the artist's personal, passionate, disinterested way. How great the need no one knows better than the man who has succeeded in teaching us to recognize and not forget its primacy.

Carl Sandburg

EVEN when his jaw hangs loose and he shovels 'em under at Austerlitz, goddams the grinning kings and kaisers and czars, and guffaws something which goes great at lawyers' assemblages, we love Carl Sandburg. We love him because he is himself the lover, taking his chance with life. The very quarter-formed verses cluttering the pages of *Smoke and Steel* make us in some fashion to see him the man whose breast is ever welling with stuff he has half playfully, half impassionedly, to give out away from himself to things. He is never so bleary that he lets us quite forget the great hours when he has taken it in lavish scoopfuls and put it under and about and above the cursed black tools of pioneer enterprise, the dreary objects amid which we dwell, and created out of the inanimate steel and loveless dirt the living thing America. Us they warn off the land, stripped stark hills, railway cuts, mounds of slag, sinister outposts of the encamped enemy; fill us with malaise and with restlessness. All that prevents us from embracing the earth we subsist on gathers about them and fortifies itself inside them as in bastions. We cannot circumvent these brutes. Sandburg, however, has been making us to be at home here in the west, and let down upon the soil the tents of our inwards. What Whitman was about in the Manhattan of the Civil War era: burning the mists off the befogged land, permitting the grim and homely objects to come into him and fuse with him there; that, Sandburg has been doing in his Chicago of the new century. He has been laughingly, extravagantly daring Fafner in his den; feeling life through smokebanks and silos and gashed palisades; feeling through them the elemental human chewing with teeth, stamping with hoofs on the ground, twisting ore into iron bars and zooming steel. And we, because of that feeling, penetration, mingling, dare, in turn, approach these harsh forbidding things. Because a man has experienced through them, their destructiveness has begun to go. The stuff gaily poured about and into them by the poet has softened their hard sides.

Through Sandburg, as largely as through any living human being, the map of the central States begins to have some of the cloudy mysterious poetry, the immanent romance, it had in the eighteen-twenties and -thirties. The continental chart begins to show faintly colored spots. Names like Omaha and Medicine Hat and Kenosha, homely flat-ringing names, begin to sound more richly, more delicately, through him. It will not be alone the words Milano, Brescia, Vicenza, Padova, Venezia, that will in the future inscribe poems on railroad trainsides. Sandburg has been feeling wonder and song in the towns of the middle border, where winging beauty

Carl Sandburg

never before was felt. The man respects and loves sincerely the rocks and rills and woods which Americans have always dimly wished to respect and love and not to exploit; known they needed to, and never quite come to love and be good to. Names of homely, dun places fill him with exquisite reverberations. The sense that a mystery is about to be unveiled upon American ground has, strangely, returned on him again. He perceives resting upon the ravished countryside the unearthly light of the future. Verses come:

> Here the water went down, the icebergs slid with gravel, the gaps and the valleys hissed, and the black loam came and the yellow sandy loam.
> Here between the sheds of the Rocky Mountains and the Appalachians, here now a morning star fixes a fire sign over the timber claims and cow pastures, the corn belt, the cotton belt, the cattle ranches.
> Here the gray geese go five hundred miles and back with a wind under their wings honking the cry for a new home.
> Here I know I will hanker after nothing so much as one more sunrise or a sky moon of fire doubled to a river moon of water.

And we feel roots beneath us in the soil suddenly; feel the tie ineluctably come to be between us and this new world earth. And we know, suddenly, madly, ridently, that we are glad to be here in the west; know full with power that here where white man has never yet lived himself all out we can live and live ourselves to the full. Through the rifts stabbed momentarily by this man in the dense pervasive fog we, too, glimpse faintly, dizzily, something that we would go and kneel down upon: hard, cheap, untilled, American soil that is nothing other than holy land.

Sandburg is adjusted, relaxed to his raw Chicago, his sad wild America. A stanza—

> The prairie sings to me in the forenoon, and I know in the night I rest easy in the prairie arms, on the prairie heart

—speaks the achieved fear-freed man; smiles the fulfilment of body and psyche amid this metallic landscape of industrialism; marks life flowing into him stilly unbeknownst like waters into a reservoir by night, filling him unbesought with wet. He has been "born on the prairie." The most of us here in America are merely foaled. We drift aimlessly in the currents of air that circle the globe; strain away to some otherwhere. But for Sandburg, the magnetic pole of life has situated itself in mid-America. He does not see, as most of us see, the old world while standing upon the shores of the new. The sun strikes the Mississippi valley directly in his gaze. The Mississippi valley is always for him the space atop the globe. The globe does not roll over and show him Sweden or Tahiti. For him it stands still: prairies running east to the Appalachians and west to the Rockies, the Windy City in the midst fixed adamantine like Jerusalem. He

Carl Sandburg

does not have to travel back to Europe to feel his root-fastness. He knows it here, amid the very inhuman pressure of Chicago; knows that his quick has contacted the earth from which all man strength springs; feels the great kindness which the woman power in the soil, the male power in the erections upon it, have had for him and have for him still. This is the miracle of his days; gift of the most lenient gods. Once he was a homeless man; son of immigrant Swedish day-laborers; heavy with old resentments and old blood-guiltiness; a fierce sensitive lad among fields and belongings which wouldn't own him, among buildings too high for his human tallness; trying to find a way to have it all become one with him; soldiering in the Spanish war, going to jail in Pittsburgh; becoming newspaper man on labor in Milwaukee; becoming secretary to the socialist mayor; getting facts for newspapers about strikes, murders, conferences. The feeling of life arrived and stored in him must have come about gradually at first; ephemerally for long; elusively perhaps some evening for an instant on a breakwater over Lake Michigan, or on some late night car, or at a touch of ember in the November sundown. Till finally something rough and tall and slugging as the skyscrapers themselves made itself plain within; something quite as high as these brutal thrusts of masonry, able to hold them back and laugh at them for cubs and make them laugh back, unwillingly. And then, an empire, spreading its breadth, must have lain inside wide as the prairie itself, containing

Port of New York

within the thrust of its borders rivers and wheat-lands, snow and smoke, towns and simple people, apple and radish red, and old things which never grow old. And where he went he must have gone with strange wonderful knowledge of the hearts of many unseen women: of some prairie girl lonely, singing, dreaming, waiting; knowing Pocahontas' body,

> lovely as a poplar, sweet as a red haw in
> November or a pawpaw in May;

seeing Adelaide Crapsey with her "rain-shattered mouth of blue pansy,"

> her head flung between
> her naked knees, and her head held listening
> to the sea, the great naked sea shouldering a load
> of salt;

till between him and the men who came before him with "ax and rifle, plow and horse"; the driven men whose pain went into the making of the things we are, whose aches dug the earth through æons; the forgotten men of yesterday and forgotten men of to-day, there was oneness:

> Finders in the dark, you Steve with a dinner bucket, you
> Steve clumping in the dusk on the sidewalks with an
> evening paper for the woman and the kids, you Steve
> with your head wondering where we all end up—
> Finders in the dark, Steve: I hook my arm in cinder sleeves;
> we go down the street together; it is all the same to
> us; you, Steve, and the rest of us end on the same stars;
> we all wear a hat in hell together, in hell or heaven.

Carl Sandburg

The process of the recognition of an inner through an outer thing has turned Sandburg to an artist. No clever mentality proposed his work to him. He did not find it needful to challenge Fafner, to will his vision. He does not, in the midst of a "Chinese" lyric, deem it necessary to insist upon his love for his "democratic queen." He apprehends the western scene not intellectually, but with his entire man. Streets and skies, jumbled harsh sites and fields of cornflower yellow have sensations for him. The prick on the skin of the eye and ear wakes the fibrous, rich, strong-taloned life, the Swedish iron in his blood, the hairy hankering galoot, the dark, thick, warm substance that speaks in his bass voice like a 'cello playing. He sees

the smokestacks bite the skyline with stub teeth;

. . . chimneys shaking on the lumber shanties
When the coal boats plow by on the river—
The hunched shoulders of the grain elevators—
The flame sprockets of the sheet steel mills;

Railroad trains at night—with a smokestack mushrooming a
     white pillar;

—The iceman with his iron tongs gripping a clear cube in
     summer sunlight;

Macabre and golden the moon opening a slant light,
A triangle for an oriole to stand and sing "Take me home."
A layer of thin white gold feathers for a child queen of
     gipsies;

71

Port of New York

—Curves of fire, the rough scarf women dancing,
Dancing out of the flues and smokestacks—flying hair of fire,
  flying feet upside down;
Buckets and baskets of fire exploding and chortling, fire
  running wild out of the steady and fastened oven;
Sparks crackling a harr-harr-huff from a solar plexus of rock-
  ribs of the earth taking a laugh for themselves;
Ears and noses of fire, gibbering gorilla arms of fire, gold
  mud-pies, gold bird-wings, red jackets riding purple
  mules, scarlet autocrats tumbling from the humps of
  camels, assassinated czars straddling vermilion balloons.

He hears the ground-bass, the breathing and sputtering of the "tall bold slugger set vivid against the little soft cities," "Eleventh Avenue racket," "all the crazy wonderful slamming roar of the street." Sometimes it is the twisting of steel muscles, the groaning of metal and granite he hears. Sometimes it is the timbres of human voices, the tone more than the words; the accents and rhythms of speech chucked by "detectives, newsies, temeos, niggers," by the "Jew fishcrier on Maxwell Street with a voice like a north wind blowing over corn stubble in January," by the "caller calling in the railroad station," by "gigglers, God knows gigglers, daffy with life's razzle-dazzle," by men screaming "we'll get you yet, you sbxyzsch!" And the sheer noise, the banging of the jazz, the "rhythmic oompa of the brasses," colored and emphatic and cruel phrases, raging and gorgeous slang of the American streets, saturate him, thrill grim, rough, sardonic joy up in him.

72

Carl Sandburg

And, once his being brims; once he is full of song and thanks; shot full of pain and love, these sparks connect with the strong, homely, racy vocabulary of farmboy and journalist and lover of poets stored in his brain, coalesce with other phrases, and come forth free-swung in whispered declaration or dithyrambic flood. In a raw, sad-hued, fumbling American world, these molten and sprawling expressions stand part of the landscape; no less of home than the autumn coloration on fields, the voices of the men and women in them, the look of the cities. Chicago is like some of these poems; as loud, as grim, as northern and western in color. They are of all the life in feeling, in imagery, in shape, in the way they fling forth, in their very inflections. What Synge did with the language of the Gaelic peasantry, this lean, slouch-hatted, stogy-smoking newspaperman is commencing to do with that of the American townspeople. Woven into the substance of passionate expression, into the music of intimate and sorrowing moods, of sardonic and robust, into love poems and jazz fantasias, there sound raucous and tender the accents of the vulgar, slangy, crude-colored speech. There is a poem of Sandburg's which commences:

All I can give you is broken-face gargoyles.
It is too early to sing and dance at funerals,
Though I can whisper to you I am looking for an undertaker
  humming a lullaby and throwing his feet in a swift and
  mystic buck-and-wing, now you see it and now you
  don't.

73

Port of New York

Another commences:

> I cannot tell you now;
>   When the wind's drive and whirl
>   Blow me along no longer,
>   And the wind's a whisper at last—
> Maybe I'll tell you then—
>   some other time.

There is one that runs:

> Listen a while, the moon is a lovely woman, a lonely woman,
>   lost in a silver dress, lost in a circus rider's silver dress;

and one that ends with:

> Galoots fat with too much, galoots lean with too little, galoot
>   millions and millions, snousel and snicker on, plug your
>   exhausts, hunt your snacks of fat and lean, grab off
>   yours.

Not merely popular phrases, but whole verses of folksongs
are incrustated into these rhapsodies. In the title-poem,
"Smoke and Steel," there is a sudden ironic quotation of
an old log fire song; and we hear:

> You may put the damper up,
> You may put the damper down,
> The smoke goes up the chimney just the same.

The result of a formula, of course, this Americanism is
not. Sandburg does not set out deliberately, like some
of the men, to write poems in the native idiom. He has

74

Carl Sandburg

no prejudice. The mood writes English, writes American; passes freely from one to the other. Among his many poems on death, and Sandburg is the blood-child of the twilit northern peoples shadowed always with the knowledge of corruption and decay, there is one which goes:

> Death is stronger than all the governments because the governments are men and men die and then death laughs: Now you see 'em, now you don't.
> Death is stronger than all proud men and so death snips proud men on the nose, throws a pair of dice and says: Read 'em and weep.
> Death sends a radiogram every day: When I want you I'll drop in—and then one day he comes with a master-key and lets himself in and says: We'll go now.

But there is also a song of the softness of death which begins:

> Under the harvest moon,
> When the soft silver
> Drips shimmering
> Over the garden nights,
> Death, the gray mocker,
> Comes and whispers to you
> As a beautiful friend
> Who remembers.

For, being an artist, he finds himself quite naïvely using the raw material life throws about him.

75

Port of New York

We love Carl Sandburg; no poet since Whitman has created the shapeless, polyphonic, nascent thing America more than he and made poems more gladdening and necessary to us here. And yet, it is in no more than a couple dozen of pieces that he has really done his work. No more than a couple dozen contain all he has had in him to say. His four volumes are made up very largely of incomplete forms. Little he gives us is ever entirely without some hoarse magnificence of language, some subtle play of assonances, some savor of the folk-life on the American prairie; and yet it is spots of coruscating color, flashing lyrical starts set in the midst of much unwrought and unglinting matter that come far more often than do accomplished wholes. Too often one finds Sandburg stepping over tree-tops where he ought sturdily to be treading the ground. Certain of his pieces, "Aprons of Silence," for example, are merely the commencements, not the totality, of poems. He is more successful in the shorter forms than in the longer; in pure lyrical movements like "Broken-Face Gargoyles," "The Great Hunt," "Follies," "Loam," "Feather Lights," "Handfuls" and a few other intimate things. The best of his long poems, "Prairie" and "Smoke and Steel," are in truth collections of short lyrics more than single wholes; although in both cases the drifting, hazy, moveless forms are justified by the subject matters, the American cornlands and the fume-banks over factory towers. Something like a unity does establish itself in

76

Carl Sandburg

"Slabs of the Sunburnt West"; but the intensity and the freshness are smaller in quantity; and everything is a trifle deliberately a "slab" of something. But even among his smaller and tenderer pieces, the perfect things are too few. It is not only the loose-jawed pieces of the shovel 'em under, I saw a man eating soup, type that vaguely irritate. In some of the compositions richest in meat he will sometimes sustain himself for three or four verses in drawing the relentless line, and then collapse and loose quite what he was on the point of fixing. "Death Snips Proud Men," "Band Concert," and "The Sins of Kalamazoo" are instances. In other cases, unable or unwilling to thrust farther, he creates an artificial conclusion by repeating with slight variations the opening lines.

Sandburg is a poet because of the unforgettable times he has given himself like a lover to things and let things come into him and mix with his essence there. What has limited his effectuality; all the while kept uncertain the vein of genius he has in him; and held him from blossoming fully into the major lyrist whose embryo he carries about inside his frame, is a certain unwillingness he must have to let life come full at him. There must be something ultimate in him he is afraid of having stirred. Too often we find him putting blinders on his mind; intercepting sight with the thick smoked glasses of sentimentality. Particularly does he put them on in the presence of human beings. Certain simple types he knows

77

Port of New York

well. Or he could not be a poet. But there are other
types, more sophisticated ones perhaps, whom he does not
know; and against whom, for some reason, he does not
venture to try himself out. Hence, an undue hurry to
accept the emotionally pretty legends about them and
leave the hound-mind inside him blinking sleepily in the
sun. The working-man, for instance, is a "martyr."
There are many poems of Sandburg's assuring us he is.
Critics wring their hands and complain "propaganda."
The truth this "martyrdom" certainly is not. The poet
has refused to give up some pet protective resentments in
the act of seeing people and confessing neither martyrdom nor guilt, but life. During the war the hand of
the American herd rested dangerously heavily on Sandburg's neck. He goddamned the Kaiser in best style;
Steichen's lieutenant-colonelcy impressed him; he cannot
yet get out of himself what he really started to feel about
the mess; he doesn't quite manage to dismiss the sergeant in Belleau Wood who said, "You bastards, etc.," to
somebody or other. But it is not merely working-men
and soldiers whom he does not want to look at. There
is a mid-American diamond in "Cornhuskers" which
begins:

> They are crying salt tears
> Over the beautiful beloved body
> Of Inez Milholland
> Because they are glad she lived,
> Because she loved open-armed, etc.

78

Carl Sandburg

The dedication of *Smoke and Steel* calls Steichen "Dreamer and Finder, Rider of Great Mornings in Gardens, Valleys, Battles." Grieg, "being with Ibsen, Björnson, Lief Ericsen," dreams "Morning, Spring, Anitra's Dance" "at the door of the new stars." There are others.

In other instances, where perception has managed to take place, its promptings are not obeyed. Then, the poet does not think his thoughts to an end and open himself completely to the light. He is found going soft and letting himself down easy. The "nurse mother" appears a little often and calls something his "dreaming heart," and that successfully blurs the outline. It is on these rocks that "The Sins of Kalamazoo," one of his best pieces, goes aground finally. For four and a half pages Sandburg continues sardonically, keenly, picturing Kalamazoo through himself and himself through Kalamazoo; and the poem is an essay, a novel, an autobiography. But, finally, the perception goes; the picture is lost in washy fog. Sandburg has gotten down to where the principle of life in himself, in Kalamazoo, in America, has to be produced; and there suddenly we find once more the "nurse mother"—

> The wishing heart of you I loved, Kalamazoo.
> I sang bye-lo, bye-lo to your dreams.
> I sang bye-lo to your hopes and songs.

Nor does Sandburg ever seem to catch himself at these evasions. His mind seems to be doped when they occur;

Port of New York

it seems to be doped when he comes to revise his poems for final publication. For this reason, a good deal of the volume, *Smoke and Steel*, seems like the contents of a reporter's note-book. It is always to be hoped that the more carefully selected contents of *Slabs of the Sunburnt West* mark a veritable and conclusive awakening of the long-dozing critical faculty.

Whether Sandburg will indeed develop further; whether he can become a harder, more concentrated workman and the major lyrist he potentially is, we do not know. There is a weariness in *Slabs of the Sunburnt West*, a wish to evade feeling in *Rootabaga Stories*, that has a disquieting look; and although we find ourselves persuaded that both are nothing other than the blinders Sandburg is perpetually putting up between his mental eye and life, we cannot be so certain as to dismiss the possibility of a sunset actually taking place over his poethood. We will be disappointed if it proves true that the amount we shall ever have of Sandburg is already contained in four volumes. We need lives lived to the full amid the crass matter of the land. We need men letting the lights of the bosom out complete upon the new chaos of machines on the American continent. It is not Paris we want; it is more New York, more Chicago, more Kalamazoo, Omaha, Kenosha, more loop, more gumbo and gravel, more armature spiders. And more will come, eventually; but it is as yet a difficult thing to believe that it can come without the assistance of Carl Sandburg; and

Carl Sandburg

a melancholy one to look forward to its coming no longer through him.

And still, few present American writers are more sure of living than he. Were he not to write again, he would stand his ground. Sometimes, from out the earth, men drag up a battered primitive effigy, some old stone fish-god with nose bashed in, leg and arm lopped off; so strong of outline, nevertheless, so harmoniously conjoined a sequence of forms, that before it the heart stops, and then beats again with joy. The poet Sandburg is such a piece. Because he breathed, it will ever be easier for men to breathe in American confines. He has given the American folk a voice. Men will need his song while men walk by skyscrapers. They will need his wild laugh and great dreaming tenderness. They will need his chant of elemental man-power, "great nail holding a skyscraper through blue nights into white stars."

Marsden Hartley

THE breath of a rare apartness informs every rectangle of canvas or glass decorated by Marsden Hartley. There is no brushstroke of his that does not exhale, elusively and still poignantly, as certain herbs their spicy nimble fragrances, an happily distinguished spirit. Like a warm flower half hidden by lush grasses, the presence glints from his clamant shields of color, meeting with light reassurance the eye when first it falls upon the great drooping curves, the prim angular shapes and flaunting areas of this simultaneously stiff and violent and whimsical art. An unaffected fastidiousness of nature has disposed these large shapes in relations at once singularly formal and full of circumstance, and yet elegant and easily original. Spontaneous daintiness, analogous to the quite instinctive expressions of natural grace and charm made in the arrangement of their garments by certain veritable fashionables, in the folding of a scarf, the tilt of a hat, the deportment of a stick, has given sudden, unexpected, quaint twists to these importunate masses. The native delicacy runs in the airiness, the relaxed elevation, with which the pigment is brushed on. One feels it aquiver in the color fancies, in the fresh and pungent opposition, say, of this verdurous dark of balsam sprig to this cool muslin white;

or in the delightful spot of that wistful silver-blue flower-bell-shape amid those funeral blacks. A thousand niceties and fancifulnesses body it forth; in a single form, at the very least, it suffuses with its precious ray all the material, the material of the poet and essayist as well as that of the painter, upon which Hartley has laid touch.

It is in the form of a tactful recognition of the cardinal limitation of his medium, and of a perfect deference to it, that most oftentimes the element of distinction of spirit manifests itself in his work. That which Cézanne declared to Renoir had taken him ten (or was it twenty?) years to discover, the difference existing between the arts of painting and sculpture, this Maine boy, with his inborn fineness of feeling, seems from the first of his career to have well sensed. Trust in his intuitions, the condition, surely, of pure feeling, made him to ascertain instinctively the character of the medium before which he found himself; made him to recognize its inevitable bi-dimensionality, and to comprehend quite simply that in a painting the tri-dimensional universe of our experience must be rendered as a convention, and as color, in its interrelations, can express it. And, honoring the individuality of his material as one might respect the sensibility of another personage, Hartley has been prevented by grace from doing the violence done to his art by so many less sensitive painters. It is practically never that we find him invading the province proper to the sculptor, in the manner of certain of his fellows, and attempting to make the

Marsden Hartley

flat surface of the canvas render a tri-dimensional reality co-extensive with space as we know it. He has always given us painting.

He has always painted flatly, subtly; left one perfectly conscious that it is a surface he is decorating. The volumes of space he translates into the idiom of surface; a feat doubtlessly permitted him and other painters by the circumstance that the eye, so it seems, knows only two dimensions, and that perception of a third is performed strictly by reason as result of experience. Planes, to be sure, break his canvases, represent spatial extension. This regal white lily with its wickedly horned leaves, erect between butter-yellow draperies, is felt as a volume against that lustrous purplish-blue sweep of bay, as that is felt against the curve of sandy shore, and the shore in turn felt against the rim of violet peaks and they against the white-clouded summer sky. This copper bowl is heaped full of stiffish bananas, globular pomegranates, and luscious figs as a bursting pod is crammed with seed. But there is no imitation of nature in the representation. You are not snared by violent lights and shades into believing you have before you the solids of sculpture. You are left, by the subtlety and lightness of the painting, in wide-eyed awareness that each object is the symbol of a volume, and that every plane is sheer as a sheet of tissue-paper.

What Hartley achieves—and every painter who finds his way to the conception of his work primarily as decora-

tion, and employs to effectuate himself the subtle, thin,
butterfly painting comparable to that of the later Cézanne
—is nothing other than art itself. For, in playing his
game of cards with the entire deck, as it were, laid face
upward on the table; in accepting frankly and honestly
the conventions of his art, as Copeau, say, accepts his,
desiring that the audience forget never that it is in a
theater, and that the stage is a few boards across some
wooden horses, that the protagonists are actors wearing
costumes, and the scenery painted stuff, he succeeds in
establishing a tiny universe sharply defined against the
great limitless chaotic outer. He sets up distinct limits to
which everything in the canvas, every line, every brushstroke, every shape, and every hue is related, and through
which relationship it begets a special significance. On
the materials of the exterior cosmos he establishes a
little sealed world declarative of his own inward human
order. And through this superimposed order he manages to escape from the literalness of the facts with which
as the product of a material universe he has to deal; and
succeeds as does every artist, in making objects register
the double significance which they have for him, at once
the animal, and the man product of civilization. The
Forest of Arden of the Shakespearean comedy, because of
what mankind owes to trees, is both the cool woodland
good to the primitive human organism worn by the con-
straints of society, and the free wild world of poesy uncontrolled by the powers of the state and church, and

Marsden Hartley

necessary to the man desirous of finer living. And so, in the paintings of Hartley, these great dark pears, for instance, bedded upon hospital-white linen on a background of severe dry black, are both the magnificent fruits shown against ascetic noble stuffs, and the entire world as a certain grim experience of life has proven it to the painter. In their doubleness, they satisfy the entire organism.

It is also in the intricacy and subtlety of his manner of composition, that the peculiar refinement of temper of Hartley manifests itself. Had he been a musician, it is most likely that his nature would have led him to something approximating the close, delicate, evanescent harmonies of Debussy and Ravel, rathermore than the more primitive tone-resistances, the kind of clashing oppositions preferred by certain of the Russians, by Ornstein, and by some of the members of the Groupe des Six. It is the similarity of objects, the inner resemblances, which he appears in his painting to stress, not their mutual repulsions, and differences. He seems to find pleasure in recording the analogies between objects and colorations superficially very dissimilar. Things apparently singular in shape and hue, will be approached to each other, and shown of a family. The broad defined color areas found in so much of modern painting appear in Hartley; but instead of being used in a sort of powerful clash, a powerful play of elemental forces, they will be approached and delicately worked into one another. In a painting based on rose, white, Yale blue, and saffron, one discovers the white suffusing the rosy area and the azure; the blue stressed in the rose and the yellow; the white faintly touched with pink. In another, Hartley produces the black in his white, the yellow in his deep violet, and the violet in his yellow. In this practice he is utterly opposed, for example, to Georgia O'Keeffe, who seems to feel instinctively the mutual resistances, the stubborn opposition of forms and things entirely to each other, and to achieve her composition through a juxtaposition of contrasting color-areas, a sort of counterpoint of exclusive and resistant forces. Hartley, in forgoing this sort of primitive robustious clash, gets a sort of intricacy and refinement of effect characteristic of the work of advanced, Alexandrian civilizations. One finds him quite unconsciously using color schemes that recall certain of the Byzantine mosaics shown in the Louvre: tawny, pungent yellows, dusky violets, milk-white and blue-black. It is characteristic of him that while in certain of his more capricious, playful, less serious and intense compositions, we find him using, boldly, primary colors; in his greatly more serious, sustained, and developed work it is in colors that contain great admixtures of black, and that make one feel the sable underneath gold and green and Tyrian red, that we find him expressing himself.

And even when one can lay no positive hand upon its local form, and when, elflike, it seems hiding always behind the bush to which one has not yet come, one gets innumerable secret intimations of the fortunate presence

Marsden Hartley

of a rare distinguishedness. It is, indeed, all pervasive.
For it is no fruit of conscious effort and patient study, but
the inborn quality of a personality; elevating with its
breath each manifestation of individual life, pervading
even passages of grief and world-weariness and death-
wardness with its ray, as some impulse in a widowed lady
in the utmost of her dejection might make her unable
to resist daintily scalloping the crust of the pie she was
baking. It is the element of a being not only fallen right,
and in the mould of a certain physical delicacy, but grown
among people to whom decorum is not ungermane, latent
only when it appears absent; and among whom the quality has been nurtured midmost all dourness and spare-
ness of living. There have been in New England many
persons, humble, half-conscious souls, perhaps, in whom
something analogous to this instinctive refinement has
lived and recorded itself in some sweet bit of handiwork,
in the twist of a chair-back, the moulding of a cornice, the
design of a sampler, a piece of embroidery, the decoration with naïve flower-fancies of a piece of wooden furniture. It was a delicacy much the same, was it not? that
gave the prose of Hawthorne its abiding and native virtue.
And in Hartley it appears again, born and nurtured, as-
suming once more in its plenitude and variety the form
of genius.

An ability to maintain itself perfectly in compositions
informed by a breath of restlessness and violence and

harsh imperiousness shows it for what it is. One finds it merged and yet not lost in statements that are as like to smash walls and scatter fragments of plaster and lath as an exploding grenade. For, if it is a giant's power which one senses active in the most of Hartley's paintings, a magnificent largeness of conception and stride, it is also a giant's power which has not quite attained the balance and harmony necessary to it. There are few of the man's works which, for all the handsomeness of coloring and somberness of passion, are completely developed organisms. Certain exceptions there no doubt are, one or two in each of the series he has executed. But they are rare. In the vast number of his canvases, it is the rule that only certain portions are stated with the magnificent fullness, the dash and distinction proper to the painter. There remain always other portions which have been left strangely devoid of great interest, blocked in rather more than calmly produced. A group of dark pears, a rubber-plant, a New Mexican mountain, a calla lily, will be painted with relish and verve. But the rest of the canvas, which under the brush of a Renoir or a Cézanne would have been no less important, will by Hartley be left half alive, treated with an irritating scantiness of attention. In consequence, most of his work is not quite finely balanced, exhales a sort of spirit of violence and restlessness which at instants recalls Van Gogh's. The developed portions for want of counterweight advance a little too far. Minor planes are like to be dismissed with a grand

Marsden Hartley

cavalierly offhandedness. Large phallic shapes brandish themselves over the spectator as heavy crucifixi might be brandished, in all dignity and still with indubitable fanaticism, by zealous priests over dying sinners or burning heretics. Great full-sailed flaunting shapes take possession, with a certain insolence not entirely obliterated by grace, of the entire situation as might a person who manages by insistent manœuvers to replete with his own person the scene to the exclusion of all others.

It is to an incomplete consciousness that we are obliged to refer this absence of fine balance in Hartley's gorgeous pieces. Consciousness of a great brilliance there exists, without a doubt, in him. His extraordinary thematic invention gives incontrovertible proof of its presence. His senses are quick; he is unceasingly getting, from everything to which he exposes his eye, crisp, pricking sensations. He is always doing something original. The influence of æsthetic models he shows very little; that of Ryder and of Cézanne remains confined to the early and less important mountain pieces and the still-lives of the period when cucumbers fascinated him. His motifs are taken freshly and directly from the life about him. His eye is intensely sensitive to the identity of the spot in which he finds himself, translating automatically into shapes and colors the peculiarity of the scene, the singular atmospheric effects, the caprices and magnificences and variations of nature. There are certain craftsmen who paint a tree of Florida and a tree of Labrador in a single

mode, a single key. But Hartley, despite the stiffness
and formality of presentation innate in him, the stiffness
of a head somewhat painfully held aloof by a chokingly
high white collar, never fails to record the genius of a
place, no more than in his essays he fails, despite his nonchalance, to express the identity and charm of the poets
and painters he describes. To go to New England mountain country in fall-time is to see early Hartleys strewn
up every furry hillside and 'round every blue-black lake,
so perfectly has he translated into impressionistic spots of
pigment the cool wistful blue of the skies above daintily
pricked forests wine-colored and golden, the waiting
stillness of the royal decline. Certain still-lives executed
in Paris reflect the sour coloring of the stonework of the
French capital. It is Bermuda with its pinkish stucco
houses and its sands and sails and vapors that comes to
us out of the severe, geometrical, conventionalized series
of 1916. In his large flamboyant Germanic set, Hartley
has gotten electrical colors and shapes, sorts of abstrac-
tions of uhlan uniforms and patriotic demonstrations, ban-
nered thoroughfares, military musics, and Kaiser fanfares
which record the frenzied Berlin of the early months of
the war. And New Mexico, with its strange depraved
topography: earth-forms fitting into each other like coup-
ling organs; strawberry-pink mountains dotted by fuzzy
poison-green shrubs, recalling breasts and wombs of clay;
clouds like sky-sailing featherbeds; boneyard aridity, is
in the pastels and the oils done in the southwest.

Marsden Hartley

Only the painter has not immersed himself sufficiently deeply in his material. He has not been able to lose himself in his "object." It has not presented itself to him with the marvelous insistency with which it presents itself to the great artist. It has for him nothing of the single saliency which the characters of his novels have for a Balzac, say. The circling of interest between his own breast and the thing before him, with the result that the thing before him begets for him an importance quite as great as his own person, and is perceived a life with rights identical to his own; the circling that continues uninterruptedly round and round till the man almost becomes a transparency through which the light of life streams, till the man almost becomes the thing before him and the thing the man, that is for some reason broken in Marsden Hartley. The object is never visible to him as an integral portion of the chain of which he himself is a link, and like him a material in which the informing spirit of the universe stirs. The Chinese knew themselves intergrown with all creation, knew no thing not intergrown with them, and their wisdom symbolized itself in the completeness and harmoniousness, the balancedness of their expressions. The great modern Frenchmen saw the world so, and accepted it fully, ugliness and pain and beauty alike, and their wisdom became the impeccable organization, the exquisite balance that enthralls us before the canvases of Cézanne and Renoir. But to this New England work, the same wisdom has not always contributed. The object has in some fashion remained always somewhat subordinate to the worker. It has been considered essentially a tributary and inferior thing, with the unique function of demonstrating some ineffable quality which is sensed present in the person regarding far more than in the substance regarded.

It is nothing more, nor less, than the fault of the society in which he grew that hampers Hartley the artist. The relation he bears his object is one that is very typical of the American in his general contacts. It is a relation resulting, it would seem, from the attitude taken by the whole of society to the soil which nourishes it. The men who have really loved the earth they have worked in America have been rare. The feeling for the earth which is characteristic of the peasantry of the older countries, the sense that it is an organism like themselves, which has to be nourished and developed and enriched and cared for so that it will increase, the whole desire that makes "grow" the soil, that, has been felt in this land until recent times only by the poor Indian. His dances and rituals were motivated very much by the knowledge that if he put himself in harmony with nature, nature would put herself in harmony with him. But the Yankee, it is a common fact, has always ravished the earth. He has always approached it with the wish to get from it with little effort what he could, and not to give as much as he got. There has been no love in his intercourse with it. He has wanted to get away from it, to rise "above" it.

Marsden Hartley

And that attitude has repeated itself throughout his civilization as a figure in a Persian rug. He is the husbandman of machinery no more than he is the husbandman of the earth. And in his art, he withholds himself no otherwise.

The number of the peacocks in the ranks of American paint is great. Unable to employ their faculties to the full in the giving of themselves to a material, they have been led to compensate themselves for the sense of guilt, inevitable companion to this niggardliness, by seeking to win attention and admiration for themselves personally. The bravura painting of Chase and Whistler and Sargent; the brushwork which seems to insist on its own brilliance and achieves no rounding of form, was motivated greatly in this way. The so insistently beautiful voice of Henry James, which manages always to get itself noticed, in many cases at the expense of the matter in hand, forms a literary parallel of a sort. The white suit of Mark Twain, in another field, constitutes another. And Hartley is the nephew of them all. To be sure, he belongs to an age other than theirs. His time is not impressionist, but new-baroque. It has referred the universe to the human body and felt the human body in the objects present to the senses. As men have done in all baroque ages; as Greco, as Bernini, as the edificer of the Cathedra Petri in St. Peter's in Rome did in their times, so Hartley too, in his, stresses in what he shapes the sexual interests of the mind. Nevertheless, via the large cucumbers, bananas, pears, goblets, lilies, and rubber-plants in his compositions, chosen doubtlessly because of a physical resemblance to the painter himself to express his ego, there comes to us an accent not really different from that borne by the stuffs of the men of the older American school.

Where men withhold themselves from nature, nature makes men pay for the braces erected against her. Tradition and early influences may have riveted them on, may have struck the stem of life a fatal gash; in some form, in blackness and weight and fear of the world the passions find their outlet. The mournfulness which informs many of Hartley's pictures, and which is never far absent from any, even the most fantastic and extravagant and capricious, is the state of a rich energy ready for use and prevented, through the habits of the civilization in which it finds itself tangled, from employing itself in its appointed fullness. Novel to America, particularly to New England it assuredly is not. That Ryder must have felt something of the same all his life we guess from the sombreness and shadowiness of his pictures. The particular mordancy which it assumes in the mind of Hartley, a mordancy perhaps more excessive than any which even gray and gloomy American painting has hitherto displayed, may result from either the fact that the more sensitive organisms feel the deprivations more poignantly, or that something in the constellation of society itself is changing, and generating in the artist a greater power and

Marsden Hartley

a greater capacity to feel pain. Some of the sadness flows, it cannot be doubted, from the wretchedness of circumstances in which every poor devil who has to gain his living in America by selling pictures of high distinction and great originality finds himself. Still, it is not the material miseries that have given life this savor on his lips. His is assuredly the world-weariness of the creature built to dive deep, who for some cause has never been able to take the headlong plunge.

It speaks as heartache, as still yearning out of the early mountain pieces, wistful as little blue flowers come up through the snows. These are like moments of warm trickling overflow that might descend suddenly on an unhappy creature as a bend of the gray road he was traversing showed a vision of far, serene blue hills. It sings a swan song over the world in its pictures of grim insuperable mountains standing high, while at their feet there dies in colorful sunsetting the New England autumn. It gives its cry of hunger and resentment and anguish in the great dark landscapes, with their "proud music of the storm," their chalk whites opposed to great belts of black, their wildly running lines and mad shapes of dull gold and night-time blue, their cruel white forms crowding and crushing the central wretched, bending one. It smoulders in the rich, gloomy still-lives, with their stiff, heavy forms of oldest gold and darkest rose on abysses of velvety sable. With the chill of death on its breath it murmurs in the funeral black folds amid

97

which sad blossoms and broken chalices are set, in the
morbid beauty of langorous white callas. There is grim
and tragic resignation in the great dark pears upon their
magnificent white. In the not unnoble wanness of certain pictures of the abstract Bermudan series we feel it as
it might be in the heart upon a day when all ran not so
unsmoothly, and when still it sounded as far thunder
through a dappled sky.

A lessened tragedy pervades the works produced the
last years. But less muscularity has been brought into
play in the creation of these works, it is evident. The
passion, the intensity which spoke grandly from the dark
Maine and the dark still-life series, is not heard quite as
distinctly. Slightly more superficial aspects of things are
registered. Enormous strides, it cannot be gainsaid,
have been taken by Hartley toward esthetic perfection
since last he painted Maine. In Berlin during the early
war years, in painting large on canvases larger than those
to which he was used, he seems to have developed enormously his control of the medium. For, when he returned to the decoration of canvases the size of the ones
formerly handled by him, it was seen that much clearer
and more fluid forms appeared, that the painting of white
in particular had become delicious. His sensuousness has
developed also. All the love of solid magnificences germane to the Englishman with his houses and his horse-
guards has risen in the blood of this, his lineal descendant.
The newer canvases and rectangles of glass speak a mar-

Marsden Hartley

velous delight in exquisite textures, silks and woolens and velvets, spices and gorgeous blooms and sweeping draperies, a voluptuous life of the touch. And a sort of delightful whimsicality has put in its appearance, too. It is a sort of quaint humorousness, reminiscent of the extravagant conceits, the cerebral enormities of Emily Dickinson, another New Englander. (What a pair they would have made!) In Hartley's art it takes the form of capricious inventions, blue and yellow bananas tumbling like circus-clowns; light complicated rhythms; a form of cold dandified blue whirling while on it there tumble contrariwise three fat rosy pears; quaint conceits of painting that cause two brown silk window draperies to fall like the skirts of the Boston dames of a generation ago; little patterns of paper dragons, chocolate drops, gardenias and swagger-sticks on a background of red that throbs like a circus-drum. But some grip there is one misses. The painting is too much merely a beauteous flow. It is a little as though the artist had made a compact with life, had agreed not to permit himself to feel deeply for the sake of avoiding the stings.

But such compacts can have no durability. Some day, perhaps some day not so far distant, Hartley will have to go back to Maine. For it seems that flight from Maine is in part flight from his deep feelings. It was down east that he was born and grew and lived a great many of his years. There dwell the people to whom he is closest akin; there is the particular landscape among which his decisive experiences were gotten; there every tree and mountain wall is reminiscent of some terrible or wonderful day. And when he has to make his peace with life, it is to this soil, so it would appear, that he must return. Here are his own people; the ones he must accept and understand and cherish. For among them only can he get the freedom of his own soul.

Marvelous Hartley! There can be made no scrutiny of this body of work which cannot be summed up in the exclamation! In face of all the shortcomings of this art, sometimes apparently as numerous as the names on Leporello's list, the words cry themselves out. For, in view of all the deficiencies of this product, there still inevitably returns upon the spectator with all the freshness of sousing spray, the rare quality, the exquisite distinguishedness of what has been put down. It may even be true that this handsome painting of still-life scratches a subject rather more than veritably penetrates it. Nevertheless, for what there is there, let the stars be praised! Even when there is no power, which is rare, there is daintiness aplenty. There is always fastidious originality of conception. Who other, indeed, than Hartley could have set down a thing like this with quite that distinct elegance, that happiness of fancy? One returns always to the Hartleys. With joy, the fine breath, the airy distinction, is greeted. One returns not once, but over and over again. They are the most charming of companions. They have a sort of discretion, for all their peacock-like

Marsden Hartley

habits. They obliterate themselves; then, another day, they dawn again, and delight with their distinguished presence. The men who march in procession holding up the shapes made by their hands that the gods in pity may grant them a long life after their bodily death, carry, the most of them, objects larger and rounder, shinier and heavier, than does this man. He has to show only a slight thing, a handful of blue fruit. But it has bewitching singularity of shape. It has airy distinction, inexplicable glamour. It holds with ease a place entirely apart.

William Carlos Williams

THE poems of William Carlos Williams are good biting stuff. Lyric substance has gotten a novel acidulousness of him. Scent bitter like the nasturtium's, and like the nasturtium's fresheningly pungent, mounts off his small spikey forms. The sharp things make gay dangerous guerilla upon the alkalis coating the brain. Corrosive fluid destroys the properties characteristic of ubiquitous Huyler's; leaves crystals of valuable salt. Poems startle with suddenly brandished cutlery. Poems writhe with the movements of bodies vainly twisting to loose themselves from fixed scorching points. Certain waver indeterminately, blankly, high up in air. Certain murmur faintly, turned in upon themselves. The tone achieves grotesque modulations. It falls unceremoniously from plane to distant unrelated plane; drops out of stars to pinholes; takes queer, off, sour, turns. Words shock with the unexpectedness of their thrusts, scratch voluptuously an instant, sting with soft sudden fangs. Notes are hammered staccato. Queries and ejaculations enter like bird-shot discharged from the muzzle of a Winchester shot-gun. Color-words come; black, yellow, green, white; but what they impart tastes not of fruit-pulps, but of mineral traces in clear spring-water.

103

Port of New York

Williams' writings are laconic acclamations of the courage to swallow bitter-flavored medicines, to bear unflinchingly the pain of violent cauterizations. They are the forms wherein a poet has given deep sober thanks to the principle by means of which he has managed to maintain his own spirit intact on a steep inclement bank of life, some Greenland on the verge of the Arctic circle. And the homely magic he wishes to hold before men's eyes is light-hearted self-irony, relentless impersonality of regard, sense of the comic and grotesque in his own career, bald matter-of-factness, willingness to stand evil smells and not run from them. Life has tempted this man with the dope of candies; urged glucose on him, cheap substitute for absent sweetnesses. For the world he inhabits is not liberal with satisfactions. It is a world of lowish climaxes and thin releases; whether from premature agedness or retarded youth, one does not know. Monotonous gray of repetition, of usedness, unrolls its scroll day-long across the firmament. At infrequent intervals, slits are cut in the drab-hued curtain. Rose quivers awhile like the ballet of pink slippers with gay pom-poms descending the stairs. A day hops like a yellow bird in April branches. Through the night from afar a sprig of tower-lights hangs against profoundest blue and utters the salutation of joyful cities. Two hours of golden promenade arrive: Columbus' first walk on new-world ground "among the trees, which was the most beautiful

thing which I had ever seen." The streets end in the
sun, and there is

> . . . blue mist
> in the distance
> with grapevine trellises
> with grape clusters
> small as strawberries
> on the vines . . .
> . . . and ditches
> running spring-water
> that continue the gutters
> with willows over them.
> The reeds begin
> like water at a shore
> their pointed petals waving
> dark green and light.

But the colors are not permanent nor intense enough to
change the aspect of the world. They are merely sufficiently satisfying to keep the organism in motion. That
is all.

> Winter is long in this climate
> and spring—a matter of a few days
> only,—a flower or two picked
> from mud or from wet leaves
> or at best against treacherous
> bitterness of wind, and sky shining
> teasingly, then closing in black
> and sudden with fierce jaws.

Port of New York

No gradual suns nurse the small hardish buds on the black branches, melting their green and tight condition, gathering warm color and sweet flesh until the earth is round and drunk with curving greenery and clustering juicèd fruits. And when blaze of July strikes them finally, it arrives upon them with such cruel suddenness that of the unopened things many shrivel and char upon their stalks, and few come to radiant maturity. The gray remains; the earth is month-long scraggly and bare, decked meagerly with a few single separate objects selected by the poet's subconscious from off the Jersey flats: a shad-bush on the edge of a clearing, a solitary track of foot-prints in the snow, a fire in an ash-can, pools left by the tide, the swirl of wind and the river,

trees
always in the distance, always against
a gray sky.

Truly, a weather-condition which encourages indulgence in <u>dope</u>; and one very prevalent through these United States, to judge by the number of institutions devoted within their bounds to the manufacture of candies of all kinds. Genius has given Williams a hardier, cleaner adjustment. This M.D. has developed the stay of esthetic perception. He finds release in seeing. A certain quantity of perfectly selfless sympathy is in him. Children exist for him. There are women in labor. There is a bone-wearied, exasperated woman in bed.

106

William Carlos Williams

There is a young man with a bad "pump." The doctor is the confessor, to-day. There is

> . . . a band of
> young poets that have not learned
> the blessedness of warmth
> (or have forgotten it).

The first impulse may still be:

> You sullen pig of a man,
> you force me into the mud
> with your stinking ash-cart!

Inevitably, the music changes to

> Brother!
> . . . if we were rich
> we'd stick our chests out
> and hold our heads high!

Sublimation of brute desires has made the world less fearful. Flash-like recognition of his proper grotesquerie, dissonance, bondage inside the persons of others; scenes, rhythms, words, oaths dawning tantalizingly upon him, have made the circumstances of the poet's own life less painfully pressing. Capacity for identifying himself with people in their own terms has made him, on one plane, a successful physician, diagnostician, healer. It is his own health for which he is fighting in other bodies, careless of their cries and cringings. On another, it has made him

107

an artist: turned his existence over to him as stuff for contemplation. For he has found himself lifted onto that plane where men become object to themselves with all the rest of the world. He has viewed himself dispassionately, as though he himself were one of his own cases; placed himself with a not unkindly irony against the remainder of the universe and gotten the exact proportion; applied red-hot irons despite his own fears and outcries to his own gangrened wounds; doused himself with cold water whenever necessary; laughed at his hysterical alarms and abrupt starts; controlled the Madame Bovary inside himself; perceived the effect which he has been having upon those in touch with him as well as the effect they have been having upon himself. He has seen the laws operating in his own life, forcing him to receive the world in certain painful forms. There is no blame laid on time, custom, environment for his leanness, as there is blame in the writings of a poet related to Williams, T. S. Eliot. Williams is aware that if the sum of appeasements in his heart resembles most often the bank-balance of a hand-to-mouth existence: held generally near the two-hundred-dollar mark; occasionally dangerously far below; only rarely up near four hundred dollars, the cause, if there is one, lies in himself. It is

. . . the madness of the birch leaves opening
cold, one by one

and nothing other.

William Carlos Williams

Because of this singularly mature capacity for insight, Williams' writings have a truthfulness wanting those of certain of his fellows'; wanting, despite the presence of great excellencies, those of T. S. Eliot. His poems give the relationship of things more justly than do those of the émigré's. Williams, for example, does not repeat Bunthorne's lament that "nothing poetic in the world can dwell," nor represent his spirit as a drowned king. Kings do not appear upon his horizons, or Christs crucified. He does not have to cast a grandiose and egoistical veil over the world; and see in it the Judas to his genius before he can approach it. He can creep close to the lean thing which exists and see it dispassionately. He can give himself, William Carlos Williams, much as he is, without either simple or inverted pride; give himself in his crassness, in his dissonant mixed blood, in absurd melancholy, wild swiftness of temper, man-shyness; Americano, Jerseyite, Rutherfordian; give himself with a frankness, a fearlessness, a scientific impersonality, that is bracing as a shock of needle-spray. The fleeting patterns, the fine breaths, in which destiny manifests itself, contain excitement enough for him. Insight probes

> the guts of shadows;

catches subtle acidulous shades, delicate movements of life. Carl Sandburg perceives

> . . . an ocean of to-morrows
> a sky of to-morrows;

109

Port of New York

but it takes a maturity as great as Williams' to be able to put the finger on anything as unobvious and fine as the vision contained in *The Nightingales:*

> My shoes as I lean
> unlacing them
> stand out upon
> flat worsted flowers
> under my feet.
> Nimbly the shadows
> of my fingers play
> unlacing
> over shoes and flowers.

And what exists for him appears in its own tone and color; finds appropriate verbal imagery and rhythmical accent; nicely weds vulgarity with lyricism. A poem begins:

> He would enjoy either
> like the others
> to buy a railroad
> or
> in his old clothes to
> chase his wife to
> some such outhouse
> as they have still on the farms . . .

and we feel lightly the hawk-and-spit of the American mouth. The crass, unvoluptuous, vitriolic language of *The Great American Novel* has definitely local color. It

William Carlos Williams

is of the American suburbs as *Ulysses* is of Dublin. And verse and prose both realize the existence of the Sunday-afternoon family motor drive, of the Pullman plate-glass window in the parlor wall, and the lump of rock-crystal on the mantelpiece. It is seen not as in the best-sellers, superficially. It is seen from within. Williams gives the subjective form.

And, in moments of felt power, in moments of conscious toughness and sharp will, he breaks "through to the fifty words necessary," and briskly, laconically, like a man with little time for matters not absolutely essential to the welfare of the universe, brings into clarity the relation existing between himself and the things seen by him. Curious harmonies of bitter and sweet, of harsh and gentle, of sluggish and swift and sharp and soft in word-color and rhythmical pattern; nude finely viscous little curves of music in which every line is a decisive stroke, render the ironic, contained, humorous dance of the spirit amid the objects of a ramshackle makeshift universe. Life chants because it can master pain, and move about through disillusionment like a man going erect and self-contained through mean sites, and musing and dreaming in

> —back streets,
> admiring the houses
> of the very poor:
> roof out of line with sides
> the yards cluttered
> with old chicken-wire, ashes,

111

Port of New York

furniture gone wrong;
the fences and outhouses
built of barrel-staves
and parts of boxes, all—
smeared a bluish green—

Spring dances like Strauss' *Till Eulenspiegel* with mordant buffoonery above the hopeless dullness of things. Intelligence planes sovereign over yards in a fury of lilac-blossoms. Sore, battered, frozen, life outlasts the cold, struggles to its feet despite the weights upon it, lifts itself like the chickory on bitter stems; blossoms like salvia on ash-heaps. It has come finally face to face with some incapacity of its own; but among the wrecks it finds a piquant sprightly music:

If I when my wife is sleeping
and the baby and Kathleen
are sleeping
and the sun is a flame-white disc
in silken mists
above shining trees,—
if I in my north room
dance naked, grotesquely
before my mirror
waving my shirt round my head
and singing softly to myself:
"I am lonely, lonely.
I was born to be lonely.
I am best so!"
If I admire my arms, my face,

William Carlos Williams

my shoulders, flanks, buttocks
against the yellow drawn shades
who shall say I am not
the happy genius of my household?

It knows its power to live in deserts; knows it can make much out of next-to-nothing; hang on by the skin of its teeth:

I bought a dishmop—
having no daughter—
for they had twisted
fine ribbons of shining copper
about white twine
and made a towsled head
of it, fastened it
upon a turned ash stick
slender at the neck
straight, tall—
when tied upright
on the brass wallbracket
to be light to me—
and naked,
as a girl should seem
to her father.

With pride it feels the return of animal health, the good tickle of the beast-skin:

It is cold. The white moon
is up among her scattered stars—
like the bare thighs of

Port of New York

the Police Sergeant's wife—among
her five children—
No answer. Pale shadows lie upon
the frosted grass. One answer:
It is midnight, it is still
and it is cold—!
White thighs of the sky! a
new answer out of the depths of
my male belly: In April—
in April I shall see again—in April!
the round and perfect thighs
of the Police Sergeant's wife
perfect still after many babies.
Oya!

And with joy we receive the reassurance brought by
these pieces, take the signal of imminent habitable land
they give. The trip from the old to the new world upon
which we are all in spite of ourselves embarked has gotten
most of us not to a city spreading "its dark life upon the
earth of a new world, rooted there, sensitive to its richest
beauty," or about a temple where "the tribe's deep feeling
for a reality that stems back into the permanence of remote
origins" has its firm hold: achievement of American civilization. It has brought us it seems no further than a
low smoky shore looking rather like the Bayonne littoral
from the Staten Island ferryboat on a sunless winter's
day: a slatey weed-garden of wharves, gas-tuns, church-
spires, chimneys, gash-like streets, habitations set against
ghostly blueless hills. And we have been standing at

William Carlos Williams

the rail, how often! undetermined to disembark our baggage; uncertain whether the shore before us is indeed solid earth upon which one can walk and nourish oneself, or merely a fume of strangling smoke; worried by the picture of a silly journey undertaken to a spot which is not firm land, and can never support the whole weight of man. But while we have been standing, somebody excited ashore has sent up some wild signal rockets through the gloom; and we see the scarlet spikey flowers abloom on the cinder-piles, and the little human habitation stand snug and whole in the shadow of vats and chimneys. Life goes on, behind this forbidding wall. The jumbled piles lose their dreadfulness. They have been shown rough customers enough, but beings among whom a sturdy pair of legs can navigate, and a stout brace of lungs breathe up. And we know the journey has led us somewhere, at least, and begin moving up our baggage.

Margaret Naumburg

MARGARET NAUMBURG's orientation has been neither to stone nor pigment, tone nor words. Life has made her prefer the diminutive human being as a medium of expression. Very early in her career she felt herself powerfully drawn to the revolutionary movement in education. Directly after graduation from Barnard, and while on her way to London to work in social research under Sidney Webb, she read Montessori's book; in an hour, she saw, in place of a process of stuffing, education become a method of laying hold on the fundamental realities of life. Curiosity, interest, imagination were focussed, definitely. From London in September she went to Rome; went to work in Montessori's laboratory; felt the deep living vision of the woman, and saw, also, to what an extent the Doctoressa had become untrue to her intuitions and fallen into slavery to fixed technical processes and routines of education. In 1913, Margaret Naumburg returned to New York with the intention of developing an educative medium of her own and conducted, during the winter 1913-1914, a class for very young children in the Henry Street settlement. During the seasons 1914-1917, she conducted two groups in the building of the Leet

117

School. Since 1917, she has had a school of her own on West Sixty-eighth Street.

Nevertheless, it is to the artists that she stands closer than to the people of her own profession. It is apparently only that the medium in which Margaret Naumburg works sets her apart from the creators commonly dubbed artists, and makes the little institution which serves as her work-shop seem a sort of place different from those upon the globe where wood or stone are expressively hewn, or images built in color upon canvas, or words or sounds composed into novels, poems, sonatas. The difference, indeed, is not of kind, only of degree, perhaps. The young directress is a sort of poet among the educators; and the two plain tall houses on the gray New York block are one of the spots, where, as in the glass-roofed studio or silent chamber of sculptor or poet, the thundering world comes whole.

Like the Alberich-cavern of Brancusi or the hastily-improvised dark-room of Stieglitz, Margaret Naumburg's school-house is "a place without walls." The horizons lie vasty round it. Landscapes stretch into the four quarters of life, penetrate pearl and bluish distances. For what has come to be inside the place has flown direct from a complete rejection of the values of brownstone, four-story, bourgeois New York; and from a complete faithfulness to the conception of a free, warm, aristocratic life and to a culture based upon the whole personality. The tiny human being cast into the turmoil of nature has

Margaret Naumburg

always made to rise, to some degree, inside this woman, the positive sense of what the human being is capable of achieving in integrity, in dignity, in loveliness. She has come to feel it not only through special and selected children from cultured and friendly surroundings; through the marvelous little creatures who go riding in Central Park in camel's-hair coats, their straight blonde hair smooth down their backs. And she has never felt it with her eyes exclusively at rest upon the forms of expression and release common to the art-life. Every sort of child, it seems, the harmed as well as the whole, the troubled as well as the bright, the handicapped as well as the privileged, has helped make grow in her the certainty of the capacity of many different sorts of personalities, on many different planes of intellectual advance, and through many different activities, for rich and high and beautiful existence. Despite the sorry history of man, despite the crumbling world; with a tough stubbornness which seems to grow more intense the darker the night and the more reactionary middle-class America becomes, she knows the wonder and fire and solid loveliness of the powers dormant or tangled in the child, knows into what good thing life might flame were they coördinated and released. There is a sort of stamp of the foot and defiant *quand-même* in her. And everything she lives and everything she sees in the four quarters of the globe, beauty of life and beauty of stone, fulfilments in love and fulfilments in art, psychoanalysis and the phi-

Port of New York

losophy of conscious control, music, dancing, and modern painting, in some mysterious fashion seem to bring her back the more intensely into the circle of this feeling, and feed and enlarge and clarify it inside of her.

The feelings which come to life in Margaret Naumburg are anything but original with her. Everybody has had their like; old-fashioned people have had them when, for some reason unknown to themselves, they have called the newborn "God's child," and placed the ownership of the small creature outside the circle of men and close to the power which flows in all things and is contained in none. There can scarcely be any one who had not felt, in the still hush and wonder which descends upon him in the presence of the infant, the wonder of life's infinite power of re-creation, and the mystery of the identity and selfhood of things. And yet, the form which it has taken in this schoolmistress is new; new to America, certainly. In her, it has become aggressive, clear and intense to the fighting point. She knows the incapacity of the child to develop, unaided, the living green with which he enters the world, particularly in a convention-bedeviled society. She knows how readily the integrity, the creative potentiality, which every being brings into the world, comes to constitute, under repression, undirection, unrelease, the fuel upon which the ugliness and sick fear of the world grow fat. The human being is poisonous in proportion to the amount of his unfulfilment. And in America, a world is stupidly bent upon repressing, smashing, misdirecting every new spirit, every living human green, into the mould of the accepted, the established, and the tried. The destructive process commences in the home. And the school, instead of checking it, continues it with deadly efficiency. The cheap values of the business world dominate education. The child is submitted to what exists outside, and not within itself. Stress is put on physical and material increase, not on mental and spiritual development. The fine body is encouraged; the fine mind repressed through malnutrition, to the common level. Hence, Margaret Naumburg finds herself moved to intervene between what is new and untried and experimental in the child and the machinery unfriendly and destructive to it. For the sake of life itself, she finds all of herself moved into creating an environment nourishing to the spirit of the children and capable of protecting it, as the glass protects the delicate vernal shoots, until they have become sufficiently powerful to meet the world and oppose to the old forms their very own.

So she has made a free school. Techniques, mechanisms of education, are all made flexible by the feeling she brings to her work. The place is free of dogmas of all sorts. It is with the wish to release the individual essence that Margaret Naumburg comes to her task. And with the empiric fact, the individual child, she begins. For her, each child is a separate and distinct problem, requiring its own method of approach, its newly furbished armory of levers and instruments. She stands, as every artist stands, the balance of two dogmatizing extremes. To her right, there are the academicians among the educators. These have formed their theory of education, their routine, independently and averted from the special case which every child is. From what they believe to have been the experience of the past, they have abstracted certain laws; and these laws they set out to follow systematically in every instance, quite independently of the individuality of the child. However much these academicians may seek to relax and make more flexible this routine, their faith in this one fixed and fundamental discipline remains inviolable, and to the utmost of their capacity they submit every one of their charges to it. Probably at heart these educators are of the sort of men who are obsessed by the belief that the impulses of the infant are naturally destructive, and that alone the intellectual routine which man has developed in the past can save the youngling for society. So, in their effort to make the new creature conform to the old world, and adjust him quickly to what is already here, they take from the child what is most valuable to it, its proper principle of growth, and produce the type of undeveloping, bored person with which our world is heavy and stale.

If Margaret Naumburg stands far removed from these schoolmasters she stands equally far from the greater number of those who constitute the flaunting red wing of education. These latter have discarded, or would discard, completely the influence of the past. Like her, they wish to commence with the empiric fact of the individual youngling. Like her, they recognize the pricelessness of the individualities of the infants born into this world. But, unlike her, in fear of the harmful influence of the past and of all inherited technique, they have resigned, or believe they have resigned, all influence upon the children entrusted to them. If they give tools and other implements into the hands of the children, they withhold also, in fear of impinging upon the characters of the new generation, all the instruction in handling them. Indeed, these experimentalists are themselves much nearer the established order than they quite wish to believe. They, too, are acting upon a preconception. In their eagerness to escape the influence of the past, they have erected a theory that there can be life without influence, without touch of subject and object. They wish to believe that even the simplest parental solicitude is not a sort of influence; that handing a child a ready manufactured implement is not a sort of interference. Their educational method like their fathers' is not built upon feeling. For were there in them this sensing of the whole of life through the child, there would come into them also a confidence in their influence upon the child. A faith that in some mysterious fashion the feeling awake in them contained both themselves, the child, and something greater than either of them taken singly, would assert itself. There would flow in them a general consciousness of what the state of creativity to which they wish to help the child really consists and a general sense of the direction in which the small feet were to be helped walk.

If the mistress of the Walden School has in her mind any system or course of instruction, it is there tentatively: a scheme to be tried out against any new fact encountered by her, and modified at the behest of experience. She is not in love with her theory. In her practice, we never find her seeking to force her medium in order to try to make it submit in spite of itself and substantiate her preconceived ideas. Her machinery is perfectly flexible. Every year her school is new. Programs of instruction may be drawn up carefully each fall; they remain perfectly flexible nevertheless and subject to improvisations. If Margaret Naumburg is in love with anything, it is certainly with the truth of each experience. If the life of the child is to be released, if the spirit of her charge is to vibrate in harmony with something felt in her own bosom, she knows it must be released in its own proper fashion and be made to vibrate in harmony with its own individual basis. So her chief care is to preserve in each child its own identity. She is the listener, her ear close to the material she would shape; the artist, eager to hear the proper voice of the object, to coax forth from the diminutive human the personality she knows intuitively to be latent there. It is the coöperation of the interest of the child she knows she has to secure. She is aware there is in every one the curiously aggressive principle, analogous somewhat to the digestive function. By means of this principle the personality relates all the stuffs with which it comes in touch with itself, and grows in power without forfeiting its integrity. Whenever this principle is not functioning, there can be no absorption of what is brought to the pupil; for the amount of what can be really assimilated and made useful is proportionate strictly to the out-giving capacity of some channel of expression established in the child. Once established, however, the individual expressive power, the power of transmuting to an experience every event, will make the child of itself reach out toward the stuff which its teachers are capable of bringing to it; will make it project its interest deeper and ever more deeply into a world that offers it so many sources of pleasure. And learning, itself, usually inflicted with pain by an outside force, will be invited by something within the child, and be received no longer as a dead but as a related, living, colorful substance.

So the infant who comes for the first time into the two narrow four-story houses and sits round the low tables with his pinafored compeers, is left to listen for the promptings of his own individuality. Other schools might command some form of activity of him. This one waits, and is content to wait with patience for the moment when the little dreaming, exclusive, resistant world strands on some coast of reality, and the child evinces an appetite for plaiting rafia or drawing with crayons on paper. He is surrounded with the sort of materials which he is physically capacitated to manipulate. But he is left to obey his own young intuitions in selecting among them. When he begins to choose, there is help for him, for he is surrounded with teachers who have some esthetic feeling, and can assist him when he calls for instruction. And, as the child grows, and becomes able to handle more complicated media of registration, the outlet of representation is still the center of the educational system of which he is a portion. The many facets of reality with which the children are brought into contact, are made personal experiences through it. Pictures are drawn, words written, quite spontaneously by these children about the material presented to them in the form of a lecture or in the course of a sight-seeing visit. Pictures are drawn and words written about history and open-air markets alike. The oldest group of children in the school, hopefuls about the age of eleven, as a result of having undertaken the marketing for the school lunches, conceived the idea, quite independently, of doing a book "for other children in other schools," concerning "where food comes from." The child, under such conditions, then, has not remained merely the passive recipient of knowledge stuffed into him, a storehouse in which separate bundles of matter have been left. By virtue of the channels dug in his willing soil by his creatively orientated directress he has created toward the multiform material brought to his consciousness; and made of the events in which he has participated in his school house a very personal experience.

By means of this mysterious aggressiveness and inquisi-

Margaret Naumburg

tiveness lured out of the pupil the old dry course of study is made a living substance. The subject-matter is no longer an arbitrary melancholy complex of mathematics, geography, history, spelling, civics. It is become a single related interpenetrated thing; life in many slightly different aspects, but palpable as the same substance under its many various appearances. For as the awakened interest of the child goes out to the various forms of knowledge of itself, it finds them not as isolated cut departments, but as matters inherently related to whatever he has already learned. He finds the base for the new experience in his own past. The class which keeps the market-books for the school, for example, uses mathematics, but not as a sort of terrible and compulsory riddle game. It uses it as a clearly understood means, and the end irradiates the means. The market started the wonder of the group over the different sorts of foodstuffs available for the table in the city proper and began its speculation over the point of origin of the various edibles. A point of entry into geography, in particular toward the dry subject known to us of this generation as "physical geography," a thing of brown and green charts and trade-winds and New York state producing apples and hay, was begun under the most happy of auspices. Various markets were visited. The children saw Italians, Greeks, Poles, Jews, Hungarians, Germans; talked with them; and in conseqeuence, an inquisitiveness concerning the immigration problem, the problem of the movement of peoples, of the history of America itself, was inflamed. The subjects, then, do not have to be forced upon the pupils by the "teacher out of the machine." They are quasi-introduced by the alerted minds of the pupils; invited by small intelligences eager to receive information, and learn in what manner source books and other reservoirs of data are to be employed. The teacher is given more opportunities than he can fully accept. The mind is become a sort of little leaping fire, catching onto any inflammable substance it can touch and nourishing itself thereupon. One does not doubt the statement of the director that the children in the school outgrade those educated in the traditional fashion by years.

But if the individuality of the child is preserved through its expressivity, and its powers educated, the individuality is preserved as well through another contact. This is the contact with the group of children its own age. For it seems that the human being has to have these two touches, one of himself through materials, and another of himself through his fellows, that he can bloom and grow. The starved individual has nothing to give his group, and can get nothing from it. To be strong in oneself is to be strong in one's relationships; a give and take is effected that feeds the powers. The pupils in the fine school on West Sixty-eighth Street learn to form spontaneously a free part of a group self-constituted for the production of a playlet, the discussion of a topic pressing upon the minds of the young parliament, and the expedi-

Margaret Naumburg

tion of any commonly assumed business. The two contacts of the inner life seem to arrive almost simultaneously in the child who has been permitted to orientate himself in self-registration; and seem to maintain themselves through each other. One sees the progress of the two distinctly in comparing at any time the group of two-year-olds with the group immediately above it. In the lower group the power of concentration onto play, onto manipulation of materials, onto a story told, is feeble; and the tots sit about, so many mutually exclusive worlds, indifferent to each other's tempers and outbawlings, and filled like two business men their coevals with jealous exclusive desire for ownership and possession. In the higher class, however, the organism has begotten the power to direct attention more sustainedly in a single chosen direction. The children have also begun to lose their insensitivity one toward the other and are able to coöperate in the building of little houses and in all sorts of infantine works which require for their performance a union of several wills. And the double contact continues, strengthened, the way upward through the school, until, in the oldest group, one sees the hopefuls, whose strangely individualized water-colors hang about on the walls, carrying on discussions with syndical gravity, giving a play with charming forgetfulness of selves, playing in a "Kindersinfonie," or cooking a meal with far less friction of personalities than must occur in the kitchens of even the most velvety managed of Ritz-Carltons.

Port of New York

And, like the children themselves, these various groups manage to preserve their identities and singularities. No two of them have followed the same course of progress or passed the same point in similar fashions. They have each one of them produced their own ways of expansion and expression. With the same material their hands have achieved entirely distinct results. The plays composed and presented by one of the groups show a single character, a romantic, mystical strain. They are full of color and dance. Those composed and presented by another of the groups show a character entirely dissimilar, and full of irony and sardonic comedy. The difference of character has even been expressed in the manner in which the scenery has been painted, in the nature of the color schemes that have been chosen.

It is not difficult for the layman to ascertain the degree to which the school has been successful in producing the individualities of its many charges. The scholar's washings and drawings are there to show it at first hand. The exhibition of these products held during the winter of 1921 at the Bourgeois Gallery was primarily an exhibition of children's views of the world. The pictures were no dictations from adult brains convinced of what a child ought to do. They were representations perfectly true to the naïve and inexperienced vision of the fledglings. One saw girls, landscapes, pots of flowers, as the ten, eleven, and twelve-year-old feels them to be. There was design before there was versimilitude. There was the

130

registration of feelings about things, not of facts concerning them. The children had influenced one another, it was patent. Ideas were caught as ideas are always caught where people are experimenting. But no adult mind had pressed upon these small artists to alter their abstract and rapt vision in conformity with the adult world. And the work, like all good work, was the by-product of living; papers dropped in the hare-and-hound chase of life, revealing to the casual observer in which direction the happy runners had sped.

Besides, there is the atmosphere of the school house itself to further establish the success. The white rooms of this world of childhood are among the few deeply refreshing places in the city of New York. For they revivify with the color and vibration of such rooms and houses and spots where folk are living utterly truly to themselves. The complete faithfulness of the infants to their own natures, their own senses, comes to the visitor with the sudden cleansing and tightening that issues from all healthy growing life,—the jungle or the forest or the cathedral pile. One feels, in the presence of these busy, eager, unconscious younglings, one's own inner self. They are working to satisfy themselves. They are not calculating what folk will say of them. They know nothing of fame or money or adoring women; they work. It is not necessary to go to church, or to go to the country, or to go to Paris, to feel this trumpet call to the expression of one's own heart, while this school is open to view.

Port of New York

Never does the place display Margaret Naumburg. It is no frame for a self-exposition. The institution is focused on the children; on the theory of education. You see the children and the educational process. It is easy to remain unaware of the size of the effort which sustains the machinery. Nevertheless, once the interest has penetrated surfaces and looked behind the scenes, it is a very large and ardent human force, possessed of a very unusual tact and persuasiveness that meets the eye. There is no sense minimizing the toughness of the material with which the young directress has for many years succeeded in grappling. Most artists, while they are at work, have merely to struggle with themselves in the effort to create a harmony of elements. While she is at work, Margaret Naumburg has to struggle with elements outside herself. All education of children is really an education of parents; for which reason many people believe all education an impossibility. And still among a group of parents, Margaret Naumburg has succeeded in maintaining sufficient of a harmony to enable her to make her fight for freedom of the personality. Indifferent, suspicious, timorous people have been wrought to sympathize with hopes and fears they did not heed; persuaded to undergo with their children the adventure of liberation. Teachers with something of the point of view of the artist have been found to work along with the group and to work out their own lives through the contact as the children themselves work out their own.

132

Margaret Naumburg

It is with mixed feelings that we behold Margaret Naumburg at work. We have little but wonder for the generosity and deep beauty of the spirit she brings to her enterprise. But, side by side with the wonder, there pervades us a sense of pity over the destiny of her school. She works in the most frail, infirm, and ephemeral of media. Her art of teaching is like the dancer's: essentially the incandescence of a moment, untenable and fleeting. It cannot survive her and bring influence to bear on succeeding generations. Her school goes when she leaves it. Her technique like that of every artist is incommunicable. Like theirs it is the secret internal balance, coördination, and rhythm, of a rare and harmonious nature communicating itself to the material with which its possessor plays. It is the vital breath of a person capable of finding the all in many chambers of life, and therefore capable of making her chosen medium expand towards the skies. And though others may try to take up her work and continue in her way, it is not probable that their results can be as fine as hers. Persons as richly soaked with age-old culture as Margaret Naumburg, as beautifully endowed with courage and vitality, and as passionately aware of the eternal values do not come often to the field of education. They do not come often into life.

Kenneth Hayes Miller

ARTHUR B. DAVIES is the painter preferred of the American patroness of arts; and the choice gives her away sadly. It seems she goes forth not to the dream growing out of a reality, but to the dream erected at the expense of reality and over a reality left shoddy. This is what her preference confesses. The poesy pervading her favorite's canvases is not readily to be set apart from sentimentality. Poet, indeed, the painter is, in his earlier and in his later personal work; poet even in hours when he is a trifle over-busied laying thorns beneath the simmering kettle. The delicate fantasies in color stem from lyrical states of soul, and bear, elusively, in their wan and charming parts the rhythms that gave them birth. Light musics sing in suave and wistful shapes and rims. A faint golden stilliness tones the pictures, a faint luxurious breath. And Davies is an artist in the narrow sense of the word at least, full of taste, handling his material with a veritable if somewhat evasive charm. He has a happy virtuosity, great sensitivity, and erudition. No American painter, Max Weber alone excepted, senses more keenly than he the qualities in paintings modern and antique, and gives better proof in his own work of the keenness of his criticisms.

135

Port of New York

Alas, that his jeweled things should savor so strongly of illegitimacy, and wake in us resentment because of the emotions they distill!

But these tender harmonies have an unavoidable trace of sugarplum. It is all too lily-leaning, too wistful, willowy, and waning. We could wish the lute might more speedily regain her jaded cry, and the ache of the roses be answered. The dream brushes elusive lips on that calm marble front of hers; and the nicely painted nipples and parts have a lingering suspicion of pink taffy. There is much ostentation of nudities and concupiscences of things and breasts; but no woman-flesh in the paint. All is virginal and charming and decorative; safely guarded and awfully refined. What we are shown are pagan animalities, friezes of gods and naiads and embattled warriors; but what we feel are rapturous pages out of the days of a dreamy, wealthy, and esthetic spinster. All is tender, poeticized, sentimentalized, sterilized. It all takes place in dreamland. There are the moods of revery-tinted promenades on sunset terraces amid the spreading plumages of peacocks. There are the lights and falltime leaves of bracing walks in Westchester County on blue October days. There are lawns outside music room windows in the pale moonshine of New England summers. And no hot fecund surge of feeling dares assert itself. A delicious regret is left, memories of singing evening skies; and the wan birches whisper, "You have known it. You have lived."

Kenneth Hayes Miller

Very flame never drives this color forth. The ecstasy lies too near the surface; carries with it no sense of roots. The style is essentially external, unincorporated with the central being of the painter; not something so much of the man that it cannot possibly be divorced from him. We feel no great reality of any kind. The style remains always the result of the forest of Barbizon men appreciated with a sensitive eye, of Piero di Cosimo appreciated with a sensitive eye, of Picasso and the Chinamen appreciated with a sensitive eye; but none fully penetrated and assimilated into the bone and blood of personality. Abraham Walkowitz it was who called Davies' later segmented surfaces an adjustable cubism; image of pianola, to be coupled to the instrument and uncoupled from it at will. So with the song which Davies sings. It has the quality of a remnant of elegaic songs and moods of another day which did not feel the sharp edges, burning color, and pounding pulse known to us. The musical states of spirit seem part of the accepted romance lingering among the subjects which inspired them, apparently as really rooted as the trees among which they breathe, intruding between us and park scenery; importunate, insistful, refusing to budge before the labor of a lifetime has been spent uprooting them. Davies is an artist and Rossetti and Burne-Jones were amateurs. Still, the American's languor remains something of an afterglow of the pre-Raphaelite ecstasy and swoon; far more ably communicated; nevertheless less innocent because of its

137

untimeliness; more self-indulgent and sinister. Which necessitates somewhere a basic reality ugly for want of fire and clarity and heartiness. Life lived beautifully from the bottom up, lived up in truth and wonder, would not have fruit in pallid, unrealistic bloom, nor threaten to carry us so far from ways of truthful living.

No hidden unaired reality lies under the etching and painting of Kenneth Hayes Miller, no indulgence in illicit revery. The man's art forms the healthiest of companion-pieces to that of Davies. We turn to it with relief for the acidulous corrective it supplies. For Miller is essentially blood-brother to Davies; he is a Davies in better, harsher form. He and the pseudo-Greek both come out of the dry American background. Both have in good measure the American daintiness and learning; and both seem to feel something of the hereditary difficulty in leaving the wet of life come close to their skins. But the transcendentalism of Miller has taken the better turning. It has not made him fall into the hereditary duality, as it seems to have made Davies fall, and left him with a bloodless dream and a wingless reality. Miller's eyes fall on what exists about him, and if he apparently has not found a reality merging imperceptibly into dream as the stony slopes of Alps merge into their caps of shining everlasting snow, neither has he been driven to still his mind with the opiates of phantasy and dreamland. Something within is satisfied by a few plain joys of life. The juice runs red in beefsteaks and, if the panorama of the universe is

Kenneth Hayes Miller

not everlastingly shot for him with prismatic color, if something of the gray of mediocrity lies over much of what he sees round about, the gray nevertheless is never so bleak that fortitude and irony and salt cannot throw lights throughout it. Often the entering sun finds painful and ugly shapes. It finds harsh, swordlike, and bitter grasses strewn plentifully among the sweet. It finds perspectives stretching gently, sadly into solitary distances. But always it finds the shagged good aërated stuff of life as it is lived.

Miller's paintings and etchings live with this honesty. It is possible the flight does not occur with great wildness in his art. The aeroplane may not oftentimes leave the ground, nor the feeling be the warmest and most abundant. Basic truthfulness, a genuine appetite, are manifest nevertheless in his painting. The objects upon which the rhythmic forms are founded are real to the painter. He has had his hands on them and around them and felt the curvatures of their surfaces and the irregularities. The paint carries the truth of the palpation. The canvases bring a sense of immediacy, of life about dense and un-rationalized, and realized through the breast and arms. We have the sense of the rhythms and weights of some of the bodies of these shoppers and singers at pianos as though we were dancing against them. The paintings are full of rondures reported through the hollow of the hand; the round of a furred cap fitting upon a woman's head; the solid of a head fitting into a hat; the solids of forms played over by lightly sheathing silk. The painting of a woman pinning her hat is full of slippery wet, of bodily form received through all the senses. If they have nothing else, Miller's great instinctive dryads have organs, at least. They could bear children, these bathers. And whether his subjects are women or marshes and hills under infinite gray skies, the immediate foregrounds of his canvases are always dynamic and replete. The forms surge directly from the lower edges of the canvases with positive sculpturesque mass. The bathers press their somewhat muscular and Swedish bulks directly toward the spectator.

The most perfect of Miller's work is to be found in his etchings and his landscapes. No American painter has done better things with the human figure in paint; nevertheless, for all the appetite and large feeling for form which he has brought to them, his painted bathers and shoppers are not entirely satisfactory throughout. Some exceptions to the rule exist; one remembers an immense reclining figure with two smaller nudes seen in the semidistance; and the form of the reclining woman has a Veronese and Venetian-like amplitude and magnificence. There is a clear, perfect nude standing in a bare room by a rubber-plant. There is a stout woman in gray singing at the piano, opening her mouth in half intense, half flaccid fashion, and the painting brings one in some way a sense of the monotony and eternal second-rateness of existence; nature taking the lives of her creatures and pour-

Kenneth Hayes Miller

ing them out carelessly; floods of energy shaken forth, nothing very noble, very intense, very tragical happening withal. Some of the latest figure paintings have a rich, sad singing quality of gray. Scarcely any of the figures clothed or unclothed is without some amazing articulation of parts; magnificently given haunches and stomachs. Passages of strongly rendered color-sensations appear. But the greater number of Miller's nudes leave one slightly irritated. He has not ever entirely fused pigment and the human body. The forms are never quite complete. A promenader is given three-quarter way with marvelously felt amounts in sleeves and haunches, with marvelously given palpabilities under cape and furs and silken blouse; then the column breaks off and turns wooden in the face. The flanks and folds of skin of a sitting woman are rich and fluent; then the arm goes dead and a hand is boneless as a hunk of meat. Renoir is suggested, but the opalescence and fluidity are missing. Miller's tendency to overmodel is too frequently apparent. Parts leave the realm of painting altogether, walk into sculpture. In both defect and corrective we feel the not entirely successful struggle with the blood. That is natural, for it is not to be overcome in a generation. Miller commenced in the Ryder tradition. He was a friend of the old dreamer. His glamorous and poetical portrait of the ancient mariner reveals the depth of the blood-sympathy which bound him to the painter of the lone little barks on the ocean. Later, Renoir came as a

second great influence, let in, doubtless, by a gradual
crumbling of the Puritan's Chinese wall against the laughter of the flesh; and to the gray period there succeeded
one of tapestried color and butterfly brushstroke. But the
wall is not entirely broken in Miller; at least, not when
he tries to approach the living satin in paint.

For some reason unknown, he has better luck in the
medium of etching. Whatever the cause, the massive
feeling of rhythmic form and the eastern daintiness of
line interplay far more uninterruptedly in his black and
white. The powerfully articulated and counter-thrusting
masses are given with tendril-delicate strokes. An whole
nature breathes freely in all its honesty, irony, and refinement in these proofs. And, even more curiously, the sensuous feeling which is somewhat lacking his figures over-
flows his landscapes with their pink and orange and green
tones at once acidulous and warm, cold and sweet, salt and
rich, their lushness of form and fluidity of movement,
their delicacy of brushmanship. And just as there is more
essential feeling of woman in the draperies of the shoppers
than in their flesh, so too there is more genuinely feminine
presence in the cloudlands and hills than in the figures.
Entirely surprising the fact is not, since women are so
like to mountains. (However well you know them, the
articulation of their forms always comes as something of
a surprise; you never know just how it is they go; and
they lie there in mysterious earthfastness, strong without
moving.) But why it should be given a painter to feel

Kenneth Hayes Miller

the song of woman-flesh so much more swimmingly through the smooth and stubbly protuberances of the landscape than through the body itself, that is known to God alone, who alone can sound the mysteries of the Yankee soul.

Miller has done important work as a teacher, too. He is without doubt the best, and perhaps the only really successful instructor in the art of painting in New York. We do not have to attend one of his classes at the League to know the reason. It is to be known quite plainly through his etchings and paintings. A tonic principle is at play in them. They adjust us lightly to the streets of the new world; and if Miller is so successful in getting people to paint, it is because behind the instruction in method there breathes, as there breathes through the dabs of pigment, a realistic, unchimerical spirit. Their well-nigh moral impulse draws us ever back to his paintings. The color, the form, and texture rid us of the burden of fraudulent idealism which lies heavy on each American back. They make us cease striving to produce out of ourselves perfections which do not lie in us; for they marry us with a certain good humor to the queer, mediocre, lusty creatures we are. The gray feeling in the landscape is not so much the gray of disillusionment as it is the grisaille of stoicism. They reduce our self-conceit, for they make us think not unwell of our everyday selves. They tell us much of the basic grimness and futility of human existence; but they make it easier for us to turn with a good heart to cultivating our little garden plots. The robustly interacting forms give us stomach. The delicate tendril lines, the light motes of paint give us happy hands.

Roger H. Sessions

WERE the queen of music a light divinity, like as not the last past months Professor Sam Eliot, Jr., of Smith, would have been hearing her play all sorts of nice little things to him upon her harp. Being not one of the looser, but of the graver Olympians, it is probable that she has merely been leaning over him from out a window in heaven and addressing some hallelujahs and *salves*, *gaudias* and *pax vobiscums* from the pipes of a concert-organ; fluting rapturously upon him many a brilliant morning, and encircling his front many a sunset hour with tender-breathèd thanks. Some marvelous expression of her gratitude, assuredly, she has been making him. Few of late have been kindlier than he to her congregation upon the earth, or more deserving of her smiles. Not himself of the musical confession, he has nevertheless most admirably supported her cause. It seems he is a member of that race which is falling more rapidly than leaves do in November, or Nordics in the minds of neo-Hegelians: the race of American college professors who have not yet permitted the environing elements to annihilate intellectual curiosity and courage in them. In the course of the last year this young man persuaded the class about to be graduated from Smith to give Andreyev's *The Black*

145

Maskers as its commencement play; persuaded the
faculty to sanction the heterodox choice; and, most in-
spiredly of all, procured the right to invite a certain unknown young composer to supply the incidental music so
richly invoked by the dramatist. In this fashion, he built
well, placed Polyhymnia in his debt. For he made himself the immediate producing cause of one of the most
important events in the life of music in America. He
made himself the midwife to an event which commences
a new time in it.

We have proof that, at length, for the first time since
the colonization of the Atlantic seaboard, an whole creative musicianship has appeared among the Americans.
The audiences which assisted at the three performances of
The Black Maskers in Northampton in June heard an
incidental music poorly performed, muffled by the two circumstances that it was sounded from behind the stage,
and by a scratch body of instrumentalists; and nevertheless thrilling and winged. Only those of the auditors
quite shut in sensibility could have failed to perceive,
through the muffling matter, the living stuff of tones.
Music was there; there was an intention which transpired,
even off the instruments of amateurs. The nine numbers
supplied by the composer brought perfectly to Andreyev's
drama the extension through music required by him. They
are a re-creation, in a sister medium, of the play itself;
flowing from a vision of it so profound and exact that it
seems the composer must have stood while composing close

Roger H. Sessions

to the point at which the dramatist stood when he made the dialogue. From these pieces, we receive a joy and satisfaction not incomparable to that which we receive from the score of *Pelléas,* from the *Psalms* of Bloch, the Möricke-songs of Wolf, or from any other musical composition in which a composer has actually created toward a poet: stood upon his own shoe-leather, and enormously enriched with his proper life-blood a literary expression. They have indeed the wild sinister pulse of Andreyev's dolorous phantasy, the sardonic and anguished cries, the flow of inky depressive current. Their tones utter, too, the chaos, the sorrow, the baffled frenzy of the mind which can no longer harmonize its visions, its many cruel, irreconcilable truths, and lies disrupted in doubt. The music has the indefinite, vague outline of bitter, endless revery, of Hamlet-like melancholia streaming densely, silently through rocky wastes and mocking perspectives underneath a sky eternally charged with murk. Lorenzo calls his musicians to play; and what sounds from their pieces gibbers and cavorts and shrieks like humiliating, destructive thoughts that will not down. A wedding-procession is organized; and wedding music is played fraught with the atrocious cries and furious irony consequent to a suddenly shattered dream, a suddenly yawning abysmal vision. More than the words, the music of Lorenzo's song curses life and confesses Satan. Music comes full of chill metaphysical brooding; deathly beautiful with the wind from out the inhuman spaces of the universe; stark and black with the sense of crucifixion. And last, while the flames of death beat back the storm of black maskers, the orchestra chants and exults and is transfigured with the cleansing, releasing, resolving deed.

A psychic maturity, freshness of spirit, living culture, and technical control have opened into the realm of music in America. The music to *The Black Maskers* is no happy hit such as many slight talents make once in their lives; accidents likely as not never to repeat themselves again. The author is an artist. His workmanship declares him marvelously in control of his resources, capable of producing hard form which reveals itself the larger the more it is heard. Broken as it sounds, elusive and mysterious as it is in outline, full of abrupt brutal resolutions and strange new sounds and sudden suspensions and blinding blurs, his work has a fine clarity and solidity of form. There is not a consonance in the work; the ideas are subtle and delicate; nevertheless, we do not go lost in this free, ultramodern style.

A living flow informs the structure. The clangorous and ironic passages subside naturally into the weeping, dolorous, soft ones. Nor has the music form in the American manner: at the expense of robustness and vibrancy. There is great strength in the movements; powerfully pulsing rhythms; long melodic lines that flow and continue and extend in beauty; no padding, no waste. The orchestral dress, too, is masterly. There were twenty-nine or thirty instruments playing; the score calls for no

Roger H. Sessions

more; yet musicians in the audience found themselves deceived as to the number and character of the components of the band. One, an expert, went behind the stage looking for bass-clarinets and contrabassoons; and found merely clarinets and fagots: the brilliant handling of the lower registers of these common instruments had caused the mistake. Indeed, perhaps only one element which might have been present in this art was wanting. That was the absolute individuality of style. Not that there was any plagiarism or even derivative material in the score. Except for some moments, mostly in the final fire-music, when vague resemblances to Moussorgsky and to Bloch appear, the music is never reminiscent. It merely wants that final sharpness of contour which the musics written by composers in the fulness of their maturity beget. But taking into consideration the youth of the composer, we see that it could not possibly have put in appearance at this early time. It is thoroughly normal, even by the laws of genius, that it should have absented itself.

Roger Huntington Sessions, the composer of this beautiful, moving work, is indeed still in his twenty-seventh year. He was born in Brooklyn at the close of 1896; but Hadley, Massachusetts, has been the residence of his family during nearly three centuries. Whether or not there were musicians among his ancestors is not known. There were clergymen, however; his maternal grandfather was Episcopal Bishop of western New York. Sessions ma-

triculated at Harvard at the age of fourteen; was editor
for a while of the Harvard Musical Magazine. After
graduation, he went to the Yale Music School to study
under Horatio Parker. He remained three years in New
Haven; then received the appointment of instructorship
in theory of music and orchestration at Smith College.
While at Smith, he found time to come to New York and
study under Ernest Bloch. When the Cleveland Con-
servatory was organized around Bloch, two and a half
years ago, Sessions accepted an engagement as instructor
in the theory and history of music, and has been associated with the institution since. A number of compositions preceded *The Black Maskers*, among them a symphony. But the Andreyev music constitutes an Opus 1.

The hour which strikes in it leaves us still a little
stunned. Only a brief while since, we had been wondering
whether the arrival of a musician with enough of chaos in
him to make a world were truly possible in America; wishing indeed for the tone such an apparition would give to
life, and nevertheless scarcely daring to expect to encoun-
ter it in our own day. Signs of an efflorescence in the
musical life were not wanting. Many young earnests of
future performance had been made; and some were more
than promises, merely: respectable and heartening performances. Nevertheless, the ripened, sovereign inner
force was not yet present. Itself is such a miracle that one
could not predict its arrival. And yet, that golden gift is
among us to-day. About it, the musical life reconstitutes

Roger H. Sessions

itself; gets a new gravity and solidness. It comes, as it must inevitably have come, as the voice of the living young people in a compromised and shoddy world. No Indian or negro or bastard Scottish tunes. Absolutely, no red, white, and blue. Rathermore, something remotely allied to the gray on gray of Russia. In it, the morbidity of the race whose most celebrated theatrical scene is Hamlet with the skull of Yorick, and whose favorite poem for a century was the *Elegy in a Country Churchyard*. In it, too, the repression, the over-withdrawal of the New Englander exposed to a winter which is too raw and long, and a summer which is too intense and abandoned; and which breaks, when it does break forth from him, in blood and pain and laceration. But, more than with any inherited trait of soul, the music of Roger Sessions is suffused with the state of those for whom the world to-day is dangerously near a vast bare barrack, and on whose lips the savor of life is brackish. It speaks their hundred ironic, conflicting, pensive, crisscross moods. And we feel strangely at home with it, strangely rich and released.

We cannot tell as yet whether Sessions' gift is primarily for the theater. The two best of the numbers in "The Black Maskers," the painful chaos of Lorenzo's thoughts in Scene III, the prelude to Act II, symphonic as they are, were inspired directly by the vision of the play. But the fact is not of necessity significant. The composer may find himself more richly in the absoluter forms. In any case, the machinery is not the matter of first importance. Sessions goes to a great career, whether it is to the opera, or the ballet, or the symphony that he goes, or whether it is to all three. It is we who are to be congratulated. He himself is good luck.

John Marin

MARIN is fast in American life like a tough and fibrous apple tree lodged and rooted in good ground. It goes infinitely well with him here in western light and clay. His branches bear fruit. Hardy *pyrus malus*, he is restlessly, unconsciously busied transforming the materials amid which he stands, dayshine and moisture and minerals, pigment and water and white sheets of Watman paper, into the fresh, firm, savorsome pulp of his art. Each year he gives himself anew in liberal windfalls, strewing on the soil about him his explosions of tart watercolor: slithering suns and racing seas of the coast of Maine; wet, fishy poems of headlands and pine-pinnacles and rain-gusts in which the rocky strength and almost Chinese delicacy of a sensitive and a robust nature have been completely, miraculously, released. And fruition in diaphanous washes, in pounding cobalts, and gritty earth-browns is as simple, as uncalculated, as integral a process with him as that of breathing. Works come into him as buds to the stalk, as breasts to the young girl. To Marin, as to the stilly laboring apple-tree, nature has lent the principle which makes the production of astrakans or bell-flowers or spies to the one, of images built in aquarelle upon white plinths to the other, the sole manner of existence possible to either. Neither debates nor questions the ultimate importance of pomes or water-colors. For both, the way of reaching fulfilments meet their individualities is widely open. And while there is a sun in heaven for them, and a little potash and phosphoric acid in the soil, they of instinct go their course, and give profusely of their lives in flower and in seed and in scented, acid-clean flesh.

Round John Marin, there move many sad, disgruntled beings, full of speech and lamentations. They are of the color of those who write in a book called *Civilization in the United States*. In words of many syllables, they bewail the fact that, in America, soil is poor and unfavorable to human growth, and men are rendered incapable of letting life pass clarified through them. But Marin persists, and with what ebullience and high spirit, in the rocky ungentle loam! He sings, whether men want his plastic harmonies or no. The incentive is from within. Men may not want his brilliant granitic wash; and still, he spreads his sensitive tips to the daypour, and meets each season with fresh vision. He requires so little pruning to preserve him: some bread, some paper, some tints. All else necessary to him comes with the sun. He is a favorable environment. Stieglitz and 291 Fifth Avenue have been a home for his spirit for the reason he has been able to use them; to take nourishment where nourishment is to be found. Nourishment for his spirit is spread with overflowing liberality upon shore and ocean, here where

John Marin

American Civilizers find so little to make song rise in them. Everything can produce in Marin his lyrical states of being, his sudden, rhythmical, flashing visions: a street-corner in down-town Manhattan, a sachem pine on Maine shoreland, summer-green hills in Delaware County, sand and fog and breakers of Stonington, a thousand unnotable niches. An outward push is leveled always from this bosom upon the overwhelming metal tons of the world. The menacing piles are thrust backward, held at arm's bay, by the force issuant from within. A skyscraper has but to jab its giant thumb into falling skies, or rapids of traffic to course under wedging walls and jagged mason-ries; a squall has but to comb the waters of Casco Bay as clawing fingers comb tumbling tresses, or sunset splinters to pour javelin-like over spruce-tops; fall blue to crowd over hilltops, or a shower lift its veilings and reveal bush-green new-laved, and the singing intensity, the sonorous beat, is present in his body. Feelings are up, lofty as the Woolworth Tower, wide-reaching as the expanse of run-ning sea, one and sovereign as the single spruce alone above the islanded bay, mystical as a rose-fluttered bridge extended into immeasurable warm distances. Something within imitates joyously the play of elements one against the other; the countermovement of towers and skylands; the landscape thrown violently to one side as the eye fol-lows the upward thrust of a tree-trunk; the rocking of the bluffs about the put-put in the billows; the fountain-wise fall of the leafage over the beech tree's column.

Port of New York

In those electric moments of vision, the objects present to the painter's sense are suddenly caught in the terms of a magical wash. The tangled shapeless world has suddenly given way before a delicious and contrapuntal water-color, rivulets and pools of aquatint, blank hard white meeting vibrant thick green and crushed tender rose, red celluloid lightenings, nuggets of somber and mystical color-ore. And the substance at play within the four outlines of his white oblongs is psychic matter running unclotted, squeezed as from a sponge; all open, all loose, all free. It courses in utmost relaxation. The water-color of Marin is a dance, a frolic, a tender wayward romance. People ask: "Is he entirely serious?" And, indeed, he has a perfect levity and nonchalance. If in Marin there is a creature with a great peaceful span in him, a serene inviolate open where a single tree stands as chieftain above a far-flung demesne and the ocean lies blue and infinite, fantastic strains of Puck nevertheless play in his blood. If in his skin there sits a being who perceives life much as the old Ionian seers perceived it, feels a cosmos composed of sand and fire, air and water, fire drawing water into floating mist, water returning to earth again in warm rain, endless mystic glittering cycles of life and death, there is also inextricably commingled with this visionary a person who scrubs his wash upon the paper with elfin freakishness; a Marin who is a sort of boy igniting water-color squibs; a timothy among the other

John Marin

grasses; a leprechaun who might have larked in the train of Titania and Bottom.

And the tangled world has made way for exquisitely balanced form. The water colors of Marin are life working absolutely within the limits of an esthetic medium. They are color. They are series of hues which condition each other's presence; hues appreciating one another and depending one on the other. Marin has a very certain and subtle sense of the values of prismatic color. His oppositions of tone are positive, and yet delicate and unobvious. A streak of dreamy crimson will wander out by the edge of the sheet; and for an instant we imagine it the caprice of the painter, merely. An instant later, the long mark has fused with the remainder of the edifice, and is felt holding in place the central shape of dusky green. Little Chinese wisps and shivers of tint dot his papers, little unobtrusive phantastic marks that seem to have strayed in by chance, but that in truth plot the central rhythm of the expression no whit less decisively than do the larger masses. Continual sudden oppositions of color shake on the movement of the works. They progress in quick wild leaps from color to distant subtle complementary hue. They pass with sudden delicious shocks from one texture to another, from shaggy surfaces spattered on the paper to smooth satiny brushes and flows. They pass from round to flat, from streaks which look like microscopic mountain ranges to streaks smooth as lake water at even. And the form of certain of the pieces which Marin has produced during the last years is solid as though the water-color were something hewn out of a front of rock.

It is a man's implicit confidence in his senses; a man's complete truthfulness to self, principle of fecundity in humankind, which, married to a delight in playing with water-color, has brought this shower of little masterworks upon the world. Marin seems of a single piece. No fear of sense breaks him, thrusting a floating baseless mind between him and the testimony of his senses; making him seek to force his experiences to conform with preconceived theories. Feeling and thought are one in him inseparably. Whistler, Winslow Homer, Cézanne, the Chinese, are forgotten when he works. He applies his wash with the directness of impulse that is supposed to be discoverable only in the work of young children. Conception and execution are so closely allied in Marin that they appear almost identical. His works are immediate realizations; expressions produced by one right in the middle of things and feeling them through every pore. This man, too, paints from the navel and addresses not the brain but the navel. And only because there is no schism in him between hand and brain has he mastered his medium. For water-color is a means which precludes hesitations. It is a means which demands, perhaps as much as any other medium, rapidity of decisions. It will not wait for long calculations. It requires a sort of instantaneous dis-

John Marin

charge of energy; a concentration and complete unification of resources, for its service. It is an epigrammatic language making very laconic statements of complex truths without, necessarily, minimizing the importance of the truths. It demands a very sharp simplification; it is a chink through which one glimpses mountainy vistas. The satisfaction it grants is the satisfaction of a great economy, the satisfaction of nature cheated, and a small space and a few shapes and lines made to contain un-crowded a multiplicity of things. And so much is Marin water-color's man, that he seems to be able to summon all his powers right on the spot before the singing landscape; to render the soarings inside him as one might jot down in a notebook during a minute-long pause in a stroll some phrase which had ducked up in the course of mus-ings. And when he turns to the medium of oil-painting as he has recently commenced doing, he continues the swift technique of the wash, the sudden intuitive leaps, and merely produces water-colors with somewhat more body, thanks to the weight of the oil itself, than water permits him to obtain.

And on his Watman sheets, Marin records what his eyes perceive, just as it is perceived; unconcerned with what records itself, or is supposed to record itself, on other retinas. His vision is strange; but he trusts his senses against those of other men. And so the rapid movement of objects against each other in our vision of nature appears upon his paper with utter directness. He

gives, first of all, the apparent movement in things seen
from the windows of bodies in rapid motion. He gives
scenes as they move by us outside railway trains; telegraph
poles slung backward, middle distances marching ahead:

> The sheep in the meadow
> Tossed back in a scare.

He gives the world as it appears from the motor-launch
heaved about on the waves: ocean swells and fir-crowned
bluffs engaged between them in a boxing-match. He puts
down a world out of focus as it seems in a suddenly
leveled glance into distance: the center of vision alone
clear, the peripheries blotches and indefinite masses of
color. The world is there, just as it is perceived before
the reason steps in and adjusts it with old experience: a
series of lights and planes and shapes. But Marin's world
is not only a world perceived from the platforms of objects in rapid motion. He gives the movement created in
things by the eye itself even when the body is stationary.
For the healthy eye stirs about in its socket continually;
and in so doing, creates balancing contrary rhythms in
what it falls upon. If, for instance, our glance runs up
a tree-trunk quickly from its base to its crown, the landscape behind the trunk will appear to throw itself violently to one side. While we walk, slowly, the middle
distance of the landscape begins to move in a direction
opposed to that taken by the receding objects of the foreground, and all the while the far background begins a

John Marin

march of its own, opposing the movement of the middle distance by taking, though at a very much slower pace, the same direction in which the foreground moves. We are continually casting things before us and behind us, upward and downward, with our eyes out of some need of the body; and there are never less than two planes, and generally more, in motion about us when we walk abroad among rooted objects. And this perception of movement reported by his eye is the basis of Marin's form. He knows precisely when he has daubed upon his paper the scratches and spots and swirling lines, the texture and color-progressions which record his impressions of three-dimensional movements of objects caught by the swiftly traveling eye. Because of this perception he stands among the great realistic discoverers.

Through it, to-day comes off the turbulent street and stands clarified and significant upon the walls. It is the very excitement of the present hour which, caught by the painter in the tranquillity of his salt Maine, is fixed in the brisk counterpoint of washes. At the core of the marvelously stained sheets there resides, of course, like a sweet kernel in a nut, like a whiff of the Atlantic in a breeze, the element of race independent of all external influence. It is the quality which was resident in the man from the instant of his conception, we suppose, and which undoubtedly would have realized itself in every age and in every land in somewhat similar an accent. There is a delicacy, a charm in Marin which is French, certainly.

161

Port of New York

No German would have seen the Dolomites as Marin saw them in his series of 1910. Besides, there is a nervousness, a fine dash and roughness of edge, in him, that is Yankee. His excitability is essentially that of a people submitted to violent and sudden thermal changes, wintry January mixed with soft languorous spring twilights, sudden summer heats in March, perpetual wrestling matches between arctic and tropic oceanic streams. Moreover, his wash is curiously different in tactile quality from that of Europeans, particularly from that of the recent French masters. None but one American-born could have rubbed this pigment and made it into the peculiarly tempered. color it is. It strikes a western dominant with its salt and slap. Something Walt Whitmanish abides in its essence. There is richness of touch; sensuality, even, crushed out like fruit juice, in Marin. But it is a richness economically emitted, athletically held in rein; a sensuality not repressed and sour, but chaste and not easy.

The place, the milieu, is present, too. Marin has seen his two points in space, New York and Maine; particularly perfectly the latter. People familiar with Casco Bay and Stonington who have never before seen a Marin water-color have been known to point to some of the most "abstract" of his representations, name certain headlands, coves or islets and give the pictures the same titles given them by the painter in his catalogue. And, still, fused with the inscrutable elements of race and place, there pulses in every one of Marin's spurts the tempo of

John Marin

the modern world. In each, through notations of rapid movement there beats the frantically accelerated age, life flying onward through space with such rapidity we can scarcely glimpse it as it thunders by; climax of life succeeding climax with indecent unceremoniousness; generations being littered every four or five years; an era of sudden developments. Scarcely any other plastic rhythms outside musical art express as do these a lightning momentum. Here, particularly in Marin's New York, all is sudden upheaval, spasmodic earthquake from the abyss of society, a thousand maddeningly conflicting tugs, London Bridge falling down, Wall Street a clattering shamble. For, in this age, men are commencing to find themselves forced to make mental calculations with the rapidity of electric current if they will remain functioning. We seem called upon to show a power of abrupt readjustment like that once shown by primitive animal life in the days when climate made immense sudden springs. And Marin appears to be one of the individuals who possess elasticity sufficient to acquire, quite undeliberately, the new technique of living. He understands with a sudden intuitive leap, reaches his goal he knows not how, and yet with all the elimination of slow human processes, in complete certainty.

In the short space of a decade and a half, another poet has been given America. The development of John Marin has been a rapid process, extended over no more than fifteen years. In the exhibition of over a hundred of his works held in the winter of 1921-22, there was included a water-color which is scarcely emerged in feeling from the Whistlerian tradition; and the sheet was painted as recently as 1908. Like so many American masters before him, Marin found himself comparatively late in life; he was well on in the thirties when he quit the architect's office for the life of art. During the first few years, his expressions were, in comparison with the dense, mightily rhythmical pieces of the recent years, lyrical and soft in character. As in the early Stieglitz photograph, one feels in them a being peeking through a silver mist. The mood registered is often one in which a wound is felt a-healing: there has been a deep hurt, one guesses, but it is no longer serious; the world, so warm with rain, so tender with opalescent mist and watery sunshine, is there to show that it was long ago, and forgiven, and of no serious wrong. And the head must have been lifted, and very gently, very whimsically, there must have come over the painter that it was, after all, a crystal, dancing world: not boisterously, not noisily, with a sort of little inner leap, and a smile upon the mouth.

But, commencing about 1915, the Marins began to come stronger in color and in tension. There can be no doubt that the experience of 291 Fifth Avenue, particularly the experience of the back room, where the painters sat about the iron stove and warmed their feet and thrashed violently through æsthetics, helped considerably

John Marin

in this development. Marin, who did not so passionately care for thought, was forced to reason. The problems of his art began seriously to engross him. The images commenced to be built upon the white paper as on a plinth. In particular, the effects of saturation with one or two spots began to make itself felt. Marin has had the courage to renounce much for the sake of achieving depth. He has found in himself the patience to set his soul still in one or two spots and permit absorption to take place. Marin has not traveled far from New York since 1908, the year of his Dolomite trip; Grantwood and Stonington have become his two poles. He has concentrated on a comparatively few motifs; the New York of the paintings of 1921 was anticipated a dozen years ago by studies of the promontories and chasms of lower Manhattan, and by the very much skeletonized etchings of 1913. And if each one of Marin's water-colors seems the fresh attempt at the solution of a problem, the problems have a certain patent homogeneity. In result the painter each year has been able to bring to his work a greater complexity of knowledge and feeling.

Till the full-throated being called by Henry McBride the Beethoven of water-color, began to have being. Thirteen years, then, have seen the growth of a delicate Whistlerian into one of the few important artists America has produced, and into one of the few great living painters. And the process of development in strength continues in a sort of geometrical progressivity. Each year Marin surprises with manifestations of rich power intenser than those of the year preceding. Each year one feels him at the limit of his capacity; and the next year he comes down from the east with new surges and reaches and color-counterpoints. The lad has long since made way for the man. The powerful sea-pieces and majestic sailing-ships carry the weight of a complete maturity, a full development. One comes each year to feel spectator to the unrolling of a larger future. We have a poem of fecundity indeed.

Arthur G. Dove

THERE was much talk of American earth one April day in 1921. It was the day the show of younger painters was hung in the Pennsylvania Academy. And in that brief hour of confidence and expansivity, while the hanging committee freshly come over from New York inspected the preliminary arrangement of canvases on musty sacrosanct walls, one racy earthen phrase recurred in many mouths. The painter who conducted a newspaper cub from color complex to complex graciously attempted a description of the common unconscious ideal drawing the American artist, and of the symbolical act in which the generation might come to fruition. And he spoke of a "kiss" planted upon American earth. The brush-brother manœuvering framed pieces in a corner, and demanding more advantageous positions for the works of synchronistic comrades, found time, nevertheless, to echo the phrase. He, too, confessed to perception of a movement in American men toward passionate homage of the soil. So likewise did the youngling making loud and fervent affirmation that the painting on the dun canvas before him was color for the reason that it had color-areas "like a painting of the Renaissance." Hue might be form or might have no other power save that of accentuating form: the final act of reconciliation of the living with those who had lived before them on the ground on which they stood, figured on his lips, too, as an embrace bestowed the soil.

It is possible that the speakers expected no corroboration from the spots of color on the sour walls. It is possible that they had projected the date of the happy nuptials somewhat over-generously into distance. For they did not turn to the exhibition and receive the veritable corroboration with which it could have furnished them. And, there is no doubt, most of the pictures would have stared at them in blank incomprehension. No comfort was to be gotten from them. Nevertheless, there *was* inside the place in that hour one picture at the very least which would have reinforced their prognostications and shown that the movement of root-taking and home-fixing was, even then, under way in American life. There was present a brown and blue pastel of Dove's; and there is not a pastel or drawing or painting of Dove's that does not communicate some love and direct sensuous feeling of the earth. There is not one that does not bring us with a queer thrill close up to some of the gross and earthy substances from which we moderns involuntarily shrink; and lay our hands gently upon hairy animal hides, and rub them over rough stubbly ground, and pass good gritty soil through fingers. They bring to the nostrils the healthy pungence of pastures and of barn-lofts. We are no longer afraid; *that* has been overcome; and we rejoice in the warm udders of the

Arthur G. Dove

cows; laugh at the grace of the young calf close to us; rub the palm over old pieces of used wood and palp their rough sides. Even when some sort of blanket seems to separate us from the object, and the life of the painting itself seems a trifle muffled and dull, we are never left entirely without the gratification of some chaste and robust animalism, some solid feeling of the soil. Dove begins a sort of "Leaves of Grass" through pigment.

For Dove brings the beginnings of an whole man to his art. He brings a spirit which does not separate any one function of life from the others. It does not know noble and ignoble organs. Hence, it has the power of making all of its bodily functions sweet by relating the whole of life to that function. And it has the power of making the whole of life rich and sensible through feeling which does not spring from the head alone, but from the breast and belly and reins as well. When this man paints, the pressure on the brush in his hand carries the weight of the body as a whole, and the life of the body as a whole. He has always a fund of robust and delicate animalism to express. He has dark, pungent, gritty hues in his palette; dark subtle schemes and delicate gradations of earth-browns and dull shadowy greens and dirt-grays and in-testiny whites that seem to flow from the body's fearless complete acceptance of itself. Sensitive realizations of metal-tones break through this somber palette; strong vi-brant renderings of coppers and silvers. But the ground-tone remains umbrageous and grim and sometimes even

169

dour. And Dove's compositions are built up of abstract shapes that suggest the body's semi-consciousness of itself: of intestine-like shapes, shapes of fern-fœtuses in May, animal udder-forms, forms in nature which doubtlessly had a fascination for the mind unafraid of its own body, and recorded themselves under the lintel of consciousness. It is not from the head that these lines and masses are pushed. It is not from the head that they are willed, and limited, and arranged. They gush forth spontaneously as breath. They are easy and free as the swing of a body relaxed in motion.

For Dove is very directly the man in painting, precisely as Georgia O'Keeffe is the female; neither type has been known in quite the degree of purity before. Dove's manner of uniting with his subject matter manifests the mechanism proper to his sex as simply as O'Keeffe's method manifests the mechanism proper to her own. For Georgia O'Keeffe the world is within herself. Its elements are felt by her in terms of her own person. Objects make her to receive the gift of her woman's body in disruptive pain or in white gradual beauty. Color, for her, flows from her own state rather than from the object; is there because she feels as she does and because it expresses her feeling. And the world rendered by her brush as line and shape and color upon canvas is transfused utterly, whether it comes in the guise of lake water and morning hills, or lilies burning like torches in stone tombs, or strange abstract surfaces and folds, with the

Arthur G. Dove

sense of woman's flesh in martyrdom, or in state of highness and glorification through flooding unhemmed spirit. Dove feels otherwise; from a point of view directly opposed to that of his sister artist. He does not feel the world within himself. He feels himself present out in its proper elements. Objects do not bring him consciousness of his own person. Rather, they make him to lose it in the discovery of the qualities and identities of the object. The center of life comes to exist for him outside himself, in the thing, tree or lamp or woman, opposite him. He has moved himself out into the object. The object, butterfly, cow, coal-ash, tree, flower, metal, is established for him by a certain condition of light felt provenient from it; a condition which the painter feels to be binding upon himself; and which he is not at liberty to change by the addition or subtraction of any color under penalty of vitiating the integrity of the object. And in his return to the world through art, Dove brings with him a sense of the thing as it exists for itself, deep in proportion to his experience of it. If he is generally found expressing himself through pastels, it is for the reason that the blue tones which he can achieve with them render to his satisfaction those very conditions of light recurrently established by his subject-matters.

And his work brings the shy interior life of things, most often familiar humble things: cattle, old wood, rusty pieces of farm machinery; the things as they perhaps exist for themselves. The brownish, cream-white pastel made

from the herd of cows brings the knowledge of some one
who has almost gotten into the kine themselves; and felt
from within the rich dull animality of their beings, felt
the thrust of the thin legs and toss of the horned front,
the unashamed udderful fecundity; and then given it out
again in characteristic abstraction and soft, sensitive, fuzzy
spotting. The pastel of the reds and blacks and yellows
about the gray egg-like shape comes out of the inner feeling of giant horses dragging a load up a yellow-loamed
hill, and gives in the cog-like shape and gray mass the
working of straining backs and the downward will of the
heavy inert bulk. The fawn-colors and soft whites of
the *Calf* render the shy gentleness of the new-born
beast, the feel of the skin, the secret nursling life, the
quaint instinctive flicking of ear and tail. There is an abstract goat that is almost the mysterious, capricious spirit
of the beast; tree-trunks that have in them the agony of
decaying nature; forests that are full of the dark upward
push of the great shafts and the interweaving branches,
the mysterious thrust felt by the primitive peoples of
life toward the light. And the wish to coincide with the
objects before him, to catch their actual substance, has led
Dove so far that, in one of his latest paintings, the acety-
lene lamp, he has not only given the quality of the metal
and the quality of the flame and the structure of the
machine, but made the image of the lamp the exact pro-
portions of the reality.

It must have been inevitable that the painter's feelings

Arthur G. Dove

about life should have been crystallized by the series of humble objects upon which his compositions are based. He was a farmer when he painted most of his pieces, and cows and calves and growing plants were in his mind. Besides, as a human being, it was of course that he should turn with large relief and regard animals, and get from them flashing feelings of the satisfaction of things filling inevitably a place. These organisms at least were not afeared of life. They were not at war with themselves, weeping over their sins, trying to improve themselves via the bootstrap, and filling the air with tempest and hysteria. These were calmly fulfilling the laws of their being, passing life fully through themselves. Like himself, they were all of a single piece. They had something to give which most of mankind had not. At least, they did not try to crush out of him the unity struggling for expression.

Not from any painter do we get a clearer sense of the miles laid behind by American life in its progress. We step with Dove upon a plane warmer, fuller, earth-faster than any known by the artists of the preceding era; by Ryder, for instance. Dove comes out a culture commencing to base itself upon the whole personality. In Ryder, the old Puritan dividedness still obtained; the fugitive state from body and earth; the duality of body and soul. That is passed in the new man. We walk amid a lusher, sunnier earth. And we have the certainty of it in spite of the fact that Dove, in a sense, is less the artist than the old man was. Ryder was more complete, more mature upon his plane. He gave what he had in its own form. Dove remains a sort of cub of a brighter world. What he has achieved so far sets him among the important living Americans; but his achievement is still rather more the prelude than the symphony. Dove is a man who has for various reasons never been able to give the power in him the chance of manifesting itself in all its altitude. Some blanket between the full man in him and the earth has not yet been entirely cut. But the high powers are recognizable even when they come wearing veils. The young swans are fledged gray; and for a while they dot the stream with their sober quiet hue. They grow into the maturity of white.

Sherwood Anderson

THEY pass us every day, a gray and driven throng, the common words that are the medium of Sherwood Anderson. In the thick ranks of the newspapers they go drab and indistinct as miners trooping by grim factory walls in latest dusk. Men's lips form them wherever in all the land talk is, but we mark their shapes no more than we mark those of the individual passengers in the subway press, the arm and overcoat jumble, each tired night at six. The objects symbolized by them lie in the range of vision of those who make each day the city trip to the office and workshop and back flatward again. They lie in the range of those who ride dully into country towns over dusty roadways, or work about their barns or in their fields or inside farm cottages. But the walls of the city thoroughfares do not impinge on us, or on the men who talk, or on the hacks who write. The earth and board sides and fences and plantations remain in a sullen murk. And the words that signify the things and their simple qualities remain in millions of voices dreary dead.

Story tellers have come with banner and hallo to lift them out of Malebolge, to burnish them, to write English, and have washed them to no more scintillance than has the tired crowd of Christmas shoppers in the Chicago loop. Dreiser himself sought to point and sharpen them, to set them together as squarely as dominoes are set together in the backrooms of German saloons. He merely succeeded in forming a surface like that of water-logged, splintery beams, unfit for any hardy service. It was only Brontosaurus rex lumbering through a mesozoic swamp. In American novels, the words remained the dreariest, most degraded of poor individuals. But out of these fallen creatures, Sherwood Anderson has made the pure poetry of his tales. He has taken the words surely, has set them firmly end to end, and underneath his hand there has come to be a surface as clean and fragrant as that of joyously made things in a fresh young country. The vocabulary of the simplest folk; words of a primer, a copy-book quotidianness, form a surface as hard as that of pungent fresh-planed boards of pine and oak. Into the ordered prose of Anderson the delicacy and sweetness of the growing corn, the grittiness and firmness of black earth sifted by the fingers, the broad-breasted power of great laboring horses, has wavered again. The writing pleases the eye. It pleases the nostrils. It is moist and adhesive to the touch, like milk.

No rare and precious and technical incrustations have stiffened it. The slang of the city proletariate has not whipped it into garish and raging color. Even in his pictures of life on the farms and in the towns of Ohio, Anderson is not colloquial. Very rarely some turn of language lifted from the speech of the Ohio country folk,

Sherwood Anderson

gives a curious twist to the ordinary English. The language remains homely, sober, and spare. The simplest constructions abound. Few adjectives arrest the course of the sentence. At intervals, the succession of simple periods is broken by a compound sprawling its loose length. Qualifying clauses are unusual. Very occasionally, some of the plain massive silver and gold of the King James version shines when Biblical poetry is echoed in the balancing of phrases, in the full unhurried repetition of words in slightly varied order. But the words themselves are no longer those that daily sweep by us in dun and opaque stream. They no longer go bent and grimy in a fog. Contours are distinct as those of objects bathed in cool morning light. The words comport themselves with dignity. They are placed so quietly, so plumbly, so solidly, in order; they are arrayed so nakedly, so four-squarely; stand so completely for what they are; ring so fully, that one perceives them bearing themselves as erectly and proudly as simple healthy folk can bear themselves. Aprons and overalls they still wear, for they are working-words. But their garments became starched and fragrant again, when Anderson squared and edged his tools. They leave us freshened as gingham-clad country girls driving past in a buggy do. If they are a little old and a little weary, they hold themselves like certain old folk who wear threadbare shawls and shiny black trousers, and still make their self-regard felt by their port.

Port of New York

It is the vague uncertain elusive music of folk in America that comes through this medium of words. Body of feeling in a groping struggling shoot of the Ohio countryside marshals the phrases, compels them into patterns, and makes the words pregnant with their real and transcendental meanings. In this writer, brother to all the dumb chaotic folk produced by two centuries of the pioneersman's life, the desire of the race is full a-cry. Sherwood Anderson was born among the men who had sacrificed, that they might take root in virgin land, much of what the centuries had warmed to life in their forbears across the Atlantic. He grew in a corn-shipping town of post-Civil-War Ohio; grew among people who had forgotten the beauty laboriously accumulated in Europe; grew ignorant of the fact that beauty made by human toil existed anywhere on the globe. Around him, too, everything was quantity, not quality; everything urged to small, cold ambition. He lived the days lived by countless other smart little boys in this meager civilization; volunteered to fight Spain and typhoid in Cuba; spent the money gained in soldiering in acquiring a little education at a fresh-water college; worked in factories, in bicycle-foundries; set out, driven by the universal goad, to become a successful business man; did become a successful business man. And still, in Anderson; in this creature sprung from out the raw American millions, desire for finer, rarer, larger life sings as it sings in every up-

Sherwood Anderson

springing, aspiring stone of Chartres. Its low voice is louder in him than the hysterical American mouth with its fictitious tumult and assurance, its rhetorical trumpeting of the high state of women in Minneapolis, the efficiency and hygienic charms of clothing-factories in Cleveland, the invigoration of the struggle for existence in New York. It will not down. It is too strong; it will not go to sleep in consenting in what happens to be powerful, or blind itself to the relationships of men and women the country over. Nor will it let itself be debouched into abdicating in favor of an interest centered entirely in children, or into the dream that possession of a house full of spick furniture and nickled faucets will suddenly make life flow sweet-colored and deep; nor ring bells of self-satisfaction to God for the reason that he has created a universe in which every one or every one's offspring can climb to the top of the human heap and become a millionaire. Cultures struggling for birth overcome the tribal fears in the man, make him tender, nervous, and musical with true feeling, quivering in readiness for motion toward the new life. Desire for new worlds, striving to connect with facts and objects at every street-corner fill him with tentative attitudes, tear at bonds, subside in pain, whisper promises of large movements and spaces. At the rear of his brain there murmurs always the liquid flow of worlds in progress in every living being. What Anderson veritably lives in Chicago and suffers and desires is known to him; what his muddy-streaming compatriots have done and still are doing to him; what his joys are, and what his pains. The man perceives the world and in perceiving it transcends it. A quiet stream, a deep black brook with whispering trickle, faëry of starts and gushes carries life like a Niagara.

Wherever he goes, in Chicago, out on the sandy foggy plain without the monster town, in the tiresome burgs where he sells the ideas of the advertising man, the state of life in him, the echo of the inner columnar movement of his being, is audible above the roar. It is ever near the surface, ready to spurt. The most ordinary objects glimpsed from an office-window high in the loop; the most ordinary sad bits of life seen in the endless avenues, a tree in a backyard, a layer of smoke, a man picking butts out of the gutter, can start it making gestures. A cake of cowdung rolled into balls by beetles, a flock of circling crows, milk turned sour by hot weather, give Anderson the clue of a thin gray string and set him winding through his drab and his wild days to find the truth of some cardinal experience and fill himself. The premature decay of buildings in America, the doleful agedness of things that have never served well and have grown old without becoming beautiful, the brutality of the Chicago skyline, open to him through a furtive chink some truth of his own starved powerful life, his own buried Mississippi Valley, his own unused empire. Or, the health that is left in the fecund soil of the continent, in the great watered spread of land, the nourishing life

Sherwood Anderson

of forests and plantations, is powerful to make known to him in mad drunken bursts his own toughness and cleanness and healthiness. Young corn growing like saplings makes rise and quiver deliciously and soar in him sense of his own resilient freshness, his crass newness on a new earth. Young corn makes chant in him delight in his own unbreakable ability to increase for ever in sensitivity, to transmute the coarse stuff of rough America into delicate spirit-strength, and become in the easy mid-Western shape ever a healthier, sweeter, finer creature. Horses trampling through the grain are to him certitude eternal of the ever-replenishment of the male gentle might that has descended to him intact through his muscled ancestry and makes sweet his breast; of the phallic daintiness that all the stupid tangle and vulgarity of life in the raw commercial centers cannot wear down in him and brutalize. A thousand delicate and mighty forms of nature are there, to pledge and promise him, the man cut loose from Europe, life abundant.

And Anderson's touch goes to his fellows of the road and the Chicago street. The *rigor mortis* of the sentimental Yank is relaxing. An American's arms are stretching open to the world; not alone to the world of the boy, the before-puberty world of Huck Finn. His arms stretch open to the days of the mature man and mature woman. Life begins to walk a little joyously, if a little crassly, on Michigan Boulevard. Walls are noiselessly a-crumble in Anderson. Of a sudden, he is breast to breast with people, with the strange gray American types, men and women he has seen the day previously; men and women, farmers, artisans, shopkeepers, he has not glimpsed in the flesh these five and twenty years. What happens only rarely, instantaneously only, in the most of us, the stretching of a ligament between another creature's bosom and our own, that happens in Anderson swiftly, repeatedly, largely. A visage, strange, gray, dun, floats up out of the dark of his mind. A man is seen doing something, lying face downward in a field, or fluttering his hands like birdwings. A woman is seen making a gesture, or walking down the railway track. The figure may have had its origin in some one long known, in some one seen but a furtive hour, in some one seen merely through hearsay. It may have its origin in the dullest, weariest creatures. But suddenly, the poet is become another person. He is some one who has never before existed, but now, even in a condition of relative colorlessness, has a life of his own as real as those of the strap-hanging men brushed every day in the streetcars. Anderson is suddenly become a labor leader. He is mad with eagerness to teach stupid laborers to synchronize their steps, to make them understand what it is to march in the daily life shoulder to shoulder as soldiers march, to fill them rich with a common stepping god in whom all find their fullness of power. He is a "queer" man working in a shabby little store. The more he strives to explain himself, the more incomprehensible and queer he becomes to his neighbors.

Sherwood Anderson

He is Melville Stoner, the little long-nosed bachelor of *Out of Nowhere Into Nothing;* ironically resigned to the futility of seeking to establish a permanent contact with another creature; tired to his marrow with the loneliness of existence. Or, he is a farm girl mortally stricken in her breast by the insensitiveness and cowardice of men to whom she turns for expression. Or, the face is that of the lanky, cold-footed inventor who cannot channel his passion into human beings. To overcome the profound inner inertia, he sets himself to doing little definite problems. Machinery is born of his impotence. And then the inventions break loose of his hands and enslave into a drab world the creatures Hugh McVey wanted to love and could not reach. Or, it is the face of *The Man in the Brown Coat,* who sits all day inside a book-lined room and knows minutely what Alexander the Great and Ulysses S. Grant did, that floats up before Anderson. Or, it is merely the figure of the officer of the law who strolled by swinging his billy as the author left his office. He is heard muttering to himself his feet ache; seen at night slowly pulling off his shoes and wriggling his stockinged toes.

Then, it is with Sherwood Anderson as it was with the two farmhands of *The Untold Lie* who suddenly hear themselves each in the other; hear in the other the voice telling that the assumption of responsibility to women and children is death, the voice telling that the assumption of the responsibility is life. In the people suddenly known to him through the imagination, Anderson recognizes the multiple pulls of his own will; hears speak in the men known the same pulls; hears in those bodies a voice, and in his own body the self-same murmur. Things long since heard in village stores, in factories and offices, spark with significance. Memories appear from nowhere, carry to him the life of a fellow forgotten long since; and the life against the childhood Ohio background is relieved and sharply drawn. Out of the murky, impenetrable limbo, a block, an idea, a shape, has been moved, and in the region of faint gray light stands outlined. What in himself he feared, what he, the fearful rebel in the Yankee flock, thought his own most special insanity, his own pariah marking, that is suddenly perceived an universal trait, present everywhere. His loneliness, that he thought a desolation all his own, is sensed in a million tight, apart bodies. His boastfulness, lust, self-infatuation, his great weariness, promptings of the messianic delusion, despair, they are suddenly perceived everywhere; they, and not the outer mask that men wear in each other's blind sight, are seen the truth. He knows people writhe; sees them, men and women, so hard and realistic, doing the things he does and then is frightened; he knows the many mad chanting voices in each fact-crowded skull. What he is beholding, what he holds in his hands before him in the shape of a scene, a gesture, a history, is the very life in himself. It is himself, Sherwood Anderson, the man who looks like a racing tout and a divine poet,

Sherwood Anderson

like a movie-actor and a young priest, like a bartender, a business-man, a hayseed, a mama's boy, a satyr, and an old sit-by-the-stove. It is himself as his father and his mother, as the people who moved about him in Clyde, Ohio, in his childhood and moved away from him, the many thousand humble and garish lives he has touched, the men he has done business with, the women he has taken, have made him.

The floating faces insist he attend upon the voice of the mind, without, within. They will not let him talk big and ignore it. His heart can no longer leap with the remainder of the country's at thought of the big beautiful business man creating with his strong mind lots of work for poor people. He can no longer turn from women in the dream of an irradiant companion, all mother, who takes the man to her bosom as the nurse the suckling, and gives with crowded hands, and wants for herself nothing but the privilege of serving in a great career. It is too late to avoid humankind with the sentimentalities of the popular authors, or the self-pitifulness of the Main Street men, the cohort of little haters. The heads will have nothing but full entry into lives, even though he perish in the effort of entering. They want the facts of the relationships of men. It is what he really knows of the truth, what he really knows of what has happened to him, what he really knows of what he has done to folk as well as what they have done to him, that is demanded of him now. Anderson has to face himself where Freud and Lawrence, Stieglitz and Picasso, and every other great artist of the time, has faced himself: has had to add a "phallic Chekov" to the group of men who have been forced by something in an age to remind an age that it is in the nucleus of sex that all the lights and the confusions have their center, and that to the nucleus of sex they all return to further illuminate or further tangle. New faces mount upward continually; sit, so he tells us, on the doorsill of his mind; are driven off by the helplessness of the American artist who has inherited no orientation in art; return and resist the cold and force him to make the effort to take them in. New faces mount up that contain more and more copiously the author, more and more copiously humanity, and demand ever finer eyes and ears.

Out of the feeling of life the style arises, the words charged with the blood and essence of the man. For quite as Anderson hears his own inner flux through the persons of other men, through materials and constructions, so, too, he hears it in the language itself. Strange and unusual words do not have to be summoned. He hears the thin vocabulary of his inarticulate fellows not only as concepts of concrete objects, but as poems charged with transcendental significance. Words are bifurcated in his mind; while the one wing rests on the ground, and remains symbol of the common object by which generations of English speakers have managed to make themselves and their offspring survive materially, the other points

Sherwood Anderson

into blue air, becomes symbol of the quality of inner life engendered by the material preoccupations. Corn is the support of the body on the American prairie; man and beast lean on it; Anderson, born and bred in corn-shipping villages, hears in the word that symbolizes the nourishing stalk the overtones of all the delicacies and refinements that bodily energy produces in him. So, too, with the words bowl and coat, that have a dark and grim resonance in his heart. The necessity of preoccupying themselves with the production of the simple tools of existence had a most definite result on life through the relationship of men and women; and Anderson knows his own life a thing at the base of a bowl, an immense feeding trough, withheld from contacting the living world by its high rims. He knows that he has within him a brown coat, that in this conventionally tinted stuff he sits wrapped all his days, cannot wear bright colors of the mind, cannot get out of this felt garment. He knows that when in writing he searches for touch with his fellows, he feels his way blindly in the dark along a thick wall, the wall left in men when they broke from their own traditions, and came into the presence of other men who too had broken from their traditions, and found no way to contact.

Anderson's artistic progress has consisted of the growing faithfulness with which he has given form to his feeling of materials, particularly the material of words. His last allegories and stories chime with overtones of prose, simple words symbolic of the inner state of the protagonists no less than of the outer. At first, in the two early novels, *Windy McPherson's Son* and *Marching Men,* the verbal quality was fairly thin. The author was forced to rely far more on a crude symbolism of action to manifest his inner music than on his medium itself. Still, particularly in the latter book, the inner voice was gathering strength. The language in which the mining town is described in the earlier chapters communicates something larger than the life of towns of the sort. It gives powerfully a sense of a grimy, cold, messy state of passion into which what Waldo Frank has so brightly called the barbaric tam-tam measure of Beaut McGregor's dream breaks as breaks a march rhythm into a sluggish orchestra. In the next book, *Winesburg, Ohio,* however, form obtains fully. The deep within Anderson utters itself through the prose. The tiny stories of village life are like tinted slits of isinglass through which one glimpses vasty space. The man's feeling for words, present always in him, reënforced one casual day when some one, expecting to produce a raw ha-ha, showed him *Tender Buttons,* is here mature. The visual images, the floating heads, have fleshed themselves, are automatically realized, by marriage with verbal images that had risen to meet them, and that contained, in their turn, the tough, spare, sprawling life in the poet. So this style, even more than the subject matter, is impregnated with the inarticulate American, the man whose inner dance is as the dance of a bag of meal. For in these words, the delicate inner column of Sherwood Anderson has risen to declare itself, to protest against the ugliness that lamed it down, to pour its life out into the unnumbered women and men. And, in his latest work, in the best of the stories in *The Triumph of the Egg,* and in the pieces of *A New Testament,* it works with always simpler means, begins to manifest itself through a literature that approaches the condition of poetry; that is more and more a play of word-timbres, a design of overtones, of verbal shapes and colors, a sort of absolute prose.

There has been no fiction in America like this. Small it is indeed by the mountainous side of the masses of Balzac, with their never-flagging volumnear swell, their circling wide contact on life, their beefy hotness. Anderson, to the present, has been most successful in the smaller forms. The short stories show him the fine workman most. The novels, the *nouvelle Out of Nowhere Into Nothing,* wander at times, are broken in sweep by evasions and holes. A many-sided contact with life is not revealed. The man is not an intellectual critic of society. His range is a fairly limited one. There is a gentle weariness through him. And still, his stories are the truest, the warmest, the most mature, that have sprung out of the Western soil. They are the very stuff of a man; unpremeditated like breath; the stuff of a highly civilized, matured, and coördinating human creature. One has but to compare these fragile, delicate fictions with those of the classic novelists, Poe and Hawthorne, to perceive the bloodfulness of Anderson. The new man is perhaps not as finished an artist as were the older. Nevertheless, he works in flesh. He has experience; he has desire; he has wisdom. It is mature men and women alive and in action that he gives us. The two ante-bellum novelists gave us in place of flesh, as Brooks so trenchantly showed, exquisite iridescent ghosts. They themselves were turned away from their day, and filled the vacuums in which they dwelt with sinister and rainbow-tinted beams. Their people satisfy no lust of experience. Both writers have merely phantasy of a fine quality to offer in its place. Howells, it is true, experienced mature existence. But he was a provincial and handled facts gingerly. He knew his people, but he was afraid of himself and drew characters from the point of view of middle-class conventionality. And Dreiser's characters? Golems, in whose breast the sacred word has not been thrust. Anderson, on the contrary, expresses us. Life of the hour pulses in his ideas. Motives hitherto obscure and unseen are brought by him up to the conscious day. From the first he has possessed the power to create through his prose style protagonists in whom every American can feel himself. Sam McPherson is the truest of all Ragged Dicks. The quaint little mushroom-like heads of Anderson's tales, the uneducated, undignified village dreamers, with their queer hops and springs, straggly speech, ineffectual large gestures, they are the little misshapen humans in this towering ma-

Sherwood Anderson

chine-noisy inhuman land, the aged infants grown a little screw-loose with inarticulateness. The sounds they make as they seek to explain themselves to one another, as they rave and denounce and pray, lie, boast, and weep, might come out of our own throats. They do come out of our own. The author may dub his heads Seth Richmond or Elsie Leander, George Willard or Wing Biddlebaum; they may be seen ever so fitfully; the stories by means of which Anderson has created them may set them out in mid-American farmland thirty years since. But they are flesh of our flesh and bone of our bone; and through them, we know ourselves in the roots of us, in the darkest chambers of the being. We know ourselves in Anderson as we knew ourselves in Whitman. And each new novel, tale and story makes audible an hitherto unheard pulsation of the warm membranes of life.

So life has found again a way of healing. Most probably, Sherwood Anderson came in the common way to suffer from the universal wrong. A man and woman, perhaps, whom life had wounded, broke the love of growing green in him in acting on each other. Or, the passive callousness of the world of outsiders did the deed, starved the nascent gentleness in the child. The society which sheltered the growing lad was rapidly becoming industrialized. Handicraftsmen remain sensitive more readily than do mechanics. Their immediate relation to the material in which they work preserves some sort of nervous fluidity in them. But the factory was eating into rural Ohio during the -eighties and the early -nineties. And there was not, what there still is in rural Europe, the reliquary of the passionate past to buttress anything of fine feeling that remained in the injured boy. No Gothic vault, no painted glass, no soft stone and nourished earth, were there to thaw the thickening ice. There was about him only the shoddy work of men disabled as he had been disabled. Indeed, the world might have seemed in conspiracy to make permanent the wound. A gigantic machinery was in readiness to aid any and all to make themselves free of their fellows. The anarchical society, that had come into existence the world over as the growing differentiations of men made sympathy more difficult, and placed a price on Narcissistic irresponsibility, was there in its extremest form to welcome another lord of misrule. Everything in raw America stimulated ugly ambitiousness, exploitation of human beings and of the soil, sense of rivalry with all men, devastating sense of god-manhood. The two images that fortify Narcissism, the images of the marvelous mother-woman and of the semi-divine all-powerful general or business man, that prevent men from finding much in the woman save the whore, and keep their interests centered on their own persons, were in the very air given the lad to breathe.

During a period, Anderson seems to have acquiesced, to have gone the way of all mortified flesh, become a smart, competing business man, and lived as lonely as no one

Sherwood Anderson

but a wounded lover can. Only a gift of telling stories, and Anderson was famous in Chicago for his Mama Geigen story long before he commenced to write, remained to prove the old power of sympathy that he had brought with him into the world not entirely broken. Some toughness, perhaps, present with all the extreme sensibility, had saved him, given him the power to recuperate. Or, perhaps, some one near him in his first years had guarded him for a while, had stood between him and the all-present evil sufficiently long to give him headstart. One of the stories in *Winesburg, Ohio,* called *Mother,* is the incorporation of a sense present in the author of an influence stilly goading him all his days to live his life and not settle down into cheap ambition, to grow and to learn; it is perhaps to this influence that the man owes his art. And Anderson showed he had the power within him to right himself. Toward his thirty-fifth year, he became sick of soul. He commenced to feel the state in which he was living as filthy. He began to perceive that his relations with men and with women, through his sunken state, were filthy. He began to perceive that he himself was giving out poison to others precisely in the same manner that poison had been given to him, was still being given to him by his contacts. Business began to become a bore. Business men, with their self-importance and gosling simplicity, began to become ludicrous. Suddenly, it appeared to him that Chicago, the mid-West, all America, was empty. There were no people. The census reports proclaimed tens upon tens of millions of inhabitants. But there were no people living human lives. There were automatons gyrating about, repeating sentences written by unconsciously lying reporters in the newspapers. No one knew the truth. No one knew what he felt, what the man reading the newspaper next him felt. No one felt, at all. In all the crowded streets and tenements of the titanic town, there was the unpeopled waste of the antarctic night.

Sickness of soul took Anderson away from business. Simultaneously a channel leading in an equally divergent direction opened itself for his energies. The gift of story telling began taking an intellectual route. At odd hours, after business, in railway trains, he began to write. And, lo, in the process of writing, the old wound began to close. He commenced to touch people again. He commenced to enter into lives. The people he met, the people he had rubbed against, were no longer adamant impenetrable surfaces to him. They began to open themselves. They began, when he met them casually, in all the ordinary ways of intercourse, to give him something nourishing to his sense of beauty, and to take from him something he needed to bestow. The sense of dirt, of whoring, of infinite degradation, began to pass in his labor. For the business of seeing people without romanticizing them, of drawing them without putting himself below or above them, but merely by feeling their lives in all the dwarfishness and prodigious bloom, is to Anderson what it is to all

Sherwood Anderson

men, an act of love, and, as love, subconsciously initiated.
The old godhead that shines in the eyes of every new-
born child revives itself through that labor of art. The
business of seeing folk clearly, steadily, wholly, is a
mystical marriage with the neighbor. It is not love of
one's image in the partner; it is the love of all men and
women through the body of a spouse. For its motive is
the preservation in another of an intact soul.

It was not a thing, this power of feeling truly, that
sprang full armed in Anderson. It has rather been a
gradual growth, a slow, patient learning. The current
of life in the country was against it. The current swept
inside Anderson himself. We see him, at the close of
Windy McPherson's Son, flinch from drawing the relentless line; loose his contact with life, and return into the
phantasy world of the American imperviousness. *Marching Men,* in its later passages, demonstrates a faulty sense
of women. Even in *Poor White,* the tendency to stop
feeling delicately, to harangue and seek to influence his
readers directly shows at moments its cloven hoof. But
the artist has been solidifying steadily in the man. In *A
New Testament* he tells us how each night he "scrubbed
the floor" of his upper room. There are miracles of
tender, fragile sensibility in *Winesburg,* in *Poor White,*
in the later stories and poems. For, in this second crisis
in Anderson's moral life, there was help at hand. He
was no longer entirely solitary in his struggle with the
habits of the country. Creatures able to strengthen him

195

were about. His mind, like the span of a Gothic arch, in springing upward, met another upspringing span and found support. It was in the guise of the most powerful outward bulwark of his mature life that the work of Van Wyck Brooks came to Sherwood Anderson. In it he encountered another conscious American who spoke his language. Here was a critic, a polished and erudite man, who brought him corroboration in his inmost feelings, and told him that nations had become great, and 'life burned high, because men had done what he was laboring to do; and that America had remained gray and terrible and oafish because men could not within her borders feel the truth. In that voice, Anderson recognized an America more real than the one that, outside and in, strove to deflect him and break his touch. What had happened to Whitman, decay for want of comprehension, was not to happen to him. He was afoot, to so remain until he could tell, in *Many Marriages,* the story of the man healed of his fear of life; no longer afraid of his white, unsunned body; willing to let men and women know him in his naked truth. Meanwhile, Anderson's pledge to himself, the song to himself as he goes his rocky road, stands recorded in *Mid-American Chants.* The little book is a sort of rude pilgrim's scrip for those who, in America, are trying to keep their faith in the work of the artist intact. And Anderson can begin writing *A New Testament,* assured that in setting down the voice of the mind murmur-

Sherwood Anderson

ous in him, he is furthering some new inward life dawning for men.

The new sensibility that is in America is only an infant. It is no more than a puny child born in the nadir of the year, a helpless, naked mite. In all the gray winter of the land, under the leaden immeasurable vault, it is a nigh invisible fleck. And still, somehow, it is there, born. You have but to read Anderson to know it well. Something is different in us since these stories and novels have commenced to circulate. Something has changed in the scene outside the rooms, in the thoroughfares through which we tread, since he began telling us the railway conductor's daughter walked down the track, the policeman went thinking how much his feet hurt him. The people in the street, the ever strange, the ever remote, the ever unyielding people in the street, they are come a little out of their drab mist, are become a little less repellent, less hostile, less remote. They have departed a little from their official forms, the forms that are imposed on them by the lie in the brain of all, the Roman lie, with its hierarchies, positions, offices, principles, duties, laws. You will perceive it the next time you pass by the Italian grocer on the corner, that formerly mealy and uninviting universe. You will perceive it when next the washerwoman comes with her basket of laundry to the door. You will perceive it when you pass the blue-coated, sallow-faced law swinging his club on the corner. They will not know that anything has happened between you and them. They may believe they see you with the old eyes. But they do not. In them as in yourself something has taken place. They have all opened a little, to let you see for a blinking instant into them. You, who have read Anderson, know it. They have all turned gentler for a second, and let you perceive inside their coats, a thing you well know. It is inside the rich fur-collared coat of the stock-gambler in Wall Street. It is inside the old army coat of the gray-faced, job-hunting, Third-Avenue walker. It is inside all men and women, that thing that you thought your own alone. It is you in diverse forms, you suffering and egoistic and lazy, you wanting to live and give life to others and exuding venom instead. It is you, dying always by your own hand, always miraculously producing again the power to live.

It seems as though the mysterious Third Person, the being who comes into existence at the moments walls fall between men and men, and dies when they rebuild themselves once more, had been given another chance.

Georgia O'Keeffe

Known in the body of a woman, the largeness of life
greets us in color. A white intensity drives the painting
of Georgia O'Keeffe. Hers is not the mind capable of
feeling one principle merely. She is not conscious of a
single principle without becoming simultaneously aware
of that contrary which gives it life. The greatest extremes lie close in her burning vision one upon the other;
far upon near, hot upon cold, bitter upon sweet; two
halves of truth. Subtleties of statement are fused with
greatest boldnesses of feeling; tenderest, rose-petal gradations with widest, most robustious oppositions of color.
Complexly varied contraries of tone she juxtaposes with a
breath-taking freshness. Her art is a swift sounding of
the abysses of the spectrum, and an immediate relation of
every color to every other one. She has the might of
creating deft, subtle, intricate chords and of concentrating
two such complexes with all the oppositional power of two
simple complementary voices; of making them abut their
flames directly upon each other and fill with delicate and
forceful thrust and counterthrust the spaces of her canvases. Her work exhibits passage upon passage comparable to the powerfully resistant planes of intricate
harmony characteristic of some modern musics. Through

199

this American, the polyharmonies of Strawinsky and Ornstein have begotten sisters in the sister medium of painting. And the modern music is no more removed from both the linear polyphony of the madrigalists and the preponderantly homophonic effects of the romantic composers, than this art from both the ruggedly but simply interplaying areas of the Renaissance, and the close, gentle, melting harmonies of the impressionists.

Painters have perceived the relativity of all color: have felt that every hue implies the presence in some form or other of its complement, its ideal opponent that gives it force; and have expressed those complements in their works. But few have dared place a sharp triad based on red in as close juxtaposition to one equally sharp based on green as Georgia O'Keeffe has done. She lays them close upon each other, point against point, flame upon flame. For her, the complementariness of these two sets of colors is natural as the green of foliage. Other painters have recognized the relation of all colors to pure white since pure white contains them all; few have had it in them to dare lay hardest piercing white between baking scarlets and the green of age-old glaciers, and make ecstatically lyrical the combination. Others have felt the gamut from intensest cold to intensest heat within the limits of a single color, and have registered it in their gradations; few, it seems, have been able to race the entire scale with such breathless rapidity, to proceed in one small area of green from the luxuriant Amazonian heat

Georgia O'Keeffe

of green mottled with dusty yellow to the bitter antarctic cold of green-blue. But it is with subtlety that these tremendous oppositions are given. They are more implied than baldly stated. It may be a chord of burning green that is felt against one of incandescent red, a chord of intensest blue against ripe orange. But most often the greens and the blues will be represented by unusual, subtle shades. They will be implied rather more than definitely stressed; the green felt through a kindred shade of blue, the blue through a kindred green. Besides, O'Keeffe does not play obvious complements of hot and cold against each other. It is more often the two warm tones in the two triads that will be found opposed in her compositions, and the two cold. Oblique, close, tart harmonies occur, flavoring much of her work with keen, pleasant, ammoniac pungency. The latitude between proximate tones, between shades of the same color, is stressed. Dazzling white is set directly against tones of pearl. Violet abuts upon fruity tomato. It is as though O'Keeffe felt as great a width between minor seconds as Leo Ornstein does. And, although she manages to run the full gamut between the heat and coolth of a tone within a diminutive area, her scale makes no sacrifice of subtleties. The most delicious gradations remain distinct and pure. Hence, tiny forms possess the distinct rotundity which many other painters manage to obtain only through bulkier masses.

A combination of immense Picasso-like power and crisp daintiness exists not alone in the color of O'Keeffe. It

201

exists likewise in the textures of her paintings and in the
shapes born in her mind with her color-schemes, and expressed through them. Precisely as the widest plunges
and the tenderest gradations point against each other in
her harmonies and fuse marvelously, so in her surfaces
do heavily varnished passages combine with blotting-
paper textures, and severe, harsh forms with strangest,
sensitive flower-like shapes. In the volumes there lives
a similar subtlety in bold strokes, a similar profundity of
dainty ones. Rigid, hard-edged forms traverse her canvases like swords through cringing flesh. Great rectan-
gular menhirs plow through veil-like textures; lie stone-
like in the midst of diaphanous color. Sharp lines, hard
as though they had been ruled, divide swimming hue
from hue. Rounds are described as by the scratching
point of a compass. But, intertwined with these naked
spires thrusting upward like Alp-pinnacles, there lie
strangest, unfurling, blossom-delicate forms. Shapes as
tender and sensitive as trembling lips make slowly,
ecstatically to unfold before the eye. Lines as sinuous
and softly breathed as Lydian tunes for the chromatic
flute climb tendril-like. It is as though one had been
given to see the mysterious parting movement of petals
under the rays of sudden fierce heat; or the scarcely
perceptible twist of a leaf in a breath of air; or the
tremulous throbbing of a diminutive bird-breast.

And in the definition of these flower-movements, these
tremblingly unfurling corollas, what precision, what

Georgia O'Keeffe

jewel-like firmness! The color of O'Keeffe has an edge that is like a line's. Here, for almost the first time one seems to see pigment used with the exquisite definiteness, the sharp presence, of linear markings. Much of her work has the precision of the most finely machine-cut products. No painting is purer. Contours and surfaces sing like instruments exquisitely sounded. There are certain of these streaks of pigment which appear licked on, so lyrical and vibrant are they. The painter appears able to move with the utmost composure and awareness amid sensations so intense they are well-nigh insupportable, and so rare and evanescent the mind faints in seeking to hold them; and here, in the regions of the spirit where the light is low on the horizon and the very flames darkling, to see clearly as in fullest noon, and to sever with the delicacy and swiftness of the great surgeon.

The sense of vasty distances imparted by even the smaller of these paintings flows directly from the rapidly and unfalteringly executed decisions of the artist. The intense oppositions felt between near-lying colors, the delicate differences perceived between graded shades of a single hue and the extreme crispness and unflagging sureness with which they are registered, carry one down into profound abysses and out through cloud-spaces and to interstellar lands that appear to have scarce any rapport with the little rectangles of canvas through which they are glimpsed. One falls from a single blue to another down gulfs of empyrean. The small intense volumes

203

Port of New York

take on the bulk of cosmical protagonists. Gnarled apples; smooth, naked tree trunks; abstract forms that are like the shapes of sails and curtains and cloaks billowed by sea-winds are each in magical fashion informed by the elemental forces that toss the earth like a baseball in their play. There are canvases of O'Keeffe's that make one to feel life in the dim regions where human, animal and plant are one, undistinguishable, and where the state of existence is blind pressure and dumb unfolding. There are spots in this work wherein the artist seems to bring before one the outline of a whole universe, a full course of life: mysterious cycles of birth and reproduction and death expressed through the terms of a woman's body.

It leads us, this painting, further and ever further into the verity of woman's life. We have scarcely a witness more articulate than that borne by it. There are sonnets of Elizabeth Barrett in this sworling, undulant color; this modern woman, too, has been overtaken unawares by an irradiation of brimming rose, and found her spirit standing up erect and strong in a translucent world. But no inherited rhetoric interposes between her feeling and her form of expression. Her concepts are not half in man's tradition. To a degree they come out of general American life; not out of analyses of Cézanne and Picasso. They come out of the need of personal expression of one who has never had the advantage of the art treasures of Europe and has lived life without the help of the city of Paris; out of the necessity of one who shows no traces

Georgia O'Keeffe

of intellectualization and has a mind born of profoundest feeling. An austerity, a fibrousness which is most closely kin to the Amerinds' pervades this paint. But, more directly even than from the plains and the cornlands and the general conditions of life in the new continent does it stem from the nature of woman, from an American girl's implicit trust in her senses, from an American girl's utter belief, not in masculinity nor in unsexedness, but in womanhood. O'Keeffe gives her perceptions utterly immediate, quivering, warm. She gives the world as it is known to woman. No man could feel as Georgia O'Keeffe and utter himself in precisely such curves and colors; for in those curves and spots and prismatic color there is the woman referring the universe to her own frame, her own balance; and rendering in her picture of things her body's subconscious knowledge of itself. The feeling of shapes in this painting is certainly one pushed from within. What men have always wanted to know, and women to hide, this girl sets forth. Essence of womanhood impregnates color and mass, giving proof of the truthfulness of a life. Whether it is the blue lines of mountains reflecting themselves in the morning stillnesses of lake-water, or the polyphony of severe imagined shapes she has represented; whether deep-toned, lustrous, gaping tulips or wicked, regardful alligator pears; it is always as though the quality of the forms of a woman's body, the essence of the grand white surfaces, had been approached to the eye, and the elusive scent of unbound

hair to the nostril. Yet, it is female, this art, only as is
the person of a woman when dense, quivering, endless
life exists in her body; when long tresses exhale the
aromatic warmth of unknown primeval submarine forests,
and dawn and the planets glimmer in the spaces between
cheeks and brows. It speaks to one ever as do those
high moments when the very stuff of external nature in
mountainsides and full-breasted clouds, in blue expanse
of roving water and rolling treetops, seems enveloped in
the brooding principle of woman's being; and never, not
ever, as speak profaner others.

For the paintings of Georgia O'Keeffe are made out
of the pangs and glories of earth lived largely. Shapes
and lines, broad single fields of tone, offer pieces of mountains to the heart, thrust windows open on the great airs
and lands. The painter has reds and greens and whites
red and green and white with all of passionate feeling of
color it seems the hollows of the heart can hold. She has
greens flameful and fiery as hottest scarlet. She has reds
serene and pure as smoothest white. Marie Laurencin
may give us the Watteau grace and delicacy of the
Trianon in modern idiom. O'Keeffe brings a spacious-
ness of feeling, sweep, tumult, and calm like the spacious-
ness of the ocean and the Texan plains she loves. It
may be the most literal representation or the most
ethereal abstraction that is rendered; and the artist
moves freely from one category to another; for her,

the two categories are single—she paints them as one. But, whatever the subject-matter, the expression releases us with the white flames which cast fears out. It is heart-bursting joy that sings, or gaunt sorrow; it is aches and blisses scooped from the depths of the being and offered to the light; it is the hours of great morning when the spirit lifts high its hands in rapture; it is white night when the firmament is a single throbbing presence and quicksilver cuts sharp rims in black and digs a golden hollow in the lake under the mountain-wall. Darkly, purely painted flower and fruit pieces have not a little sorrow; contours silently weep. Pain treads upon the recumbent figure. Pain rends the womb to shreds with knives. Pain studs the universe with shark's teeth. Other times moods play like teasing children at tag. A prim and foolish little house winks its windows, while a flag-staff leans crazy, and mauve evening clouds tumble clownishly. An innocent orange flower is out walking of a nice Sunday morning through sweet green with a new feather stuck in its bonnet. A cow in apple time curls forth its purple watering tongue of flannel and rolls the comic muteness of its impenetrable bovine eye. Then, veils of ineffable purity steam like morning mists off tranquil lake-water. The span of heaven is an arch of bloom. Pearly shapes chant ecstatically against somber backgrounds. Life seems to rise on wing, in the dumbness of utter bestowal, into a climax of seraphic hues.

Fortune appears to have endowed Georgia O'Keeffe

with two gifts which are perhaps a single one. It seems to have given her capacity of fiery passion; it has also shod her adamantine with safeguarding purity of edge. Hers is a spirit like steel-construction; all skeleton nudity and savage thrust. Burningness of life can breathe up and breathe free in her. For it rises flame-sharp of rim. Volcanic surge of feeling can find its way clean into the world. For folded in its substance there lies the whiteness of the spot where the race begins. She goes through the world upholding in her thin sensitive hands above the brushing crowd a bubble of a bowl. The world is rich for this woman because of the unfaltering swift selections of her deep unconscious principle. And it is from the white integrity with which her being is bound that the tremendous decisions which constitute the art of Georgia O'Keeffe proceed. What she herself within herself is, where she is woman most, becomes apparent to her, because of her artist's vision, in external objects. There is no manner of deepened intercourse for the artist which does not become for him a correspondingly approfondized sense of his material. There is no piercing of the rind of nature at any point that is not a simultaneous piercing at many points. There is nothing really experienced which does not become esthetics for him. And, since O'Keeffe knows life as it comes to the passionately living; knows by the side of attraction, repulsion; by the side of life-giving, death-dealing; by the side of birth, decay, she sees scattered over the face of the world, in autumn

Georgia O'Keeffe

landscapes, in baskets of fruit, in flower-cups and mountainsides the symbols of extremely concentrated feeling.
She sees shapes and hues in the powerful oppositions born
of intense passion. As few have seen them, she sees the
refractions of light on solids, the relativity of color.
She sees clashing principles lying close upon each other,
speaking the subtle, wondrous high thing she knows;
great forces brought close in upon each other, their virtue
increased through the intensity of their mutual resistances
under approximation. And, in the arrowlike tongue of
her pigment she registers them with unfaltering faithfulness, and gives the personal inner truth of her opalescent
sphere.

The American failure has been primarily a failure in
men and women. Of the two masterpieces *manqué* the
greater failure has been the woman, for the reason that it
is she who is the object of labors, the work upon which
the care of the artist has most generously been bestowed.
It is the woman who has been given the position of honor
in American society, been freed not only of conventional
restraints, but made the arbiter of education and of life.
The great privileges of leisure have gone to the girls.
And though the new world has made of the woman a
marvelously shining edifice, flowing of line and rich in
material, it has also made of her a dwelling uninhabited,
gray and chill like the houses where the furniture stands
year-long in twilight under its shrouds. For, in keeping
the male undeveloped and infantile, American culture has

Port of New York

attributed the masculine principle to the female, and divided the female against her proper intuitions. The country has men who are boys and rest sixteen at seventy; and women who are Parian glories outside and little stunted men inside. Of life based upon the whole and developed personality there is scarcely any. But the art of Georgia O'Keeffe is no art of a poor little man. With this young artist, the splendid forsaken mansion flushes suddenly with the radiance of many chandeliers, the long-speechless windows glitter with active life. She is the little girl and the sybil, the wild, mysterious, long-haired one and the great calm rooted tree. The freshness of vesture given the sex by the American adventure is not lost in her. It has merely been made glorious and swift by the woman-psyche accepted, respected, cherished. A woman soul is on the road, going toward the fulfillment of a destiny. The effulgent art, like a seraphic visitor, comes with the force of life. In blaze of revelation it demonstrates woman to the world and to woman. It summons a psychic capacity toward new limits. It veers nature once again to its great way.

Randolph Bourne

Bourne was the great bearer of moral authority while America was at war. He was our bannerman of values in the general collapse. Round him, during those hateful years, there crashed, one after another, the ruins of intellectual directorships. Philosophers, educators, "socialists, college professors, new-republicans, practitioners of literature," the great majority of those who had thought themselves interpreters of the country's effort for larger life, made haste to overturn the values they had once defended. Liberal journals pretended that the war-technique annihilating those values was indeed the expression of them. Everywhere were men rationalizing in diverse fashions their own consentment in the course destined to pervert the better will of the country, to bring Europe to final disaster and America to the brink of demoralization. Bourne stepped without pompousness into the place left vacant by the universal recalcitrancy. Amid the dissolving minds his stood like a rock in the ocean. The external pressures so baleful to the great host of intellectuals succeeded only in kneading his rebellious spirit surer an hundred-fold in itself than it had previously been. They summoned it into increased aggressiveness and doggedness; concentrated the whole of his powerful little man in a single resistant ironic point. His fine boy's head, cleared by the discipline of his pragmatist masters, became a powerful dialectical machine. Out of it, amid the shooting fires, there came the high act of the sort from which the other pragmatists and intellectuals to a man recoiled: the formulation, couched in the very terms of the present crisis and expressed with an incisiveness perhaps never excelled by any of his countrymen, of the creative will of American men.

Bourne knew his enemy. He knew with what power among his compatriots he had affair. He could not deceive himself into seeing the American participation in the European war as evil merely, as certain of the pacifists saw it, because it necessitated further carnage of men; no more than he could deceive himself into seeing that participation, as many of the liberal, hopeful, compromised intellectuals permitted themselves to perceive it, in the attractive shape of a nice trained doggy who would go fetch the world out the water and deposit it gently in their laps and there let them refashion it at their good pleasure. Before the government decided a state of war he had guessed what nigger lay concealed in the woodpile of belligerency. He had done his uttermost to dissuade the new-republicans from letting themselves be used slyly by the Administration as decoys for liberal opinion. He had opposed the repressing, illiberal, reactionary movement which was sliding the country into the trenches, with a new statement of the democratic ideal of a community of beings each one a religion to himself. In the statement, he had rejected colonialism, bastard Anglo-Saxondom and the cheap melting-pot American in favor of a transnational America; an America, itself a world-federation in miniature, possessed of a culture that was "a weaving back and forth, with the other lands, of many threads of all sizes and colors." The weeks which followed on the opening of hostilities merely corroborated his most sinister intuitions. The surge toward education, toward the release of the capacities for more impassioned living which had once thrilled the mind of the nation did not, he knew, express itself through forms as malevolent as those which began to crop up on every side like spearheads sown. The soldiers who tried to lynch Max Eastman proved only too well that "current patriotism was not a product of the will to remake the world." The American house itself was afire.

Behind the war, using the war as an instrument of aggression, was the obscure force which has kept the human being in ignorance and in a condition of servitude through the centuries, periodically recalling him to his bestial past and making him to destroy the capital of self-reliance assembled for him by years of comparative freedom. War was the "health of the state." War was the vitalization of herd attitudes. The mystical form made healthy by war, the image of the father projected onto the cultural group, had always been the instrument whereby the resources of communities had been exploited for the benefit of classes. And the capture of a community by the privileged classes had invariably resulted in the spread, in the interests of privilege, of a universal passive resistance to "the effort of reason and the adventure of beauty." America was at war, therefore, with its own forces of spiritual release; with whatever outstreaming generous forces the breasts of its people still contained. America supposed it was coming to the rescue of liberty; for its leaders said it was going to make the world a safe place. But it was deceived. In going to war, it had itself been captured by the ancient tyrannies of the old world: nationalism, patriotism, militarism, state mysticism, formulas by means of which the human spirit had been held in an undeveloped, dependent, childish condition and in the bonds of an animal past.

The dreary war years and the drearier afterworld of war, a shattered European life and an American harried by frights and intolerances and mob-fanaticisms, were about Bourne in those early weeks as though there were no time. Experience made him clairvoyant. Experience made him discover under the disguises they wore the forces which repress and withhold the human spirit from fresh, quick, significant forms of expression; made him to scent out their presence with the instinct of the animal wary of the beasts that exist by preying on its kind. For he himself, all his short life, had been in mortal conflict with the shrinking, dissipating powers of fear and hate and whatever else dissuades the spirit from its trials of

214

Randolph Bourne

strength. He had come into the dead becalmment of American life. And like the others of his group and time he had suffered in dumb blindness year-long from the curious inertia of it. The teeming world had been a great parching emptiness around him. The "bright" bustling activity of American civilization did not exist for him. It was merely a kind of thin surface; and underneath the hammering and speeding and quiver of electric wires there lay, still as an Atlantis at the bottom of an oceanic valley, a world hardened in a dull, ugly shape. And, for all the bright commercial expansion, each year seemed to harden it the more. The earth was noisy and broken with meaningless, endless, directionless activity. Iron ribs of buildings were being lifted at a thousand points into the air amid the metallic pecking of the steel-riveter; every year there were hundreds of new factories, skyscrapers, lofts, stores, hotels, garages, flats. The trains and ferries and tunnels leading into Manhattan were thick black every morning with crowds streaming into the city to work; and every night the wave swept back during hours across the Jersey suburbs, and spilt itself in thick-set leagues of houses; and every year there were new hundreds of thousands of young men and women beginning to go to work. Children were sprouting everywhere like grass from topsoil; into New York Bay the immigrant ships were bearing every month their cargoes of able bodies; there was a perpetual movement upward of general financial conditions, a rising tide of bank deposits, bathtubs, sanitary plumbing, shined shoes, college educations. Nevertheless, strangely, the air was motionless and heavy and stagnant like the air in stagnant, close August nights. No current of wind broke through the glassy calm and set the body breathing. Everything,—friends, neighbors, classmates,—was curiously pressing life downward into inertia; bearing down toward the mediocre existing form of it; patting the world of good-enough with the vigor of new lives. Every year, new hordes of youth came to fortify it with their blood; to fit themselves willingly into the dull form of it and let it grow mightier through them, and become in turn emblems of it in the forms of sales managers, bank cashiers, smart story writers, insurance brokers, automobile mechanics, advertising wizards; all admirably adjusted to the immoral, untightened thing which existed. There was always a position in some business house drawing like a magnet. And behind that, there was always a neat, approved, two-family dwelling, and behind that, a neat, approved girl of the sort the family would like. There had seemed no way.

More richly almost than any other member of his generation in the land, he had stored within him that principle of growth against which the self-repression of a community, its passive resistance to "the effort of reason and the adventure of beauty" wages a silent, incessant war of attrition. Bourne was a cripple; he was the son of unfine, conventional, immobile American society; but the

216

Randolph Bourne

seeds of fineness burned in him, and made him a wedge
of crimson into the dun, the timorousness, the cheap self-
satisfaction of his community. The whole of him was
directed towards development. The first time one saw
the man, one saw, perhaps, the crippled frame, the poor
twisted ear, and shrank involuntarily from them. They
were gone the second time; gone never again to obtrude.
Only the long sensitive Gothic face remained; the fine
musician's hands with their delightful language; the joyous, youthful, certain dance of the mind. One knew,
and women knew it no less positively than did men, that
through the appearance of this being a great vacancy in
American life, perhaps never until the moment of
Bourne's coming more than partially seen, had been filled.
During prep-school days, in college, during the first contacts with mature life one had looked hopefully over
many a spotless collar, under many a smart straw hat,
been drawn by many a sincerity and purity of spirit, and
then invariably stood baffled a little and bewildered; but
for what one had groped, and why one had been disappointed, and what it was American life seemed to lack,
that one never quite clearly knew till Bourne commenced
to move through the world. Only then was there set before one where it could be perceived the fact that what one
had been groping for so comically, and what America was
poor for the want of, was the young American who desired
not things but high experience, and who was capable of
taking the jumbled objects of American civilization and

217

converting them into nutriment for the spirit. For the man; and the thirst for high experience, and love, and art, and impassioned living; and the capacity for converting the raw of life into wisdom and humanity, embodiments of the shadowy dream, were here.

He was the democratic individual in America; the youth of a beautiful, unrealized, ever-impending plane of existence sprung in a society banked against that plane. He was the young being having need of living from his own center who came awake in a land terrorized by the conventions; bourgeois conventions giving themselves out for the laws of the universe, and proclaiming themselves from every pulpit and school-platform. In a society full of external and assumed principles, he was the man who produces his own principles from out of himself; and cleaves along a single and unswerving line in all his expressions not because of external convictions of right and wrong, but because of some powerful and clarified impulsion deep in himself. Part of a civilization of outer frenetic movement and inner rigidity, he wanted from the world not external movement, nor external symbols of power and dominion over the persons of others, but emotion, the beauty of a rich, fecund, mature personality, the growth of the power to receive high aristocratic pleasure from the simplest common stuffs of existence. And from out society, he wanted men and women living from their own centers no differently than he from his: for the reason that their truthfulness to themselves would

218

Randolph Bourne

strengthen his own truthfulness to himself, and reveal his own mind the better to him. Alongside of himself, he wanted people developing infinite varieties of character, expanding in directions perhaps contrary to his own, for the reason that to such people he could give life, and from them get it in exchange, and through the intercourse grow the larger in himself.

Hence, he had had to suffer long the punishment of hostile indifference and subtle humiliation his environment deals out to rebels such as he. He had had to suffer long from the profoundest loneliness and helplessness; the want of any corroboration of his vague struggling feelings; the want of any insight into his own condition; the want of the immense encouragement which comes from finding a fellow-journeyer. People were afraid of growing and of those who grew. Had but some voice, some book, come at the time and told young Randolph Bourne that his terrible discomfort resulted from the inertia of American civilization, from the resistance of lower-middle-class life to the life of ideas and of spiritual distinction; told him that he suffered because some thing within him was attempting to start an evolution toward fineness against the weight of society organized for business only, he might not have lost the years of his youth spent in ineffectual groping. He might have found his own way much earlier. But during the nineteen hundreds, there were no such voices and no such books. There was a thin movement of social uplift. But there was no movement toward spiritual growth; no movement toward a new form of society flowing from the soul. Literature was playing the procurer. Literature was pretending the universal dun was color of roses; pretending that the stagnation was movement upward into the sunny blue. Literature was content in being mediocre: in being part of the mediocre immobile form. There were no people. There were no individuals in America. The men who were to make that new literature of rebellion and democratic idealism were themselves, like Bourne himself, trying to coördinate their faculties in motion. So, the first twenty-three years of Bourne's life went in dazed wandering. The next five or six, better directed though they were, were passed in a semi-ignorance of what it was that repressed, and what it was that drove. Bourne felt himself alone at Columbia. He felt himself alone while traveling in Europe as the Gilder Scholar for 1913. It was only during the last four years of his life that he met on the common meeting ground the men who were trying to go his way, and through them felt himself right and knew what the seed in himself was trying to realize.

But Bourne was filled with the Lord Spring. His being had thrust outside the form of existence led around him a sort of lodestone, a guiding star of intenser richer living. And the projected values, vague though they must perforce have been, mere faintly shimmering asteroids, nevertheless had drawn him counter to the current of society and towards the life of wisdom and of art. They had

Randolph Bourne

made him go hunt whatever material for growth this world afforded; made him create out of the raw an environment in which the youth and appetite for high adventure stored within him could breathe and come to ever fresher burgeoning. It was difficult for Bourne to make his way unaided to the university; and, at the conclusion of high-schooling he took first the position of secretary to some moneyed drearies; then of musical proofreader in a pianola-record factory; then of accompanist to a toreador singing-master in Carnegie Studios who euchered him of his pay. And still, in his twenty-third year, he reached Columbia, and used Columbia. He became perhaps the most distinguished of all John Dewey's pupils. In learning to write, he developed a technique of expressing past experience and present desire in combination, thus at once making room in himself for deeper experience and greater desire, and forcing the world to sustain him in his unconventional manner of living. His first book, a defense of his own budding principle called *Youth and Life*, was published while he was still a junior. His poor body notwithstanding, he found his way to the places where gardens grow about women. With his inappeasable appetite for the personal, he found his way to young women and men in Columbia, in Greenwich Village, in the offices of magazines and advertising companies who were being thrust forward much as he; some of them queer people enough: beautiful hysterical girls, half-poets, founders of ideal communities, composers who composed in obsolete styles, old children, helpless radicals; almost abortive efforts of life to maintain itself on a more spiritual plane who, nevertheless, were far more generously human than the folk better adjusted to the American scene. And from them he learned, too. Through them, he came to feel his own enthusiasms and ideals more intensely. Like "Mon Amie," the girl with whom he used to go walking during his months in Paris, they all brought him, to some degree, a greater sense of the loveliness of "luminous understanding, personal verve, lightness of expression, the feeling of ideas and the thinking of emotions, deathless loyalty which betrays only at the clutch of some deeper loyalty." They all brought him himself.

In the last years given him he was touching life at a multitude of points. By virtue of the talisman he bore in him, he seemed to find his way with ease to the movements which, dissimilar though they seemed to be, nevertheless were each to some extent moved by the principle active in himself. He discovered new educational experiments; new path-findings in philosophy and literature; new flights in politics and musical art. To the problems of each field he seemed to bring the whole sum of his former experience, his deep intuition and sure sense of fact, sharp comprehension, quick imaginativeness and pleasure in the sensuous. And through this liberal delivery the reports of his discoveries, whether they assumed the shape of a description of the schools in Gary

Randolph Bourne

or of a review of a novel, of a whimsical account of friends, children, teachers, or a serious discussion of the future of American culture, became, almost always, experiments in themselves, new theories of facts, new keen images of reality. Bourne could speak with equal sureness, humanity, lightness on a dozen different topics; and his talk itself, like his book-reviewing, was a sort of adventure. Through each subject, Bourne seemed to touch the living, fluid principle; even politics became life when he tossed it on his mobile hands. One miniature but nevertheless perfectly authentic salon, at the very least, was started about his person; and persisted, in New York itself, while he was there to talk brilliantly and provoke good talk with his sharp ironical mind. It languished only with his death.

Just as he could enter the gates of a dozen distinct media of expression, so, too, he seemed to be able to express himself with perfect ease through several of them. Very few of his friends did not have the delight of coming in on him some morning, and hearing him, his language precise with wisdom and delicate irony, talk off some article, some of his priceless replies to Dewey, some one of his finest bits of logic, even while he was engaged in the seemingly effortless act of composition; and then seeing him step over to his upright piano and begin playing Bach or Ravel or Scriabine. Bourne could, how quietly, charm a dinner table, from his chair where he throned like a little pope, with his brilliant political

speculation; and then going to the keyboard continue offering in a different medium, and through his broad palms
and flexible wrists, the entertainment begun by his ratioci-
nations.

Towards the very close of his short heyday, each of
the many manifestations of life seemed to provide him
with a subject for aristocratic pleasures. Not even his long
depression over the war, or the doors which were slammed
in his face because of his stand on American participation,
or the cowardice of some of his radical collaborators, or
other and more personal vexations, could dull the enjoy-
ment. Life was a feast which began with breakfast and
the latest broadsides of journalistic self-delivery. It was
a feast which continued well into the night, so long as
but a human being was near. Even while he went about
carrying all the woes of all the friends being shipped off
to army camps, and was being watched as a suspicious
person because he and two ladies had taken a walking trip
along the shore of Buzzard's Bay in the midst of a submarine scare, he could still laugh at the muckers of the
New York *Tribune* with their "Who's Who in Traitors,"
no less than at the organs of liberal opinion with their
"symposiums of eloquent idealism, their appealing har-
bingers of a cosmically efficacious and well-bred war."
He had the rare gift of being able to pick up a newspaper
or weekly and open it directly to the spot where the most
naïve and absurd line of the issue was to be found. Breakfast was scarcely begun before Bourne had found at least

Randolph Bourne

one line to make the day go brightly. He even enjoyed himself, poor devil, as he lay a-choking to death and unable to inhale the oxygen conducted to his mouth. An eggnog was brought to him at his mumbled request; and as soon as he saw the saffron liquid, he began exclaiming with pleasure over its gorgeous hue. It was in keeping with his career that his last uttered syllables should have registered a delight of the eye.

From out this life, the broad flaunt of humanist colors in the crisis of war grew like fruit from roots and trunk and branch. In intercourse, in literature, Bourne had long been bearing witness to the glory of the life of wisdom. And still, so clarified was his vision of human values in the collapse of April 5th, so male the power, so sure the means of expressing them, that sometimes the man of the *Seven Arts* essays seems a being apart from the author of *Youth and Life* and *Education and Living*; even from parts of *The History of a Literary Radical*. The steps taken before the moment when Bourne became spokesman of moral authority were taken on the ground. Those taken from the hour when America went to war sound from the high bridge where men of stature march. There were only three or four; and then the reverberations ceased. But we know the clang of the stride; and whence such clangors carry. A man of power had suddenly been coördinated in powerful complete release. The rhythm of the *Seven Arts* essays is freer, stronger, lighter by far than that underlying anything previously

Port of New York

written by Bourne. Vanished is every trace of the gingerly *Atlantic Monthly* style, with its mincingness of persons perpetually afeared of stepping on eggs. Gone is the somewhat thin and colorless, if serviceable, style of the *New Republic* essays. A spirit had come out of America and stood in the place held at other times by the great humanists. Shod with irony and gay satiric laughter, humble weapons of those who combat with the intellect the beef of humanity, the sappy protagonist youth once again breathed, over a locked and chaotic and mechanized humanity, the sense of the scope and the possibility of life. This was no longer a Defense of Irony. The soul had entered into iron indeed. It had taken the language of its opponents, their solemn phrases, their mouthings of democracy and liberty and conscience and love, and, tilting them just a little out of plumb, shown in what manner these words conceal from their users their own conduct. In these bright sentences, lyrical with lucid thought, there shone like a rising sun the forces of spiritual release, widening the horizon so piteously shrunken by the war-morale, and filling it again with colors and blooms and significances.

Passion had taken the challenge. Passion gave it back again. Passion for liberty said "No"; said it louder and more angrily than it had said it before the challenge came. All along the line, "Yes" was hastily being substituted for "No." Softly, subtly, insinuatingly, the crisis was stepping up to men, and asking them whether they would

Randolph Bourne

not reconsider their language, now that the stream was coursing contrary to them. And the majority of them changed, noble freemen! and for the best of reasons, of course. It was all like William James and the Philippine imbroglio. It was wrong to annex the islands before they were actually annexed. But once they were taken, then, for some reason, it did not seem so wrong a thing at all. For the "Yes" of America to the democratic ideal, to liberty of individual development, to freedom from ancient tyrannies, in the most of cases, had never been given from the center of the being. It had been an assent given to something for the reason that this something existed, or seemed to exist, or seemed destined to exist. And now, since the stream commenced flowing away from this object; since militarism, nationalism, patriotism, state mysticism, were coming to stand in its place, assent to the successor came quite as readily. No principles stood like steel girders in a conflagration. But in a few noble men and women, the crisis encountered a resistant force; in one man, at the very least, a force so intense that, like Greek fire, it flamed the fiercer for the water hurled upon it. In Bourne it came upon a passionate love of the image of freedom. It came upon a being given up entirely in passion for freedom for growth for himself and other people; in desire for free play to all the world, the five continents and seven seas, to expand human nature in numberless and even conflicting directions. It came in Bourne upon one Anglo-Saxon American, at least, who was not as yet ready to renounce the Englishman's heritage of liberty; an Anglo-Saxon American in whom there still burnt high the faith in the variations of character through self-reliance and perfection by standards voluntarily assumed that had once made the rebellions against the spiritual authoritarianism of Archbishop Laud and against King George III's pretention to Divine Right. This passion so "nineteenth-century," as Bourne himself used ruefully to say, would not drop its arms since the battle was commencing to go against it, and fall to dreaming of an international congress of young radicals to follow upon the war when the liberal forces were going down in defeat. It was aggressive, being intense; summoned itself to ever greater effort since the house was afire at all corners. It defended, it glorified, it tried to summon men back to their allegiance to its object. In the midst of the mêlée, like the passion of a great European contemporary, it asserted in proud faithfulness its ideal. The war had brought into play another of these beings who in defending their cause defended that of every man.

The age-old desire for the release of the capacities for impassioned living pent in the human frame which spoke through Randolph Bourne during the war-time, was never caught by him and held in the shape of a formal statement of the democratic ideal. He died six weeks after the armistice; and throughout the greater part of the bitter months he was midmost, and not above the battle. It was only after *The Seven Arts* perished that Bourne, cut

Randolph Bourne

off from every channel of publicity, gave up his attempt to bring influence to bear on current events; and, going to work in the field of theory, made his deadly wonderful analysis of the State. Hence, most of his fighting was done on the practical level. The articles contributed by him to *The Seven Arts* were, for the most part, defenses of what remained of the democratic machinery thrown up at single points of the fray. They were attempts made to save what remained of the democratic attitude through sharp pitiless analyses of the situation created by the failure of the intellectuals and of the administration to control the ruin-bringing war-technique. Through these brilliant sardonic pictures, Bourne was trying to call to their colors the forces which had once made for democracy; to rouse the intellectuals from the herd-attitudes into which they had collapsed; to try and rechannel the interest of the country into a national educational service whence the herd's need of a military victory had debouched it. *The War and the Intellectuals* was a call for mind; rejection of the pragmatist intellectuals, with whom Bourne had previously been associated, for their failure to create a program for America; demand for intellectuals who could hold the authorities to a war, "gallantly played, with insistent care for democratic values at home and unequivocal alliance with democratic elements abroad for a peace that shall promise more than a mere union of benevolent imperialisms." *Twilight of Idols* formulated Bourne's reasons for discarding pragmatism

229

and all philosophy of intelligent control which does not begin with values and ideals, and therefore permits values to be subordinated in times of stress to pure technique. *Below the Battle* was a composite description of the spiritual states of two friends of Bourne's, a young architect and a young violinist drafted for military service. Through the texture, there runs, it is true, like the red thread through the rope-work of the British fleet, the glorification of the allure of "fresh and true ideas, free speculation, artistic vigor, cultural styles, intelligence suffused by feeling and feeling given fiber and outline by intelligence"; lodestars which draw the individual onward to completion. It is true that all through the writing, we are shown as on a stage, the combat of two forces existing in the world to-day, the one making for the democratic community of free men, the other making against it. The free, self-reliant, self-determined individual is set over against the herd-individual, subject to the herd authorities and orthodoxies, and hemmed round with principles which are worthless in moments of crisis for the reason that they are external. The life of art and wisdom is opposed to the life of domination over the persons of others. The clear feeling and seeing which flows from life lived from the center within, is opposed to the muddled feeling and thinking of men who have never dared trust their intuitions and live their passions out; the intellect which does not dread suspense and is not drugged with fatigue, to that which is in haste to crystallize, to

Randolph Bourne

find its little theory of the universe and then disregard whatever will not fit into it. Yet, what the specific ideal of life for which the author is fighting is, we are not explicitly told. Bourne had no time.

Nevertheless, not anything written by any of the new Americans makes more real than do these fighting papers, the sense of the democratic community of people developed by standards voluntarily assumed and perfected by completest self-reliance, towards which the best minds among those who built the country have moved. The rhythm of these writings brings it again, the sense of men free of the orthodoxies and authorities of state and church, of privilege and radicalism alike; brings it as the breeze in May transports, elusively and yet unmistakably, the breath of unfolding landscapes. It flutters from every dancing line as the rag of a standard tied to a pikehead might flutter in a battle; unnoticed perhaps of the wielder of the weapon, but flaunted by every motion of the staff. It is not a man alone that is speaking. Rather, it is a plane of being demonstrating itself through the substance of words. The light of reason seems to flow from out a beautiful unrealized world, and to make that hidden sphere more real and visible by its tremulous presence. What is expressed calls to fresher life desire for that city of the soul wherever the desire is latent. It seems to build a brave high place of stately colonnades and to extend wide and sunshot spaces around us here in the grim jumble of hard lines and shrieking metal and somber driven hordes. For it gives joyous sanction to all in man which moves toward freedom from ancient shackling tyrannies; it calls forth in beauty what the established order beats down and attends with pain. And it gives it high right not merely through an emotional appeal. It gives right to it through coldest, clearest logic. It hails it health and sanity and wisdom through proof that the life of art and wisdom is the most practical of lives in a strictly practical world; that "interest in creatively enhancing personal and artistic life, interest in the creation of cultural values" makes for greater sureness of observation and clarity of vision than interest devoted entirely to the problem of material increase. For Bourne was a man interested in more impassioned living for himself and others, a man who lived through art, a man disgusted with the continual frustrations and aridities of American life, apologist and exponent both of self-reliant humanity; and Bourne was right about the war; right from the first. This philosophical temperament was not one of those who, like the greater number of our practical young political thinkers, had to wait for Versailles to know that we were "like brave passengers who had set out for the Isles of the Blest only to find that the first mate had gone insane and jumped overboard, the rudder come loose and dropped to the bottom of the sea, and the captain and pilot were lying dead drunk under the wheel." *The Collapse of American Strategy*, written directly after the President's call for "force, force to the uttermost," gave warning that the dead weight of the war-technique was carrying the country entirely away from the purpose for which the war-technique allegedly was being employed; gave warning we were "a rudderless nation, to be exploited as the Allies wished, politically and materially, and towed, to their aggrandizement, in any direction they might desire"; and showed Woodrow Wilson well on the road which led to his eventual miserable failure. And Bourne became righter with every hour. Like a gigantic shadow thrown upon a wall behind the chunky little cripple, the war corroborated him at every point, and gave truth to his words scarcely after they were uttered. It is difficult to believe to-day he was writing in the summer of 1917, and not of 1920 or 1921, so accurate were his prophesies. The heresies of yesterday are become the bromides of to-day.

They were rapidly becoming banalities before Bourne died. Nevertheless, he failed of his immediate objective. He was not interested in being right for the mere pleasure of being right, but in rescuing his freeman's heritage and the democratic future from the hands of the mob. And the politicians, the unprincipled people, the yes-and-no people, carried the day. Probably, Woodrow Wilson never heard of his foremost critic. If any one of his advisors had his attention drawn to certain articles published in an obscure highbrow review in New York, he probably came swiftly, in the manner of the war-mind, to the conclusion that Bourne's name was really "Rudolph

Braun" or perhaps "Randdorff Boerne." The public of
action in America does not take heed of what the public
of theory is saying, particularly when the public of theory
happens to be truly theoretical and consequently truly
practical. So 1776 finally receded to 1917. Liberty became universal compulsory service in defense of repub-
lican monarchy. Democracy became pressure downward
and backward; became the ancient herd-attitudes; forceful suppression of minorities; compulsion of thought; be-
trayal of the liberal elements in Europe; a league of capi-
talistic imperialisms; starvation of millions of people in
the east of Europe; the decay of occidental civilization;
the capture of American institutions by a Fascistic mob.
And 1917 receded to 1923. Bourne only saw the commencement of the fulfillment of his bitter prophecies.
Even in the December of 1918, in the midst of the black
death, the fearful reactionary current was only swollen
to half the size it has since gained. There was still more
of a will to the change of spirit and of organization
throughout the country then, than there is at present.
There was still more of a fund of good-will and courageous thought in circulation. But since, the forces which
have kept the human being in ignorance and in a condition
of servitude have waxed fat on the energies of men.
Every obscurantism has taken courage. Every inertia
has felt itself justified. They can do anything they wish
with us. We are become like a herd of cows.

And yet, Bourne snatched a victory from the very maw

Randolph Bourne

of defeat. He is more visible to us to-day than he was
while he was alive. He seems to have left behind him
some immortal part that walks about the earth much as
he used himself to walk. At innumerable corners of life
we seem to glimpse advancing toward us the quaint little
figure in its long black cloak; so like one of the digni-
taries who parade across the stage during the march in
Carmen. When he died, we knew that perhaps the
strongest mind of the entire younger generation in America had gone. But in the few years that have elapsed
since that December day, Bourne's figure has grown to
a far greater stature. To-day, already, we know him
for one of the rarest, freest, sweetest spirits that have ever
come out of this land. We see the size of him plainly
in the bitter moments in which we realize how vacant
the scene has become since he quit it. There is so gray a
death in the many fields to which he brought the light
of his own clear nature! He was a humanist; and the
men left us are sociologists, political thinkers, professors,
and critics. We see the size of him, too, in happier moments; in some of those flashes in which, with a far sur-
mise, we know what it is to be a free spirit; what it is to
live for an idea, to "write in favor of that which the great
interests of the world are against," to work toward "the
enhancement of personal and artistic life and the creation
of cultural values." For he was the artist-fighter in the
drab American streets. It is certain, then, that his figure
will stretch as the years go by, and become ever more

generally visible. His fame and future are with the cycles of life.

For despite the mediocre world which would not heed him, he remained true to the spirit in him. He succeeded thoroughly in expressing to his time the far community of which he was a member. In his person, therefore, he has lent the world another image, another symbol and banner whereby the unborn thing which filled him, wherever and in whomsoever it grows, can come to greater consciousness, and therefore greater courage of itself, and be pressed onward toward birth. And, some day, the spring will come again to men.

Alfred Stieglitz

I

ALFRED STIEGLITZ is of the company of the great affirmers of life. There is no matter in all the world so homely, trite, and humble that through it this man of the black box and chemical bath cannot express himself entire. A tree, a barn, a bone, a cloud, have released the spirit in Stieglitz. Soilure of a windowpane has started the beat of light. Raindrops pausing on leaves have started it; and the glistening rims of cartwheels, and feet broken by bad modern shoes, and stormlight of a feverish August day. And car-horses steaming amid smudged New York snow have made pulse the light no less lambently than whitest cloudshapes breezing through shoreless blue; cloth of an old coat no less burningly than the singing downtown skyline; brick walls torn and brick walls laboriously upbuilding no less rapturously than slender fingers licked with sensitive life. Prints color of pearl, of milk, of bronze, black and platinum planes and segments of planes reveal a city-full of quotidian stuffs charged with vital significance. The photographer has cast the artist's net wider into the material world than any man before him or alongside him. Not Whitman with his running blackberry

Port of New York

vine and dung-rolling beetles; not the cubist French with their playing cards and chimney pots, newspaper and bocks and walls eaten into by words, have landed a greater catch of untried subject matter, nor seen as related portions of designs so many common immediate stuffs. Stieglitz has shoved the nozzle of his camera into hells where man's hand has rested cruellest, and caught filthy smoke and grimy skies, iron and cinders and strung steely wires. He has brought the lens close to the human epidermis, and given the pores, the fine hairs along the shin-bone, the veining of the pulse and the moisture on the upper lip. He has portrayed the people of the American streets and of the workmen's cottages, of the kitchens, the slums, the studios, the little westside apartments, and the shining limousines. He has based clear and singing prints on motives taken from every portion of the persons of women, not alone on visages and hands and rears of heads, but on feet naked and feet stockinged and shod, on ears and nostrils, on breasts and stomachs, thighs and buttocks, on navels, armpits, and the bones underneath the skin of collar and chest.

Backyards hung with laundry and cut by fire-escapes, and nourished fullness of a bright July; a foolish Victorian parlor with casts of Cupid and the Venus de Milo in the corner, and the regard of love from chaste unfathomable eyes, all alike are made to partake in a single quality of incandescence. Snaps from the hand-camera and plates from the large camera of the tripod, all are

238

Alfred Stieglitz

infinite rhythms of warm wondrous light, choral symphonies and dances of the sunpour. The tiny scale between black and white is distended in these prints to an immense keyboard of infinitely delicate modulations. Black and white become capable of registering in strong and subtle relations a universe of ecstasy and dream and anguish. The delicious variations of light utter exciting rhythms and many-voiced speech like the modern orchestral machine's. Rich brushing of the darker strings is in his deep softly flowing shadowings. The smoothness of the flutes is in the broad creamy passages; the nasal whirligigs of the other reeds in many a sinuosity. And the fiercely burning points of illumination have the pierce of the brass; impact of the horns, jagged cutting of the trumpets. Nevertheless the lucent keyboard of the photographer is better comparable perhaps to an orchestra of tones electrically generated; capable of subtler shadings than the one which we to-day possess, and abler therefore to approach more closely the dark wet quick in man. Through his machinery, Stieglitz has been able to produce a gamut more delicate than the hand can draw. He has strange pungent tones, dark creams, fawns, cobweb grays, unknown to Western art. He has photographs thrustful like beaten steel and photographs tenderer than softest flower-petals, photographs sonorous as bronze, and photographs lacier than the filagree of the frost. Infinitesimal shapes, elusive flakes, chime positively in this delicious tintinnabulation of light. One gets new eyes, new nerves in receiving these gleams, points, breaths of the silvery scale. The noble prints, so clear, precise, charged with unimaginably subtle detail and vibrantly given textures are like the writings of a needle sensitive to the gravity of man, the state of his spirit, the movement of his blood, the faintest tingling of his cortexes, as the seismograph is sensitive to the minutest vibrations of the crust of the earth.

The infinite light is the substance in Stieglitz, the living matter of the bosom taken shape. Through a piece of machinery, the ancient religiosity of the old world has found channel once again into life; the cathedral upreared itself serene in shrill American day. This is the radiant wonder of the maker of the prints and his tragedy and endless struggle, too: that in flaccid breast-choking, desiccate New York among hard little-feeling people, his spirit should have remained intense, ever-liquid, profoundly poetical, and joyous, outpouring fountainwise in exhaustless flow its living waters. There is the separation of only a generation from the humid European soil to help explain the gift; but that explains really nothing. There are ten student years in green and liberal Berlin and Munich to help; there is a family tree of old life-loving western Jews. But these facts, too, reach no further than the human body's stretch along a tower's height. Wonderful it still remains that here where the soul is universally cheap and irreverent and indifferent, this one should always be astand amid streets and peoples

Alfred Stieglitz

as the primitive religious soul stood in needle-scented pine forests when the cathedral first commenced beneath the heart: speechless in conscience of an earthborn wonder beyond itself, like the uprising colonnade of the trees. Amid pavements thrown like universal bad feeling before the feet of the world, the man perceives, everywhere, in matter never touched by the spirit finger, in American city stuffs and scrawny rats of people, electric modes of the far-reaching substance beyond himself. His breast goes forth in passion of surrender to the higher, fairer, purer presence ineffable as the dying west through forest fronds and crowns. The classical new-worlder may behold nothing but matter unrelated to himself, there to be blasted and uprooted and used in any way for any purpose. But Stieglitz knows endless variations of a wondrous stuff, fluid of firmaments, which he can never grasp, never describe for all his passionate efforts to embrace it and to say it. He sees it everywhere, in the stone, the plant, the flying vapor, and its presence is a joy and a pity and a fulfillment to him. A button is a bone; a ruffling aspen, feminine; the stones full of flesh. He sees divine stuff flickering, gasping in the human breast; and something binds him in utter allegiance to it, and takes everything he has, and holds it at the disposal of the struggling, growing principle. And it is there enormous and dense for him every moment. The classical new-worlder may behold majesty only in the moment passed, or in the moment yet to come. But for this man, a fleeting expression

Port of New York

of countenance, a sudden twitching smile, a raise of the hand, a quiver of stormcloud edge, may hold a profound revelation of life; assemble the wonder and the agony of living complete: pain lying close on humorousness and ghastly death on gleaming youth, the glory, the defeat, and the joke all together. And in the conditions of light everlastingly reaching him with all shapes and stuffs and lines; in the births and agonies of day, there is fused the marvelous meaning all things have for him; the passion for all manifestations of life; the singing and soaring of spirit stretching to grasp the overwhelming presence afloat before it, and growing rarer, stronger, steelier pinions in reaching.

If any career in America has demonstrated spirit; if any career has flowed out of a man's complete obedience to the imperative of the unborn stuff of worlds in his bosom, it is Stieglitz'. Photography, *Camera Work*, Photo-Secession, 291 Fifth Avenue, each of his forms of action has been life creating out of economy its proper unprecedented form; breasting matter immediately and traveling by air line directly to its mark. The man moves in original psychic patterns; for manner of living, manner of working, spiritual gesture, and esthetic process flow from within, produced by inner necessity. The direction is taken subconsciously, but is the more positive for that reason. A small boy in the early -seventies during vacation time carries all his lead racehorses into the booth of a tintyper in Lake George village for the

Alfred Stieglitz

purpose of having their pictures taken. The dark room intrigues him; and while the other boys remain outside, he goes in behind the curtain to see what is taking place. In the early -eighties, the same lad is a student in the Polytechnic in Berlin. He is supposed to be studying mechanical engineering, for the parental abode is positive the future of America rests in the hands of mechanical engineers. But he is spending his time indeed playing piano and playing billiards. He becomes amateur billiard champion of Germany and Austria, goes a hundred times or so to *Tristan* and a hundred times or so to *Carmen;* is moved profoundly by the naturalistic draughtsmen, Ibsen, Zola, and the Russians. The only English author who interests him at the time is Mark Twain. Goethe's *Faust* lies under his well-stuffed German pillow. One day he discovers the camera and goes to work in the photographic laboratory. The machine releases him; he feels he has a right to live, and a right to be living in Berlin. There was nothing fortuitous in the discovery. Stieglitz and his machine were affinities born. Camera and man discovered one another. Capacity for instantaneous crystallization, for dazzling flash-like selections of the unconscious mind from among the welter of materials present to his senses, is a principle of Stieglitz' psyche. He can seize his moment, the fore-moment, the moment before the raindrop falls, when it comes; even though it move fast as the rack in the heavens. Some chisel-hardness of edge exists in him; sharpness of tem-

243

pered metal which the impact of excruciating pain cannot bend. It keeps him conscious during the preparation of the moment, at the very climax of the moment; able to catch and fix the ground-beat of life in the green wound. Rarest sensibility seems to show him ephemeral gestures invisible to the rest of the world and make audible to him the faint strumming of the wires announcing messages from afar. He will await his moment through many years, carry an idea fifteen years, twenty years, longer still, in his head, until his understanding and the material circumstance are ready to cope with the problem, and the vital instant presents itself. Life appears always fully present along the epidermis of his body: vitality ready to be squeezed forth entire in fixing the instant, in recording a brief weary smile, a twitch of the hand, the fugitive pour of sun through clouds. And not a tool, save the camera, is capable of registering such complex ephemeral responses, and expressing the full majesty of the moment. No hand can express it, for the reason that the mind cannot retain the unmutated truth of a moment sufficiently long to permit the slow fingers to notate large masses of related detail. The impressionists tried in vain to achieve the notation. For, consciously or unconsciously, what they were striving to demonstrate with their effects of light was the truths of moments; impressionism has ever sought to fix the wonder of the here, the now. But the momentary effects of lighting escaped them while they were busy analyzing; and their "impression" remains

Alfred Stieglitz

usually a series of impressions superimposed one upon the other. Stieglitz was better guided. He went directly to the instrument made for him.

And he has used the machine in perfect obedience to the moving spirit. He has used it unmechanically. During a century and a half, the race of machines has been enslaving man and impoverishing his experience. Like Frankensteins invented by the human brain to serve it, these creatures have turned upon their master, and made prey of him. It is not so much the fact that men have used these implements in manufacturing that has made the slaves, as the fact that the mass production has been made easy by the use of arms of steel and iron. The lazy human being, forever asteer for methods of sparing himself the fatigue of brain-work, has discovered that although it is even more difficult to make sensitive the hand of steel than the hand of flesh, it is possible, nevertheless, to produce vast quantities of articles with machinery without applying brain-power to the processes of production. The machine is capable of repeating, an infinite number of times, a single gesture; and the monotony never wearies it. And it is precisely this mechanical use of the new implements that has harmed the human psyche. The vast quantities of necessities produced by the machine, the swiftness of production, have rapidly increased the population; the increase in numbers of people has in turn forced the establishment of criteria of quantity in place of criteria of quality. The machine has turned men mechanical. It has forced them to forego experiment and the search for finer products for the sake of repeating incessantly the few gestures demanded of them by the arms of steel. It has forced them to repeat over and over again their old experiences, to numb subconsciously the desire for self-improvement through the improvement of craftsmanship; for men cannot serve both the master of greater and cheaper production and of finer and more durable work. It has obliged them to seek to root out of themselves all interest in fresh experience, for the reason that desire, once aroused, is extinguished only with pain. It has caused them to regard objects not with the eyes of feeling, the eyes of the life-loving, earth-loving, green-and-growth-loving spirit. In America, particularly, has the machine sown decay. The human values dissolved early in the history of the country; the civilization of the pioneers was erected upon the withholding of a certain sort of feeling from the work of the hands; and it was easier here than elsewhere for the machine to suppress in men all religious sentiment for their tools and the materials upon which the tools performed labor.

But since the commencement of his career, Stieglitz has been doing with the camera exactly what the folk of the industrial spheres in America have failed doing with their implements. He has made his machine a portion of the living, changing, growing body; and the act of photography an experience. He began without preconceptions; it was of no consequence to him whether his products were

Alfred Stieglitz

"art" or no. He knew the camera gave him an opportunity of expressing himself—like sitting down at the piano; and of uttering his cry for the full human life America had promised him, the small American boy, and would not give. And he had a curious intuitive faith that the black box and the chemical bath and the printing paper could be made to record to his satisfaction what he felt about the world. Stieglitz' long struggle with the machine has been made at the behest of a passionate unsleeping need of a quality. The machinery people were content to repeat *ad infinitum* the well enough achievements of their implements. The photographer began pushing his camera beyond its known frontiers; unconsciously, in the desire to make it render his picture of things, obliging it to attack the most complex problems of plastic representation. An arm was being developed by being forced continually to adjust itself to new conditions and problems. Every one of Stieglitz' photographs is an experiment; an act of penetration into regions where one has no feet to walk, and arrives only in flying fragments. He does not repeat. Each print is the result of a complete reconsideration of what exposure, developing, and quality of paper can do toward solving the problem presented to him by his feelings. Each is the result of a complete summoning of all the strength and all the wisdom gained through past experiences for the purpose of expressing something felt in life. For the sake of achieving the vitality of a photograph, he will make sometimes fifty, and sometimes one and two hundred attempts at satisfactory printing. Like an inventor, he will work for years on a single problem until he is appeased. A negative having given a satisfactory print, he will sometimes set about making it render a print of a feeling latent in it, but not registered by the earlier proof; he has gotten as many as twelve different sensations from a single negative. Nor is the manner of presenting the stamp an afterthought. The difference of a fraction of a centimeter in the position of the limiting mat can make or unmake certain of the designs. Besides, Stieglitz is constantly photographing in his mind. Photography is something more to him than the science of the dark box. It is a philosophy of life.

Integrity, reverence for the integrity of others, has made Alfred Stieglitz have respect for the integrity of the very machinery he uses; and religious respect for the nature of his implements sets him no further away from the mechanical people of America than from the fellowship of the pictorial photographers. Where he, with his unique intensity has driven and is driving the machine to the limits of its powers of putting down the thing which exists before the lens in its own way, they have been living in Capua, taking the problems of photography very easily, and playing recreant to their medium. The camera, too, can select. The photographer can synthesize feelings gotten from many objects in the object present before the dead eye of the machine; and he has the power of intelli-

Alfred Stieglitz

gent control over the filter and bath of developers to assist in the process of selection made by his emotion from among the range of materials before him. All forms exist in nature. The artists have merely assembled them. The Italian primitives are written over the face of Umbria and Tuscany. But the photographer whose emotion has failed to make the significant selection and simplification, and who gums and fuzzies and diffuses his plates and introduces the human hand into the process of photography, is not living as his medium demands he live. He is a-run from the medium and its unique problem. Likewise the photographers who try to paint with the camera, to produce Whistlerian effects and to repeat Böcklin and Degas. They too are striving away from their machine and its ever-present pregnant moment into moments lived before them by certain individuals who etched, painted, and lithographed. Stieglitz' photography, however, has always been "straight." If, in *Camera Notes* and in *Camera Work* he showed himself willing to grant every photographer the privilege of working out his own proper idea of the new art; and has stood shoulder to shoulder before the world with men whose esthetics differ radically from his own, his own work has always been achieved by the simplest means of his craft. Perhaps for the reason that he himself has never wanted to paint and has always wanted to photograph. Never has photography been practiced so nude of tricks of any sort. During the first thirteen years of his career, he refused to "spot" his negatives, for his feeling of what photography was would not permit retouching. And in the making of none of the prints which he has exhibited has the human interfered; none are gummed, fuzzied, or diffused.

Stieglitz has rarely had the privilege of a dark-room. A bath-room; a door drawn close to a wall and draped with a blanket: a blanket tented above a table, even, have served him. But, through his deep feeling for the state of life in all things, and through his passion for the work and the relentlessness with which he has driven himself and his machine, Stieglitz, without reference to the tradition of any other art, has indeed produced an additional artistic medium, capable like any other of responding to any feeling entertained about his life by man. And he has mastered the subtlest problems of plastic representation. It has never interested him to analyze the old painters. He has merely been trying to do justice to his feelings about the matters before him. And yet the same dramatic oppositions and double-pulls of form, the same interplay of angles and curves present in the paintings of the old men are to be found in all the later photographs of the New Yorker; Stieglitz' form of proof that the masters, too, sat before nature, and were moved by a passion to represent what they saw. The earlier photographs have a form relatively simple, it is true. Their form is more a matter of composition and of balance than of rhythmic order, although spirit and exquisitely pure photographic quality are in them no differently than in the later prints. But, in

Alfred Stieglitz

laboring, and with the experience of years, Stieglitz has managed to create a dynamic rhythmic order. The more recent photographs are three-dimensional polyphony. They have convexity, and the grand double motion of penetration of background and of recedence, hollowing, opening out. The backdrops of monotone have not a whit less of life than any other of the vibrantly given textures; a figure thrown against black is thrown against snapping fecund space. And the shadowed squares and oblongs have become progressively intenser in span. Without having in any fashion sacrificed the delicacy of his earlier work, Stieglitz has managed to release himself ever more copiously, and to get larger and ever larger amounts from line and form. Linear contours are elegant, precise, and delicate as Ingres', for Stieglitz draws marvelously with the camera as few have drawn with the pencil; sinuous, dramatic, and vehement as Ingres' rarely are. In certain of the forms, we feel the weight of a man entire, and in all swiftness and lightness of motion, the rude thrust of primitive American life, the insane pressure, the wild iron clutch. Menhirs and monoliths of black and white design themselves clearly, lyrically within the white borders. Great coils of life lie brazen and terrible upon the walls. Many of the prints are sonorously sculpturesque, and recall objects of massive silver and platinum and gold, or lumps of stone and steel and wood. A head is mighty as a cannon ball. Clouds have the released energy of hillsides dynamited.

Port of New York

II

Fullness of spirit inevitably comes to express itself in combat for an idea; and the burning life of the man could not be satisfied in singing its song of pain and wonder, or in waging silent internal war on the backward drag of America; even in fashioning prints which let no beholder pass unmindful of the godhead. Some more immediate hold on the weight of unspiritual civilization was necessary to Stieglitz; and the passion in him early became fight for the idea of photography, fight for the privilege of the spirit to use new tradition-unhallowed media for the purpose of expressing itself. But if at the beginning the war was waged nominally for the products of the camera, for the photographs of the foreign pictorialists, and those of the Americans Käsebier, Coburn, Eugene, Steichen, Brigman, White, Keiley, Strand, and the rest, the fight itself was never any other than the spirit's eternal war on the letter. For if painters and public both were clinging to the letter of the classics, and denying to machine-made objects the values of works of art, it was because neither artist nor public had, or wanted to have any very exact sense of what the impulse of the artist is. If the painters refused to perceive that it was the song that the masters had expressed through color that made their canvases precious, and stubbornly insisted on holding the medium, the pigment and the violin and the piece of marble and the regular meters, sacrosanct, it was for the reason that what

252

Alfred Stieglitz

they least could understand was the driving force of song, which makes vibrant a dead material. The evidence of the photographs was there to show them, if see they could, that with the camera too a man could select, and that the photographer too could carry about with him in his mind the feeling of one object and express it through other ones. Hence, Stieglitz began doing the work of prophet and awakener—with series of related shows of pictorial photography. He made a cultural force of the Camera Club of New York; and when the organization expelled him, its spark of life went into eternal slumber. With Eduard Steichen, his friend, he opened late in 1905 the little attic of 291 Fifth Avenue, at the line where the areas of uptown and downtown moralities meet, for the purpose of giving Americans opportunity of seeing what photography had achieved in Europe and America. Exhibitions of prints were sent out over the world. But it was the prints of others than Stieglitz himself that went; for Stieglitz, with characteristic sportsmanship, gave the work of others preference over his own, and stood aside for the sake of the idea.

The quarterly, *Camera Work*, had had existence before the Photo-Secession Gallery was opened. And *Camera Work* continued to carry the idea of photography beyond the radius of exhibitions, and to reinforce the exhibitions by recording them. In time the magazine, perhaps the handsomest and most esthetically presented periodical ever issued, came to give in its fifty splendid numbers the complete record of the experiments in the new art. It contained specimens selected for their artistic value of the work of all the important photographers, American and European. And it presented the specimens in a manner which left them their full life. Many of the "reproductions" were pulled directly from the original negatives, were printed in the spirit of the original picture, and made to retain all its quality. They were in reality original stamps. The nature of the photogravures published in *Camera Work* was demonstrated very early in its existence. In 1904, the Photo-Secession exhibit contributed to the exhibition of the Société L'Effort in Brussels happened to go astray. The Exhibition Committee thereupon took about thirty of the gravures which had been published in *Camera Work*, mounted and framed them, and hung them as representing America in the exhibition. According to the criticisms published, this little American section proved the success of the show. And it was not until after it had closed that it became generally known that the American Section had consisted entirely of plates of *Camera Work*. More recently, the President of the Royal Photographic Society, J. Dudley Johnston, in making an address before the society on the development of photography, used the photogravures of Stieglitz' quarterly to illustrate his talk. Besides the pictures, the periodical brought special articles written for it by Bernard Shaw, Maeterlinck, Caffin, R. Child Bayley, J. Craig Annan, Kerfoot, Virginia Sharp, de Zayas, Mabel Dodge, Keiley,

Alfred Stieglitz

Francis and Gabrielle Picabia, and others. Later, when the little gallery commenced to show paintings, it published reproductions of the new art. It brought the record of the public reception of the exhibits by reprinting the press notices down to the imbecilities and malevolences of Cortissoz and Carey; and on its magnificent pages it introduced to the reading world the writings of Gertrude Stein, Mina Loy, Max Weber, John Marin, and Leonard van Noppen. And every sheet of *Camera Work* declares Stieglitz' passion for his cause. The very format is lyrical. The magazine is itself a piece of expression, so beautifully has the spacing, the printing, the quality of the paper, the form of the pages, the form of the advertisements, even, been handled; so generously has lover's touch been expended on every aspect of the publication.

It was only two years after the Photo-Secession Gallery was opened that its aggression was commencing to stretch over its natural territory; the little photographic gallery was in the way to developing into the wide place "291." By 1908 the battle for the photographic idea was become the battle for "modern," post-impressionist, non-representational art. Modern color, supposed to be anti-photographic, is indeed the close ally of Stieglitz' photography. The colorist in his medium, like the photographer in his own, is seeking in the phrase of Paul Strand "to use the expressivity of the objective world for the end of fashioning therewith subjective form." He, too, is working from the rhythmic pattern established in him by his relationship to the object before him. And, in place of devaluating the art of the painter, the camera indeed sets him free to work with new intensity within his potential limits; and to gain for his medium the emotional intensification which flows from the precise usage of means. There is no more conflict between the two media than between the means of poetry and of music. The struggle of the colorist is the struggle of the photographer; it is the grapple of foothold of media precisely, finely used and emotionally intensified against a world unwilling to read the language of the senses. Hence, while London and fashion and Roger Fry still ignored Post-Impressionistic art, "291" began forcing upon New York the European and American experimenters in color and clay. Chase and the other pundits were outraged at seeing the drawings and washes of Rodin shown publicly; their anguish was merely commenced. Matisse followed in his painting and sculpture, and then the essential Cézanne of the water colors. Picasso was presented as painter, sculptor, and draughtsman. Henri Rousseau, Brancusi, Nadelman, Picabia, Marius de Zayas the caricaturist too were shown at "291" for the first time. Likewise the Americans, Max Weber, Hartley, Carles, Dove, Marin, Bluemner, Walkowitz, Macdonald-Wright, O'Keeffe, the "modern" Maurer, and others. Between exhibitions of paintings and exhibitions of photography there came the first official shows of negroid sculpture and the first synthetic show of children's work which definitely established the

Alfred Stieglitz

relationship between the infantine esthetic perceptions and those at the root of modern "abstract" art.

If ever institution in America came to bring the challenge of the truth of life to the land of the free, and to show the face of expressivity to a trading society living by middle-class conventions, it was the little gallery "291." "291" was an art gallery that was itself a work of art. Exhibitions of baffling work were hung there with a white austerity; exhibitions were hung like scientific presentations of fact. And though each exhibition demonstrated the quintessential spirit of an artist, the shows were hung in sequences emotionally conditioned. The many separate shows contributed to a single demonstration that grew like a tree—the demonstration of the world hour. It was a place where the work of the heart was let be, set clear of commercial entanglements, and allowed to do its work; and where the spirit of life came alive, and windows swung through erstwhile meaningless complexes of spots and lines and shapes. It was a place where people got very hot and explanatory and argumentative about rectangles of color and lumps of bronze and revealed themselves; and a place where quiet unobtrusive people suddenly said luminous things in personal language about paintings and drawings scornfully, authoritatively excluded by others, and revealed life. It was like a play. Nevertheless "291" was a laboratory. Behind the curtain, in the back room, *Camera Work* was edited; and here de Zayas, Paul Haviland, Agnes E. Meyer, Picabia, Katharine N.

257

Port of New York

Rhoades, and Stieglitz collaborated upon the brilliant Apollinarian experiments with typography called *291*. Mats were cut; frames tried; bathroom water ran over photographic plates; and Marie, the stenographer, who was studying singing, addressed some envelopes, played the typewriter, and listened wonder-eyed. A scientific spirit was alive: people were making serious study of the components of expression, and Stieglitz was watching, with the zeal of a psychological experimenter life as it flowed into his retort and out again, observing its patterns, proving his intuitions, "registering" the psychic reactions of America of the business man, the artist, the woman, everybody who happened in. Meanwhile, other demonstrations were in progress, a demonstration on John Marin, among others, conducted for the purpose of proving that an artist in America could remain completely obedient to the promptings of an imperious, uncompromising, revolutionary spirit, and yet maintain himself beneath the statue of Commerce and Industry.

The little attic was a house of God besides. It gave all life that came into it a chance to hear itself speak, to be clarified by inner truth. It may be you went a good while ignorant that this profane space, where every spirit stuff and rag were shaken free, and anarchism and the essence of sex remained ever present, was indeed, without program, and merely of its proper nature, a church. Then, some moment when the individual staying power was near collapse, and energy dissolved and faith evapo-

Alfred Stieglitz

rated, arrived; and for a reason not quite clear, you found yourself once more going to shabby Fifth Avenue near Thirtieth Street, and getting into the rickety elevator, and then standing in the garret once again among the walls and the art. In such a moment the nature of the place was made known. You were alone among the subdued fall of day. The rumor of the whistling, rattling life which had bashed in every side of you and dissolved the inner column was still here. But at a distance, like the Fifth Avenue traffic; flowing gently, serviceably about the sanctity of the rooms. You sat on a chair, or on a packing case, as there usually was no chair; and against the gray stuff of the walls, or standing about on the floor, were strange segments of marble and strange movements of color and line. It might be Matisse or Nadelman, Walkowitz or the girl from Virginia, or was it Georgia—one never knew quite certainly in which state it was that she was teaching school? But, that day, whatever it was that stood about became another stuff, a thing which carried on curves and contours the ground-voice of life murmuring. You heard again, clearly, persuasively, the summons seated in the center of you, saw presented to you again the steep, the difficult, the daring pathway up which you had to go. The room wherein you sat breathed clean, brave toleration of your way. It seemed to demand that you be yourself utterly—for in this place nothing but that final self, that utter, inner design of the soul was revered. No half measures were good, no shrewd with-

259

holding. There was but one adventure worthy the living; the battle for the sake of the central self—the adventure of the difficult way of truthful living. For here were others giving their truths. Here on the walls were testimonies of fellow-travelers somewhere over the darkened immense far-stretching land. These were the men who had renounced other men's thoughts and other men's conceptions to creep closer to life that exists and get something of its pulse and fume onto canvas or into bronze. Here was the time, the beating now. The impulse to all honest living, from its place inside, had reached out and taken you by the hand again.

You had been a ten minutes in the gallery, merely. But for the sake of those ten minutes the place stayed open. Not alone for the sake of Picasso and Hartley, Weber and Georgia O'Keeffe. For the sake of the little outside person who came in and saw a little more deeply, and felt the stream a-trickle again. For the sake of the living of life everywhere. It stood, perpetual affirmation of a faith that there existed, somewhere, here in very New York, a spiritual America. And through the wilderness it sent its call for human beings. Not saviourism; but a prophetic challenge to the insane personalism of American life; the unconscious cry of a spirit for people to become the walking, growing, soul-faithful persons they potentially were. The challenge was to the public and the artists alike; the cry to them all to break their dead jails and enter out into the life of feeling so close await-

Alfred Stieglitz

ing them, and lose themselves a moment at least in love
of some unpersonal thing through which they might take
life and give it forth again. With nothing but his own
deep civilization to direct him, Stieglitz was asking from
out the land the free community of people, the "democratic" community living for the fair sake of the thing
which belongs to no one man, and lends itself merely
now to this one and now to that, and is owned by none.

And, for a brief space, his place did have such a company of friends. Stieglitz achieved it through shows of
art; he achieved it through his talk. The two had much
the same tendency and the same effect. . . . From the
back room, behind the gray curtaining stuff, there came
always the sound of talking going on. If you went in,
you found a number of people with amazing shapes and
directions sitting around an iron stove toasting their feet.
Bluemner, Marin, Zoler, Hartley, and Walkowitz were
sure to be present; often Steichen, Agnes E. Meyer,
Haviland, de Zayas, and Picabia. Here the lion and the
lamb, Huntington Wright and Caffin, lay down together,
and the lion and the unicorn, Huntington Wright and
Leo Stein, fought for the crown of definitions. At a table
by the window that gave on chimney pots and towering
rear walls, there stood pasting something and addressing
the company, a slight slender figure clad in a pepper and
salt business suit: gray bristling mustache, gray fighting
hair, and shining brown eyes behind glasses. Stieglitz
was on his shoe leather all day long; and if you did not

Port of New York

go into the back room, like as not he would come out into the gallery and begin speaking to you with his fierce and informal, jovial and passionate, address; and all the others trail after him from the stove and lean abstractedly about attending on whatever was going to happen. You had a burlesque picture of the disciples standing about waiting for Jesus to perform a miracle of loaves or fishes. It was very disconcerting at first, Stieglitz' talking; and the silent wisdom of the others, and their looks that gave you to know that everything which you ventured stabbed them through the stomach; and Hartley's attainment of Nirvana right in the middle of the room. And many people never quite got to like it; or to perceive what Stieglitz was doing with his memories and experiences. It would have been pleasant to have Stieglitz tell you what the pictures were, or to have him listen to your account of your reactions; and sometimes he did say what the works made him feel, or let you tell him what they made you feel. But, usually, he spoke of his life. And in the commencement, it was not entirely comprehensible why he was telling you about the assistant American consul in Berlin who cheated him and a group of fellow students at poker and then tried to clear the deed by offering him a tip on the races; or what the tale of the rich society patroness and the *Serf* of Matisse had to do with the Marin watercolors upon the wall; or why you were read the disagreeable letter received

262

Alfred Stieglitz

that morning from a painter categorically ordering Stieglitz to send him the most distinguished French pastel-crayons. Sometimes, there seemed no point to the narrative at all, or to Stieglitz' recounted retort to the museum director, and you forced a stupid grin; and then you wondered why some other visitor who happened to be listening, or who happened to be the person addressed, found a significance and laughed or nodded his head, or said some smiling thing which made Stieglitz give forth a relieved "correct." Also, much of the pithy talk appeared too persistently personal, too much about Stieglitz' own affairs; and the jeremiads on New York and the American and the "people" who had no "idea" seemed to smite unjustly you. But one never went without some gotten glint of life, some shrewd observation, some profound penetration of character. And the feeling of personalism disappeared. It was Stieglitz who was talking, exuberantly, bitterly, mischievously. It was Stieglitz who was telling of his own quixotic existence and of his father and his brother-in-law and his wife. But nevertheless a life was being used objectively, as the matter of an artist. The facts were clearly known and clearly limned, and what one saw through the flashing, deep-cut windows was the gray formless fluid termed human life. The little moments lay, deeply set, in an eternal thing. They were patterns ever present, ever repeating themselves with slightest variation through the world; moreover the eternal stuff had to do with something right before the door on the pavements of New York; running right throughout the dull and marvelous opacity called the United States. Some pattern, some tendency, some motive, were visible to the man, or becoming clear perhaps only as he talked. Maybe you left a little sore in the chest from the wild emotional impact. But though perhaps you went with a sense of defeats and terrors and tragedies lurking far nearer in life than you had ever supposed they crouched, you went marvelously freed; with courage even for the wheel of New York.

"291" had an end in the spring of 1917. For a couple of years longer, Stieglitz was to be seen among pictures in a sort of no-man's-land on the deserted second floor of the old Altman-estate building. Then that barn was vacated too. The spirit which had created the little gallery had to destroy it; for the reason that it itself remained steadfast while the work of its love was threatened with perversion. A crisis, recurrent in Stieglitz' life, and apparently inevitable in it, had put in a new appearance. At the root of the man's dream of a group of people, working together, each one preserving his own identity, there must lie some strong unconscious family feeling; perhaps the strong Jewish family feeling; extended in this case not to individuals related in blood, but related in work and spirit. All his life he has been hoping for the realization of this dream; first among his friends when a young man; later during his attempts at

Alfred Stieglitz

business, when he thought his workmen would work with him freely if he made them feel at liberty to carry things out in their own way, and trusted them; again in the Camera Club; then in the "Photo-Secession"; then in "291." And each time the hope has been taken away from him; for the reason that he has found few persons instinct with the family feeling so full in him, and capable of combining with him in a living group. "291" had found few permanent members from out the public. The public could not be gotten to create toward the artist; the true spirit of appreciation ever trickled but thinly. People wanted to buy established names, for the reason that they wished to shine in reflected splendor, to entertain ambassadors under Cézannes, or to capture brilliant investments of capital. People were incapable of interesting themselves in potentialities. A development meant nothing to them. People thought they adored Ingres and Whistler and Chinese art. But they could not recognize the classical spirit when it took the form Picasso . . . (that is, they couldn't in 1916. Since then Fifth Avenue has seen a great "light"); they could not recognize the Whistlerian charm when it spoke through Morgan Russell; or Chinese delicacy when Marin created a modern equivalent for it. A few patrons only gave to the artist in the spirit in which the artist was giving to the world; in thanks. The skyscrapers and the eternal Rockefeller seemed indomitable. But it was not because of the public's attitude that the gallery closed.

Port of New York

It was because of the smallness of the artists that it had to be destroyed. They were closing the door on freedom. The pictorial photographers were betraying the machine; photography the living issue was non-existent. And the colorists were playing against the spirit of art. Stieglitz had imported modern French painting for the sake of an idea; and the French painters and their friends seemed incapable of understanding that "291" was anything but a salesroom. The American artists with the soul-shrivelry characteristic of the new-worlder were knifing one another, or seeking to capture the laboratory for a formula, socialism, anarchism, patriotism, intellectualism, estheticism. The smart world had said "tag" to Cézanne and he was It. A new academy was commencing to form under his sign; and Stieglitz, who had first shown the essential Cézanne, wished he could place his foot squarely through every one of the beatified canvases of the beatified painter. Also, the artists insisted on considering Stieglitz a man overflowing with cash and full of an inexhaustible power of procuring the same for them. They seemed indeed to have lost all sense of the idea. For the $15,000 which had paid for the thirteen years of "291," and which had helped give a number of artists their freedom, had been found not alone by Stieglitz; and the little place never was a business.

Besides, it had done its pioneer work. The little gallery had brought the new art in. Due partly to its enterprise the great armory show of 1913 was made;

Alfred Stieglitz

and the "futurists" were introduced to the larger public. Thereupon, through the efforts of John Quinn, art was made "free" at the customs house; and all the Fifth Avenue picture dealers began showing the new Parisians. And if there was no "idea" in peace time, there was even less in time of war. The President's declaration accelerated the terrible process of suspicion, reactionary dread, moral disintegration. The violent downhill to 1924 was in full course. But Stieglitz met the familiar crisis in his own fashion. He did not withdraw. Perceiving the others recalcitrant, he merely insisted on living more intensely, ruthlessly, relentlessly in the light of his own ghost. It was the others who withdrew. It was he who was left alone, in the wilderness, once more, with his own spirit. Downstairs, before the door of the building, the little Photo-Secession sign for a long while announced an exhibition by "Miss Georgia O'Keeffe of Virginia." Then, taking the Marins, the Hartleys, and the O'Keeffes under his arm, and leaving the spars of another hope behind him, he disappeared from the public into the dark.

III

Rumor insisted he was no longer interested in photography. Suddenly there came the new affirmation. In February of 1921, through the liberality of Mr. Mitchell Kennerly, Stieglitz showed an hundred and forty-five of his photographs in the Anderson Galleries; after the

Port of New York

silence, the ancient challenge sounded forth an hundredfold more richly, bravely, sonorously. No element of this new confirmation of life had been absent from the work previously accomplished by Stieglitz through his various means; the wondrous clarity that chanted out had been in the living he had previously done. But the grasp had undergone gigantic fortification. Stieglitz had gone from the public the passionate believer not in possessions but in souls. He had gone the passionate asseverator of man's ultimate power over the arms and claws of steel. He had gone the man for whom the quality of the products of life loomed a million times larger than their physical extent; the man who believed that a spiritual America existed somewhere, that America was not the grave of the Occident; and had been making it possible with nourishment spiritual and physical for artists to bring out of the soil the human values of the land. Now, the older years seemed merely the bud. The fire was spread out, and become a blossoming form. In the space of a few years Stieglitz had done his great work. In that short while the immense artistic figure was achieved. If he had disappeared the "defeated" man who had been the first of photographers, he returned as great an artist in the word's narrowest sense as any man produced by the new world, for not Whitman or Hawthorne or James had completer control over his medium. He returned certainly one of the greatest forces for spiritual life produced by the new world. The shows of 1921 and of 1923

Alfred Stieglitz

were religious demonstrations. If ever an American man brought American people before their own life, it was this photographer with his rectangles of milk and bronze and earth. If ever American man brought American people into relation with people and trees, rocks and skies, brought the finite into tune with the infinite, it was this man of the black box and chemical bath. A weight like all the metal tons seems to evaporate in the presence of these pictures; some desired state of vibrance and release to come and laugh. Conviction that the world is old, and that man will remain slave always to the terrible machines; conviction that America is foredoomed a blasted heath out of which no straight, robust or lofty form of soul can sprout, cannot remain where these things are.

Before the lens of Stieglitz' camera, the moveless heavy woman, American life, has thrilled as from the touch of wizard's wand, and spoken from her womb in rhythms of chromatic light as other worlds in rhythms of Greco, Beethoven, Balzac. A man with an almighty passion to penetrate has gone deep into his earthly circumstance, and has joined in religious, lover's reverence for their identities with the things before him, and made them live. A spirit has given of itself to the objects, the people about it, and spread through touch with them until it has held them all contained in its own blood, uttering them in uttering its proper song and cry. Into a single living circle of relativity all people, rocks, and trees have been drawn and made to confess the single informing

Port of New York

one. The Stieglitz photographs lie at that point where the objective world and the subjective world coincide. They are true alike to fact and to the inner sense of life. The sonorous portraits belong among the great representations of people. The photographs of New York, of the hillside at Lake George, have marvelously the sense of place. Never, in any art, has the sky been given more truly, more sensitively, more inclusively, than in the series of cloudscapes. But the photographs swim no less with objective truth than with the inner truth of the common experience. Myriad moments are caught in myriad objects; myriad moods far apart from each other as the dionysiac dancing of trees is from the snake's agony in shedding its skin; as the most hideous carving and scratching of death from the sunset heavens chanting an icy November *gloria*. And the myriad things while giving out each their own essence speak in accents related and tell one story. There is the stuff of the hour of glass and steel in each of them, in their abstract and realistic elements alike. Lines, shapes and tones in interplay give the death, agony, and electric crystallizations of the world's present hour. You have to look close at some of these marvelous prints, so curiously do they resemble at a hasty glance the banal photograph; so close are they apparently to the flat stuff moving everywhere in the world to-day; so deep under the nervous fragmented skin of the after-war does the sun-god span his bow. An individual life has been used to make them; but the record is clear of egotism; of

Alfred Stieglitz

personal resentments and bitterness. The photographs give the American mode of the one life in the race; the history of the breath among men locked as men have never before been locked each one in the dungeon of his own person. They are the tragedy, humor, and triumph of the Third Person meshed struggling, tearing in the shackles of a million miserable separatenesses; and clawing his way forth into new-colored ecstasy and sweetness; into painful-tenderest blossom and ripe spirit-juiced fruit. At the bottom of the gulch of New York the march of moments begins. There is a short prelude, a European prelude with happy gentle children standing beside their ancient cottages, with solid peasants laboring in harvest fields by lines of golden grain, and pure Swiss snow-crags rising in serenest song. Then, the curtain rises upon the city we all have known, and which not many of us can leave behind entirely. There were human beings plentifully in the photographs Stieglitz took during his joyous *Wanderjahre*. But the photographs of New York are full of strange brazen human emptiness. Life is ambitious, exclusive, hard; a roaring, shrilling solitude. Stone work vaults arrogantly, masterfully, toward heaven. The new world of physical power shouts and thrusts and towers. Locomotives belch geysers of filthy smoke. Steel rails cut viciously through murk and smoky air. Lit uncurtained office windows glitter hard in the cold night, and a lonely path stretches blue and chill through trees of the park. It is a strange life, giving only hard

271

edges and stone and pavements to the breast, inviting human love no more than the masonry invites the flower, and the streets the bush. If human forms and faces appear at all, they are terribly separate, remote, passive. Aeons of time separate the nose-picking men and dwarf-mothers of *The Steerage* from the white glittering bridge with its chains of fine links. An abyss of water divides the folk crowded in the yawning mouth of the ferryboat from the foreground piles. And when people are present, they are never the ones to whom the stone, steel, and glass belong. And they come singly. A man is alone with his steam drill. A teamster feeds an old horse. In the drizzly light of April on Fifth Avenue, a little whitewing scrapes the asphalt while a caged sapling stretches bare branches to the day.

Heads, shoulders, hands, come before the lens. Nevertheless the subjective tale begun by the city piles and railway yards continues through the texts of human flesh. The photographs of the artists made during the years of "291" give the skyscraper civilization as it lies in the struggling psyche of the male. These are men, full of a marvelous potential life, full of richness out of many houses; but men caught and held and torn in the fearful psychic conflicts of our day. It seems that a new sort of fish is peering through aquarium walls of thickest glass. A man wrapped and swathed in silk muffler, fur collar, velvet hat gazes out of his sumptuous vice in fright and hopeless straining and fanatic self-fulness. A man sits

Alfred Stieglitz

rigid, strapped Pharaoh-like in a chair as though it were the electric executor in the death house at Sing Sing; impaled by a ghastly brain-light. Young Dürer slumps dejectedly; no stand-upness in this long trunk. A face peeps timidly out of a silver mist; will it come on, will it venture? Heads hold up grandiosely into aureoles of mad conceit; put up a brazen aggressive front to hide a pathetic childish inferiority; show a tired woman's visage through the hard ridges of an American "mug." A man is pressed down by the black weights of a nervous depression, carries upon caving shoulders the weight of something as though it were the great globe itself. And one butts his way ruthless and uncouth; and another seems on the point of coming to pieces, torso and legs losing connection; and still another sits, a small pricklouse in the core of an apple, concentrating entirely on his own blind self. Only one looks out warmly, faithfully, selflessly. And he is a negro.

Spirit of sex permeates the entire body of the photographs, shimmers delicate and rich in grasses and clouds. A rippling Lombardy poplar against lightly wadded skyland utters the mystery, the sheen, the glamour of the woman-gate no less than the passionate poise of a head, or female forms slipping through seething water. And the very elemental side of present woman breaks forth like strange tortured bloom in the portraits of individual women. Pictures of servant girls and grandes dames, of school-mistresses and artists, of pubescent girls and old ladies alike are suffused with the impersonal ideal challenge the woman makes the man. The prints sing with woman the unconscious caller, woman the laughter of the sea, the impulse that crumbles in smart little walls and sends hard through drooping arms. But it is not alone ideal glamours that these lights make beat. They blast and strike with a relentless inevitable demand. They bring the brute want of bread and children and children's bread that bears down on men like a locomotive bearing down a track and cannot be turned off nor be avoided. They fume with the smoke of altars that want no half-libations, but all riches and inner strengths to burn on them and pass in clouds of offering. Destruction pushes with all the main of feet and legs and loins that have massed in them the blind impersonality of nature. The dark romance, the pathos and comedy, the anguish and hot weight of woman's flesh torn by her spiritual division lie close upon each other. There are talon-like, possessive hands, that turn the crystal they are holding black. There are elegant, gloved hands demoniacally compelled ever to attitudinize before imaginary footlights. There are unconscious coquettish gestures which are full in the unripe girl and persistent in the wrinkled dying woman; and beautiful lacy gestures existing for their own Narcissistic ends. Prints are full of woman's curious preoccupation with her own person, full of the ceremonial of the hair. Eyes gaze searchingly forth with the look that is ever watching for people. Eyes which have wept so long no

Alfred Stieglitz

tears can come, lie wide with the wakefulness of an hundred endless empty vigils. And there are irrational hungry demandful eyes which all the food of Ormus and of Ind could not satiate; laughing little-girlish eyes not extinct even on the bed of paralysis; eyes that pierce out stern and judge more pitilessly than any man's. A visage moves out like a sail-crowded galleon bound into the glow of sunset. Another of cool white young American flesh has the whinny of the race-horse. There is a visage lifting laughing flowers into the flower's pathetically brief day. A young head hangs like overripened fruit with too much precocious knowing. There is a little scrawny girl with the face of a drowned being. There is an old woman full of the fading grace of a passing era thinking back woefully, wistfully; striving, at the dark extremity of life, a final time to comprehend.

One portrait gives Stieglitz' idea in boniest, most essential aspect. It is the series of almost two hundred prints made of Georgia O'Keeffe. In the young painter, rarest expression of the human spirit herself, the photographer got the model. The series of pictures, filled with high cathedral air and religious elevation, constitutes one of the profoundest records of woman's being which we possess. The many scores of infinitely poignant, infinitely tragical, infinitely rapturous moments are from the deeps of the psyche. They are moments of the race of those which glint ephemerally in some intimate, intense, decisive passage of life, reveal the trend of subterranean streams and are gone again unseen except of the well-attuned spirit. What shows itself only too fleetingly; what one cannot see, dare not see, and will not see, lies here, clear, massive as a sum and a completion. And through the array, through the many revealing perfect instants, there runs the truth of human life these latter years upon the globe as the sore vibrant modern nerves have felt it. For what goes on in the outer world is present in simplest, barest state in the intimate relationship between man and woman. What from instant to instant arises new between the man and the woman finds eventual way out into mundane affairs. So, the pictures of a single woman give the way that spirit has had to go among the tombs in a world organized against it. Hands, like aquatic plants wavering to the surface of pond-water, stretch suffocatingly to the light falling through smudged windowglass. A woman, pitiful resignation upon her face, holds up her two lithe living hands in the effort to sustain against the machine the integrity of a spirit, holds them up as though she would forgo all the world, and give up all joy, all reward, if only it be granted her that the sense of the wonder and high tragedy of existence remain fresh and unbesmirched. A torso, the hip-bone a point of suffering, stands like a gaunt tree in a parched sandy Arizona. A palm offers itself in pure frankness, candid and generous, without concealment. A baffled woeful face, a painfully twitched cloak, are sad as a pure melody of Moussorgsky's. A spirit at bay flares up a

Alfred Stieglitz

lioness threatened, proud anger poising on eyes, lips, nostrils; ready to spring. Breasts hang sensitive, sore and tired, tender from too much mortal hurt in the quick of life. A tiny phallic figure weeps alone, is bowed upon itself in weeping, while behind, like watered silk, there weaves the sunlight of creation. A naked body, white cloths draping the arms like streamers of ecstasy, stands in its moment of release, greeting some dawn no man can' see. Is it the call for death the one holy? Is it the final cry of human life for its vanished soul?

Last, playing like the heavens above the darkling earth and dying chestnut trees, floating above the body of a work an airy crown, there chants the luminous affirmation of the series of *Songs of the Sky;* and light like voices and instruments in solemn service utters *credo* and *sanctus, benedictus* and *gloria.* All the photographic science of forty years of experimentation has gone into the making of these most delicate, most seraphic prints. All Stieglitz' clarity, warmth, intensity of nature, is manifest in tenderest gradations of light and ineffable harmonies of tone, in the faëry of wisp-like delicious shapes and free-rolling, polyphonic form. The pictures are his most abstract achievement; the sky as purest interplay of shapes, lines, and volumes; almost the law of clouds. Light in them has three dimensions. An hour had arrived which made it impossible for him to photograph the human being; for a while, the human being had no more to give him. Besides, the chorus which declared **that**

277

Port of New York

Stieglitz photographed untruly and put into his photographs of people matters which did not exist in the objects, was growing louder; had even found support from among some whilom and disgruntled "friends." Hence after thirty years of observation and preparation he turned to photographing clouds. Like the photographs of people, and of the trees and barnsides, the photographs of the skies are marvelously sensitive to fact; and like the people and the stones of New York, full of the movement of to-day, of chaotic countercurrents, gestures of beginning and dying, opening and passing away. But, there is a new quality of fulgurant light in these songs of the day of man; light kindred to the music of ultimate reconciliation and freedom of the last comedies of Shakespeare. A spirit has fled from the shattered, ashen world to the skies for the ultimate time to seek confirmation for what it has dreamt amid the mechanization of the earth; to demand of the rolling, impersonal vault whether the vision of freedom, sweetness, largeness of human life, felt amid so much frustration and pain, and all of the ideal which it glimpsed so fitfully, and all the delicacy, the warmth which man's dreadful social order and man's helpless brutal self crush out, were indeed merely the fantastic lights of a spirit derailed from material course. And, in the clouds, in the heavens, in the illimitable blue, through the dead eye of the camera, it has found corroboration of its faith sustained in the desert of New York. The generous, unfolding, sweeping movements

Alfred Stieglitz

which man has called the soul, the opening, reaching, yearning, of the heart, the tender, quivering projections, dark passionate storms and chanting hours of roundness and fulfilment, exist indeed not in him alone. In things which man has not touched their patterns, rhythms, tonalities, are shown, aplay wild and fair as in the anguished wrestling brain. The movements of the heart are from a power greater than man's is. The sun in heaven may become a little thing before the menacing gases of night. Woman may seek to put stars and moon in her hair, and use the light of the sky to fertilize herself. The world may disintegrate into myriad wretched fragments of the whole which once it was; the sons of the dark may have their hands on the daypour; the breath of death may be close on every ideal form and every quality and fineness which we know. But above the universal decay and personal extinction the heaven-sweeping, heaven-storming gestures of the clouds declare that all which men has called spirit exists, a portion of some eternally abiding principle. The mornings of the human soul, amid the very creeping blackness are safe, immortal, fresh, with the law that governs all things.

Something spiritual thrustfuller than the skyscrapers, has come to stand.

EPILOGUE: PORT OF NEW YORK

THE liners emerge from the lower bay. Up through the Narrows they heave their sharp prows. In sleety, in blue, in sullen weather, throughout the lighted hours, mouse-colored shapes are stretched off Quarantine. Between cheesebox fort and fume of nondescript South Brooklyn waterfront, metal abdomens which were not seated there yesterday are submitted to rising concrete sides, masts, red iron, ferryslips. In New York harbor, always, new-come bodies foreign to it; issued from Southampton and Bergen, Gibraltar and Bremen, Naples and Antwerp; now engirdled by sullen shorelines and lapped by tired crisscrossed wavelets.

The lean voyagers steer under the tower-jumbled point of Manhattan. Flanks are lashed to the town; holds thrown open to the cobbled street. Decks are annexes of the littoral, portion of New York no less than the leagues of "L" sweeping past dismal brick over caverned thoroughfares. And through periods of many days, for weeks, even, the liners lie roped to their piersides, rows of captives handcuffed to policemen. The plated sides list obediently toward bald sheds. Only feeble brownish wisps of smoke adrift from silent smokestacks betray the incorporation incomplete. Then, one day, a pierside is

281

Port of New York

found stripped. Next day, another; two. The vigilantes stand stupid. In the open quadrangle between docks, merely a dingy freighter, and small lighter-fry. By sea-coated piles, the muckerish North River water shrugs its shoulders. The liners have evaded; fled again through the straits. Beyond where eye can reach iron rumps dwindle down the ocean.

And has it really faded from the port, the painful glamour? Has it really gone off them, the fiction that was always on the movements of the liners in and out the upper bay? Or has it merely retreated for a while behind the bluffs of the Jersey shore, to return on us again to-morrow and draw the breast away once more into the distance beneath Staten Island hill? It was on a day just like this one, year before last or last year even—and outside the window the sun fell much as it does now across asphalt grimy with a little last snow, and people came about the corner house and walked past brick walls, and motors ticked and drays banged—that the harbor of New York was somehow the inexplicable scene of a mysterious cruel translation. And nothing in the traffic of the port and in the city streets has changed. Below Battery point, the liners stand off Quarantine all through the lighted hours; and here inside the town the solid gazing houses and shadowed walls have not gone. Steel hooves ring brilliant in the lightening air. Coal roars as it slides down iron into the neighbors' cellars. The truckmen stand like Pharaohs behind their horses and yell at the chickens.

Epilogue: Port of New York

From a block away the elevated train comes up like a thunderstorm. These and the bells and the fire-escapes are where they were last year and the year before. How is it that the strange dream light should have gone off the port, and left us in another New York City?

It seemed the liners did not come across the Atlantic on a single plane. Somewhere, in the course of their voyage from the European coasts, they left one plane and descended to another. True, they were steam-packets plying in a huge oceanic ferryboat business, moving in well-known lanes through fog with smell of boilers and pounding of machines. Nevertheless, a mysterious translation took place before they reached their American terminus. If indeed they did plow over the regular surface of the globe, they also came out of delicious unknown qualities of light, and out of wafts of air lighter and fierier than any aplay this side the water. In coming, they had descended as one descends from a heaven-near plateau under blue skylands into a dank and shadowy vale. Going to Europe, coming from Europe, might abolish the illusion; at a touch of the new world earth it was upon one again, not to be rationalized and not to be expelled. But a few hours before their entrance into Ambrose channel, the mighty voyagers now ringed about with smoky land and the sullen objects of the rawly furnished shores had experienced, it seemed, not alone the fishy white Atlantic, but the clear, free, ineffable space which does not know the port. Against steel plates and

Port of New York

salt-soaked yellow, white, and pitch-black paint; about funnels and masts erect against the stars, there had lain the otherwhere than New York, the hidden side of the city moon; the unknown aspect of the flower of the moment. Rock lighter than sea-water, the visitor had swum in the space relieved of all the depressure of new world objects; the space that the gas-tuns, chimney pennons of coal-fume, smoky length of Staten Island hill would not let be seen, and stood upon like gravestones upon graves. About it with the sky and salt and ocean was the place that labors in man's behalf, and calls forth and lets bloom in beauty the stuff the new world sites repress and force back and will not let grow. Warming suns and long mild days had poured on it.

But here, in the workman bay, the mysterious water-world it seemed was wrenched from the liners, wrenched as eelskins are drawn. A bad change had been worked. Upon the very sides which had known the free untrammeled space and moved through rich elastic stuff, another vulgarer world had imposed itself. Brightness was no longer about the ship. The city horizon was the one horizon. And when once more the cables were thrown off, the departed liners seemed marine expresses less than they had ever seemed. They were exiled princes gone to regain their thrones. They had shaken from them the situation of frustrating objects and mediocre unsatisfying forms quite as they had shaken from the tired choppy waters and rims of murky brown. Experienced once again

284

Epilogue: Port of New York

was the spirit morning. The liners had left New York.

There was a sun overhead here in New York, blazing cruelly enough in the Yankee summer. But the sun which makes life fragrant and rich did not stand overhead. That sun shone far away across the Atlantic, upon the coasts of Europe. High up, one saw the European coast-line gleaming a fertile yellow and green, shining with a soft gold like Alp pinnacles saluted by the first liquor of daylight. But the sun which shone direct upon the eastern margent of the ocean struck the western slantingly and faint. New York lay in blue twilight as in a valley which the sun never comes to bake with heat. One lived, here in New York, upon ultimate edge of life, a kind of hyperborean edge midmost the temperate zone; the border of a perpetual shadow. For behind us, to the west, a continent lay submerged in chaotic pre-creation darkness. Movement, noise, rise and fall of perpetually displaced matter, all these seeming products of sun-power, were unsubstantial quite, dusty mirages of all the senses. For the very heat was not here. Or merely faintly enough to let us know what it was we wanted. Nothing moved indeed. Nothing came into relation.

The seed inside did not take root. It was a curious thing to know that one had been born here; to know that in precisely this dull red house on the avenue corner, with the precise number, say of 1186, one had undergone the experience which the Englishman underwent in his little island, or the Frenchman in his pleasant land of

Port of New York

France, or the German in deep Germany. For, when the European was born, did he not begin the process of coming into relationship with the people and the things which stood about him? Did not something in him, the free-moving particle, cleave to the sites, the walls, the trees, the waters amid which he found himself, so that forever after the sight and memory of these objects had power to bring him nourishment comparable to the nourishment the tree draws from out its rock and loam? But here one did not come into blood relation. Oh, yes, here it was very formally inscribed in the records that on a certain day in a certain month of a certain year, a child had been born a certain citizen and his wife, with the sex male; which meant that one could, legally, become President; and, failing that, vote, sit on a jury, and have consular protection when traveling. But they only said one belonged to these things here, and they to one. In truth, a red spired village seen from railway windows over German cornfields; a prim Holland garden descending from a glass-enclosed verandah; the vision of an avenue with iron balconies in Paris; these foreign things were more life-giving, more feeding and familiar to one for all their strangeness, than the corner of New York rounded regularly each morning and evening. For in the city, things were very definitely outside you, apart from you; you were very definitely over here, they very definitely over there. You were alien to them, it seemed, and for your part you could not move closer to them, no

286

Epilogue: Port of New York

more than to the people who moved amongst them; even to those of the people you were supposed to know the best of all and with whom you had spent years. It was as useless trying to feel yourself through the crowding towers of the lower town, and feel a whole, as it was trying to feel yourself through the forbidding people in the streets. The towers were not a whit less hard, less mutually exclusive, less eager to crowd each other out, than the people who had made them. They snatched the light from each other; rough-shouldered each other; were loud, anarchical, showy, . . . unfriendly; flaunting money; calling for money. Edges stood, knife against knife. Nothing ever came with the warmth of heaven to do the work of the sun and melt the many antagonistic particles. The breast entire strained out toward the place of fruitful suns. With sad wonder, one was aware of the movements of liners. For these were things which through the power of motion threw off like an old coat the hyperborean state which held them awhile, and regained climates fertilized by spirit pours.

Nevertheless, one could not break with New York. If one floated aimlessly about inside its walls, within them one nevertheless remained. The suction which drew the psyche out of New York harbor was exerted upon one only in the city. The voyage to Europe once actually undertaken, the pumping force relaxed and dwindled down under the horizon. Two weeks of the green and gold of the Parisian boulevards; and a counter-magnet

Port of New York

began exerting its attractive rays. The free, low-arching skies and Louvre flanks and chestnut avenues, what had their beauty really to do with us? This beauty was in its way as remote from us as the awful meaninglessness of the ways and granites of New York. It had its roots in a past which was not ours, and which we might never adopt. To feel it was to squander the best stuff of the bosom not on the true wife, but on the indifferent courtesan. It was beauty in America one wanted, not in France or Switzerland. It was the towers of Manhattan one wanted to see suddenly garlanded with loveliness. One wanted life for them and for oneself together. Somewhere in one always there had been the will to take root in New York; to come into relation with the things and the people, not in the insane self-abnegation of current patriotism and nationalism, but in the form of one's utmost self; in the form of realizing all the possibilities for life shut inside one, and simultaneously finding oneself one with the people. Somewhere within, perhaps in obedience to some outer voice trusted in childhood, there was a voice which promised one day the consummation. One day a miracle should happen over the magnificent harbor, and set life thrilling and rhythming through the place of New York. How it was to happen, one did not know. And sometimes, one supposed that where the immigrant ships had come in, a supernatural and winged visitor would have to appear, fall into the port as a meteorite might fall from the sky, before the new state

Epilogue: Port of New York

which had not been reached when the immigrant feet had touched earth at Castle Garden would declare itself. But it was to happen, that one knew; and within, slumbrous power patiently awaited the divine event. And in Europe, one heard, distinct again, the promise. One knew the secret allegiance to the unfriendly new world; and if it did not take the form of a red, white, and blue rosette in the buttonhole, nevertheless something like a precious promissory letter was carried underneath the heart through all the monuments and treasure houses.

So one went back over the sea, eyes peeled for the moment when the arms of the port would open up and receive one, and the sense of home be written large over every crevice and electric sign. But the welcome proved cold, and the day after landing the buildings recommenced their languid snubbing. The restlessness came back. The water world beyond Sandy Hook began to draw again. There was scarcely a place, two or three at the very utmost, which did anything for you, and urged you out into life and adventure and experiment. The city would not give and stood defiant. There were moments: the river at sundown, West Street with its purple blotches on walls, one pile against another. But one became sore so easily. One could accomplish only a little at a time; one became sore and shrank away, and found it impossible to press further. It was impossible as ever to sit before a table and work for long. One gave a little; here was a little trickle of beauty, a moment of absorption. Then something gave out, and one wanted to run off, to hide, to forget, to go out of doors, anything rather than sit before the table and press further. And, in dreams; in the dreams of many, in the dreams of a whole city and country perhaps, steamers departed for Europe, steamers silently discharged from New York harbor, great iron liners headed and predestined for the opposite coasts of the North Atlantic.

It may be that it was yesteryear they still went forth. It was not long ago. And yet, this year, it is certain they have ceased to move. The line has passed away. If any dream-voyagers stir in dreams, their bows are presented to us. The steamers, small, dogged, shoulderful, come headed America-ward. Merely a fistful of months may separate us from the time they still moved out; and sometimes it seems the time cannot indeed be gone. But it is gone. The enormous spaces that divide world from world separate us from it. The impossible thing has indeed come to pass on us. What seemed a miracle alone could accomplish has taken place. There is no one not aware something has happened in New York. What, it is possible, may not be clearly seen. But that an event has taken place is universally sure. No supernatural and winged flyer has descended into the bay. No enchanter has touched the buildings and made them change their forms. The town still stands the same; no littoral has rearranged itself about the bay. Morning upon morning mouse-colored new-come shapes are

Epilogue: Port of New York

stretched off Quarantine; and in the North River tug-boats drag the departers into midstream. Nevertheless, we could go from the world to-day and still feel that life had been wonderfully good.

The steamers no longer descend from one plane onto another when they come into New York harbor. The port is not the inferior situation, depressive to every spiritual excellence and every impulse to life, which once it was. Glamour lies upon it still; but not the painful dreamlight of yesteryear. A kind of strong, hearty daylight has come upon the port. Once, thought of it filled us with nostalgia and wander-dreams. To-day, it brings a wash of strength and power over us. Sudden, at the foot of a street, the vague wandering eye perceives with a joyous shock a loading steamer carrying high its mast as a child carries a cross in an all-saints procession. The port-nights loom blue and enormous over the leagues of massy masonries. Out of the purpling evening above office piles there comes a breeze, and in that breath there are, like two delicious positive words in an evasive letter, the fishy hoarse Atlantic. The tall street lamps in brown-stone gulches on winter nights press back a soft fog that has in it the gray rims and biting wind and tramps of all nations steering. Or, some afternoon, from a bridge train, the salt tide unrolls before our eyes; the sun casts a little orange onto the tide off Battery, and illuminates Bayonne beyond with the cadences of daylight; and the clay giants of the lower city fuse into a bluish mass. Then

Port of New York

it is almost beauty that comes to dress the slipshod harbor of New York.

For what we once could feel only by quitting New York: the fundamental oneness we have with the place and the people in it, that is sensible to us to-day in the very jostling, abstracted streets of the city. We know it here, our relationship with this place in which we live. The buildings cannot deprive us of it. For they and we have suddenly commenced growing together. A state of relation has timidly commenced—between the objects, and between the objects and ourselves. The form is still very vague. One is still alone; among people who are alone, scattered like seed or pebbles thrown. And perhaps the form is still most like the faint scum-like build first taken by the embryo in the womb. It seems a misty architectural shape taking up into itself like individual building stones the skyscrapers, tenements, thoroughfares, and people; and with the mass of them erecting a tower higher than any of them, even the highest, toward the sky. But if it is faint, still, it is none the less evident. Day after day in gray and desperate weather even, one can see its mystic aspiration above the skyscrapers of New York. Over our melancholy it rises high. It seems that we have taken root. The place has gotten a gravity that holds us. The suction outward has abated. No longer do we yearn to quit New York. We are not drawn away. We are content to remain in New York. In the very middle of the city, we can feel the fluid of life to

Epilogue: Port of New York

be present. We know the space beyond Staten Island hill is no more filled with the elixir than the air about the buildings. Other places may have it no whit less than New York; but New York has it no whit less than they; the stuff of the breast can make its way into the world here too. Something outside works with it. The city is a center like every other point upon the circumference of the globe. The circle of the globe commences here, too. The port of New York lies on a single plane with all the world to-day. A single plane unites it with every other port and seacoast and point of the whole world. Out of the American hinterland, out of the depths of the inarticulate American unconsciousness, a spring has come, a push and a resilience; and here where Europe meets America we have come to sit at the focal point where two upspringing forces balance. The sun is rising overhead, the sun which once shone brightly on Europe alone and threw slanting rays merely upon New York. The sun has moved across the Atlantic. The far coasts of Europe still shine with his light. But they shine mildly, softly, like eastern coasts in late summer afternoon when the sun commences to slope toward the western sea. And behind us, over the American hinterland, morning rays slant where deep, impenetrable murkiness lay, and begin to unveil the face of a continent. But over New York the dayspring commences to flood his fruity warmth.

It is that the values have come to stand among us. It is they that outtop the heaven-storming piles, and make the sun to float aloft and the steam to shoot like flags. It was their absence that made the buildings stand like tombstones, and life to lie inert. We never knew them here. They may have stood before, in earlier American days. But in our time they were gone. What bore their name and aped their style were the conventions of middleclass trading society giving themselves out for the worths of civilization. We had the smug safe bourgeois values of the "humanists," the pontifical allies of the anarchistic business men. But the principles which lift men out of themselves and lead them to human growth and human beauty were gone from the scene; and unrelation of all things and all people filled the land with black. For values and religion and relation rise together. So it stood until the second decade of the new century when the new orientation began. What gave it to a dozen or more of artists to find the values again here on the soil, to restate ideas of work and growth and love, and run the flag of mature developed life once more to the masthead, we do not know. It may be that conditions were favorable to the new erection. Life has perhaps commenced to stabilize itself on the new continent, and men begun to cease excluding one another. Perhaps the new world of new expression of life which should have been reached when the feet first stepped from off the boats on American soil has faintly begun. Perhaps the tradition of life imported over the Atlantic has commenced expressing itself in terms of the new environ-

Epilogue: Port of New York

ment, giving the Port of New York a sense at last, and the entire land the sense of the Port of New York. It seems possible the European war helped the values to the masthead. We had been sponging on Europe for direction instead of developing our own, and Europe had been handing out nice little packages of spiritual direction to us. But then Europe fell into disorder and lost her way, and we were thrown back on ourselves to find inside ourselves sustaining faith. Yet, whether there was indeed a general movement anterior to the work of the worth-givers or whether the movement which we feel to-day merely flows from the songs they sang and the cries they uttered, we cannot know for sure. We saw it only after they had spoken. But what we do know, whatever the cause, is that we have to thank them for a wondrous gift. For, if to-day, the values stand aloft; if to-day the commencement of a religious sense is here; if to-day men on American land are commencing to come into relationship with one another and with the places in which they dwell, it is through the labor of some dozens of artist hands. Through words, lights, colors, the new world has been reached at last. We have to thank a few people— for the gift that is likest the gift of life.

APPENDIX

Albert P. Ryder

Albert Pinkham Ryder was born in New Bedford, Mass., March 19, 1847, and died in New York City, March 28, 1917. The family of his father, Alexander Gage Ryder, came from Yarmouth. Ryder's mother's name was Elizabeth Cobb. In 1867, the family moved to New York, and Ryder had lessons in painting from William Marshall, a pupil of Couture's. He attended the National Academy School in 1871. He exhibited for the first time in the National Academy show of 1873 and continued contributing regularly until 1888. He also showed with the Society of American Artists from 1878 to 1887, with the exception of the year 1885. Ryder's creativity began to decline about the middle of the -nineties; most of his important work was done before 1893.

Van Wyck Brooks

Van Wyck Brooks was born in Plainfield, N. J., on February 16, 1886. His father, Charles Edward Brooks, and his mother, Sarah Ames, were of old New England and New York Dutch stock. Brooks matriculated at Harvard with the class of 1908, and received his A.B. in 1907. In June, 1907, he went to England, where he spent a year and a half, and wrote *The Wine of the Puritans*, his first book. Returning to New York, he was a member for a year of the staff of the *Standard Dictionary*, and subsequently for a year of *The World's Work* magazine. In 1911 he went to California, where he was married to Eleanore Stimson, and taught for two years at Leland Stanford

Port of New York

University. Then, in 1913, he returned to England as a lecturer in the Workers' Educational Association. In 1915 he entered the office of the Century Co., New York, remaining there for three years. In 1917-1918 he was associate editor of *The Seven Arts*. From 1918 to 1920 he was in Carmel, California, at work on *The Ordeal of Mark Twain*. Since April, 1920, he has been a member of the staff of *The Freeman*. He is the recipient of *The Dial's* prize for 1923.

Brooks has published the following books: *The Wine of the Puritans* (1908); *The Malady of the Ideal* (1913); *John Addington Symonds* (1915); *The World of H. G. Wells* (1915); *America's Coming-of-Age* (1916); *Letters and Leadership* (1918); and *The Ordeal of Mark Twain* (1920). He has also translated in collaboration with his wife several books, including *Some Aspects of the Life of Jesus* (Berger), *Rousseau* (Amiel), *The Intimate Journals of Paul Gauguin*, and is the editor of *The History of a Literary Radical* by Randolph Bourne. He is at present residing in Westport, Conn.

Carl Sandburg

Carl Sandburg was born in Galesburg, Ill., in 1878. His father, August Johnson, was a Swedish immigrant who changed his name to Sandburg. Young Carl left grammar school at the age of thirteen and began driving a milk wagon. He worked in brickyards and potteries; rode the "rattlers" to Kansas and pitched wheat. He washed dishes in Denver hotels, shoveled coal in Omaha, and saw active service in the Spanish-American War in Porto Rico as a member of the 6th Illinois volunteer infantry. At the end of the war he returned to Galesburg and went to Lombard College. Here he took a prize in oratory. After, he became labor editor on a Milwaukee journal and secretary to Milwaukee's socialist mayor. He seems to have commenced writing poetry about 1900. *Chicago Poems* appeared in 1916; *Cornhuskers* was published in 1918, and shared the Pulitzer

Appendix

Poetry Prize for that year; *Smoke and Steel* appeared in 1920; *Slabs of the Sunburnt West* in 1922. For several years Sandburg has been on the staff of the Chicago *Daily News;* at present in the capacity of moving picture editor. During the world war Sandburg represented a newspaper syndicate in the Scandinavian countries. His wife, Lillian Steichen, is the sister of Eduard Steichen the painter and photographer.

Sandburg has also recently published two volumes of stories for children called *Rootabaga Stories* and *Rootabaga Pigeons.*

Marsden Hartley

Marsden Hartley was born in Lewiston, Maine, in 1878. His parents came from Staleybridge, near Manchester, England. Hartley attended the Grammar School until he was fifteen; then he went to Cleveland, Ohio, and commenced earning his living as an office boy. Once a week he took a lesson in art from John Semon. His interest in art cost him his position; a scholarship in the Cleveland School of Arts enabled him to pursue his training. He had lessons from Cullen Yates; but the vital influence came to him from Miss Nina Waldeck, who taught him drawing, and gave him *Emerson's Essays*, the first book he read. By that time he was twenty-one or twenty-two. He went to New York to study at the Chase School, and had lessons in drawing from F. Luis Mora; and studied with Frank Vincent Dumont, with Chase; and had eight criticisms from Kenyon Cox, "whose humor proved always oppressive." His summers he spent in Maine. His second year in New York he worked at the National Academy of Design under Francis C. Jones, Edgar M. Ward, Maynard, Dillman, and J. Scott Hartley. Then he gave up the schools and went to live in Maine, at North Bridgeton, and Center Lovell. All his subjects were taken from Stoneham Valley. In 1909, he had his first public exhibition. It was at "291," and it gave him his freedom for many months. The exhibition brought forth a storm of abuse and vilification. In 1911, he had his second exhibition at "291," and from that time onward he became identified with the institution. He is said to have heard of Cézanne first from the lips of Maurice Prendergast, but at "291" he was introduced to the work of Cézanne and of Matisse and Picasso, who influenced him. Assistance came to him from N. E. Montross, who also introduced him to Ryder. "That was the day my imagination was fixed in the country of its abode. I became the kind of New Englander I now am, at that juncture." In 1912, through the help of "291" and of Arthur B. Davies, Hartley was enabled to make his first European trip. He went to Paris; became a close friend of Gertrude Stein's. In Paris he had direct vision of Delacroix, Courbet, Cézanne, Picasso, the "raging cubists," Van Gogh, Gauguin, the *duanier* Rousseau, and Redon. In 1913 he returned to America and lived in Bermuda, New York, and Provincetown. He showed his work at "291," and in the early part of 1914 returned to Europe; went to Paris, London, Munich, and Berlin. In Munich he came into touch with Kandinsky, Marc, and Paul Klee, and was invited by them to join the group of "Der Blaue Reiter." He exhibited in Munich through "Der Blaue Reiter." He also exhibited in the Herbstsalon in Berlin, and in Dresden and Breslau. He had a one-man show in the house of Max Liebermann. In spite of the outbreak of the war, he was in Berlin until 1916, when he returned to America, on the way "passing through Amsterdam to get another look at the *Night Watch*." He exhibited in the historic Forum Show at the Anderson Gallery in 1916. Till 1918 he was in New York full of despair. A couple of small shows were held at the Daniel Gallery. Then in 1918 Hartley went to the southwest, where he remained for two years. In the summer of 1920 he was in Gloucester, and in the fall showed a few pictures at the Montross Gallery. In the spring of 1921, through the kindness of Mitchell Kennerly, Stieglitz organized an auction of all the pictures in Hartley's possession. Hartley was in very bad physical condition and very low in mind. But the auction was a

Appendix

success beyond all expectations. It assured the painter three or four years of perfect freedom, placed him with the public and the art world. Hartley returned to Europe, to London, Paris, Berlin, Vienna, Marseilles, Florence. Then, in the winter of 1923-1924, "Piero della Francesca, Giotto, Bronzino, Vesuvius, Fifth Avenue."

Hartley has published two books: *Adventures in the Arts* (Liveright) and *Twenty-five Poems* (Paris: Three Mountains Press). He has published articles and poems in *The Seven Arts, The Dial, Contact, Camera Work, Playboy, The Craftsman,* and *The New Republic.*

William Carlos Williams

William Carlos Williams, born September 17, 1883, at Rutherford, N. J., U. S. A., son of Raquel Ellen Rose Hoheb, born Mayaguez, Porto Rico, and William George Williams, born Birmingham, England. Maternal grandparents, Solomon Hoheb, Dutch and Jewish extraction, birthplace unknown; Meline Hurrard, born St. Pierre, Martinique, of Basque stock. Paternal grandparents, William Williams, born England, exact place unknown, died in early life; Emily Dickinson, born small village near Birmingham, England. This Emily Dickinson Williams, early a widow, emigrated from England with infant son, William, landing in New York, 1858. She there remarried and went with new husband to St. Thomas, Danish West Indies, where the boy, William, grew up. William George Williams and Raquel Ellen Rose Hoheb married in New York City, 1882, moving thence to Rutherford, N. J. William Carlos, their first child, was educated in Rutherford Public Schools, Château de Lancy, Geneva, Switzerland, Horace Mann H. S., New York City, and graduated in Medicine at U. of P., 1906; interned for two and a half years in N. Y. C. hospitals; studied and traveled in Europe 1909-1910; has practiced medicine in Rutherford, N. J., ever since. Publications: *The Tempers* (1913), Elkin Matthews, London, England; *Al Que*

Port of New York

Quiere (1917); *Kora in Hell* (1921); *Sour Grapes* (1922), Four Seas Co., Boston, Mass.; *The Great American Novel* (1923), Three Mountains Press, Paris, France; *Spring and All* (1923), Contact Publishing Co., Paris, France. At various intervals, and in collaboration with Robert MacAlmon, the magazine *Contact*.

Margaret Naumburg

Margaret Naumburg was born in New York City, May 14, 1890. Her parents are of Jewish stock. Her father, Max Naumburg, came to America from Bavaria as a small child. Her mother, Theresa Kahnweiler, was born in North Carolina. Margaret Naumburg attended the New York Public School No. 87 for one year; Horace Mann School for three years; and prepared for college at the Sachs School. She matriculated at Vassar College in 1908; remained there one year, and was at Barnard College the next three. While at Barnard she took courses in philosophy until Prof. John Dewey, and specialized in philosophy and economics. In 1912 she went to London with the purpose of working in social research in the London School of Economics under Sidney Webb. In January, 1913, she went to Rome and took Montessori's training course for teachers. She returned to New York in the fall of 1913, and for one year conducted a class of kindergarten-aged children at the Henry Street Settlement. Claire Raphael Ries assisted her in music. While commencing her practical work, Margaret Naumburg continued to do work in psychoanalysis and studied with F. Matthias Alexander and with Marietta Johnson. In 1914 she rented two rooms in the Leet schoolhouse, and conducted a class of children of from three to five years of age. The second year, her class expanded into two groups and employed three teachers. In 1917 she began The Children's School, later The Walden School, at No. 34 West 68th St., with four groups and a number of special teachers. On December 20, 1916, Margaret Naumburg was married to Waldo Frank. In 1921 she ceased from

302

Appendix

active executive control of her school, but as the parents of the school-children wished to maintain the little institution, she remained associated with it in an advisory capacity. The Walden School is at present under the control of Margaret Pollitzer and of Evelyn Goldsmith. A son, Thomas, was born to Margaret Naumburg on May 12, 1922.

Margaret Naumburg is the author of articles on education published in the *Evening Mail*, the *Outlook*, the *World To-morrow*, *The New Republic*, and the *Survey*. Several poems were published in *The Dial* for September, 1923. She is at present engaged on a book on modern education.

Kenneth Hayes Miller

Kenneth Hayes Miller was born in the Oneida Community, Oneida, N. Y., on March 11, 1876. His father, George Noyes Miller, was of old New England stock; his mother, Annie Elizabeth Kelley, of Scotch-Irish. The family removed to New York City in 1888. Miller was educated in the Horace Mann School. He studied art at the Art Students' League and in the New York School of Art. He was in Europe in 1900. In 1898, Miller was married to Juna C. Ferry of Oneida. He was divorced in Reno, Nev., in 1910. In 1911 he was married to Helen Pendleton of New York City. From 1899 to 1911, Miller was instructor in drawing and painting at the New York School of Art. Since 1911 he has conducted a class at the Art Students' League.

Miller has had three large exhibitions at the Montross Gallery in 1918, 1921, and 1923. His studio is at 6 East 14th St., New York.

John Marin

The following autobiographical note by John Marin was printed in *Manuscripts No. 2:*

Port of New York

"I—John Marin—was born some fifty years ago
thereby placing Rutherford, N. J., on the map
though the blooming Burg hasn't acknowledged
Early childhood spent making scrawls of rabbits and
things (my most industrious period)
Then the usual—public schooling where as is usual
        was soundly flogged for doing the
           unusual
      drawing more rabbits on slate
          After enough flogging
one year at Hoboken Academy where the usual
was the keeping in after hours—I qualified
—a few more rabbits and a smattering of the
          now obsolete German language
Stevens High School discovered me next and next
the Stevens Institute—went through the High School
went to—not through Institute
     Of course a few bunnies were added to my
        collection but the main thing I got
there was mathematics for the which I am
duly grateful as I am now an adept at
         subtraction
—1 year business not much chance at the gamebag
        believe I was fired
    4 years Architects offices
         not much class
    otherwise they'd have discovered my—(Wondership)
        2 years blank
2 years Philadelphia Academy
could draw all the rabbits I wanted to
therefore didn't draw many
While there shot at and captured prize for
        some sketches

Appendix

1 year blank
1 year Art Students' League, N. Y.
      Saw—KENYON COX—
            2 years blank
4 years abroad
played some billiards
incidently knocked out some
batches of etchings which people
rave over everywhere
At this period the French Government was going to give me the
            Legion d'Honor   I refused
they then insisted on buying one of my Oils
I ran away to Venice
they set up such a howl that
there was no escaping
            I let them have it
Since then I have taken up Fishing and
Hunting and with some spare time
Knocked out a few
            water-colors
for which in former years I had had
      a leaning
So this brings me up to date
I might add (relating to the water-colors)
that I cannot supply the demand
      and that day before yesterday
I climbed a Tulip tree in my backyard
which was mighty hard work
those who don't believe me are welcome
to try not later than June 15—1921."

On his father's side, Marin is of French extraction. His grandfather, Jean-Baptiste Marin, came to America from the Île-de-France.

Port of New York

His father's name was John C. Marin. His mother's name was Annie Louise Currey. The Curreys lived near Peekskill, N. Y., at the time of the Revolution, and with other Tory families went to New Brunswick at the conclusion of the war. The father of Annie Currey returned to the United States.

Marin showed oils in the Salon des Indépendents of 1909, and had ten watercolors in the Autumn Salon in 1910. He was first shown in America in 1910 at "291"; and had a show there practically every year until the place was discontinued. He has exhibited at the Daniel Gallery, and in 1921 and 1922 had large life-work exhibitions at the Montross Gallery.

Arthur G. Dove

Arthur G. Dove was born in Canandaigua, N. Y., on August 2, 1880. His father, William G. Dove, and his mother, Anna E. Chipps, were of old English-American stock. Both came from Geneva, N. Y. Dove attended private school and High School at Geneva, N. Y. He spent two years, 1899-1901, at Hobart College, and graduated from Cornell University with the degree of A.B. in 1903, having elected one year of law. He was a member of the Sigma Phi fraternity. In 1903 he began work as illustrator for American magazines. From 1908 to 1909, he worked as a painter in France and Italy. From 1912 to 1918, he farmed in Westport, Conn. He has exhibited paintings at the Autumn Salon in Paris, at Alfred Stieglitz' little gallery at 291 Fifth Avenue, at the Forum Exhibition of 1916, the Anderson Galleries in New York, at Thurber's Gallery in Chicago, and in galleries in San Francisco, Philadelphia, and Rochester. He is at present living in New York.

Appendix

Sherwood Anderson

Sherwood Anderson was born in Clyde, Ohio, in 1876. John Anderson and Emma Smith, his father and mother, were of old pioneer stock. Anderson spent his early youth at numerous occupations, proving his resourcefulness at the age of twelve by obtaining the office of timekeeper on public construction work, the office having been created at his own subtle suggestion through the influence of a political friend. He saw service in Cuba during the Spanish-American War, and, returning to work in which he had now lost interest, he decided to take a course at Wittenberg College in Springfield, Ohio. Here he worked at odd jobs to pay his way.

Breaking into the advertising game, he became a manager in a mail order concern in Cleveland in 1906 and laid the grounds for his reputation as one of the best mail order copy-writers in America. Starting business for himself in Elyria, Ohio, a year later, he was handicapped by failing health and forced to return to Chicago.

Anderson commenced writing about 1911. *The Little Review* in 1915 published a story called "Sister"; it was the first story Anderson had been willing to print. Through the intermediacy of Theodore Dreiser, John Lane in 1916 published the novel, *Windy McPherson's Son*. *The Little Review*, *The Seven Arts* and *The Masses* brought out other Anderson stories. The novel, *Marching Men*, appeared in 1917; *Mid-American Chants* in 1918; *Winesburg, Ohio* in 1919; *Poor White* in 1920; *The Triumph of the Egg* in 1921; *Many Marriages* and *Horses and Men* in 1923.

In 1921 Anderson went to Europe for the first time in his life. At the close of the year he became the recipient of *The Dial's* first award of its yearly prize. Since 1921 he has lived in Chicago, New York, and New Orleans. The following books are in preparation: *A Story Teller's Story* and *A New Testament*.

307

Port of New York

Georgia O'Keeffe

Georgia O'Keeffe was born in Sun Prairie, Wisconsin, on November 15, 1887. Her father, Francis O'Keeffe, was of Irish extraction; her mother, Ida Totto, was of Hungarian and Knickerbocker Dutch. Georgia O'Keeffe was taught at the age of ten to copy pansies and roses by a Mrs. Mann. Also to draw from plaster casts. In 1901 her family removed to Williamsburg, Va. Here she had more lessons in copying pansies and roses. At the age of seventeen, she went to Chicago to spend a year at the Art Institute. She studied drawing under John Vanderpoel, from whom she learned what she knows of draughtsmanship. Next year she spent in New York, at the Art Students' League. She studied under Chase, under F. Luis Mora; attended Kenyon Cox's lectures in anatomy; and won a scholarship in Chase's still-life class. While in New York she saw the first "modern" exhibition at "291." From 1908 to 1909 she was engaged in advertising in Chicago. She ceased painting for several years; but from 1912-1914 attended the classes of Alon Bement at the University of Virginia, and was stimulated to resume her work. She was at Teachers' College in New York from 1914-1916, studying with Bement and with Prof. Arthur Dow. During that time she saw the exhibitions at "291." Through the influence of Bement, she started teaching art in schools. From 1916 to 1917 she was supervisor in the public schools of Amarillo, Texas, and next year she was head of the art department in the West Texas State Normal College. Her introduction to the public as an artist occurred in 1916, with a show of black and white at "291"; and it was with a show of her work that the institution closed in 1917. In 1918, Georgia O'Keeffe came to New York, and has resided in New York and Lake George ever since. In January, 1923, she had a large complete exhibition at the Anderson Galleries. One hundred and fifty-six pictures in water color, black and white, pastel and oil were shown.

Appendix

Randolph Bourne

Randolph S. Bourne was born in Bloomfield, N. J., on May 30, 1886, and died in New York City, December 22, 1918. His father, Charles R. Bourne, and his mother, Clara Merritt, were of English descent. His father's father, Theodore Bourne, was a Congregational minister. Bourne was educated in the public and high schools of Bloomfield. In 1903 he went to work, first as secretary in Morristown, then as proofreader in a pianola-record factory in Newark, and finally in a vocal studio in Carnegie Hall, where he played the accompaniments. He matriculated at Columbia University in 1909, and in 1911 began contributing to the *Atlantic Monthly*. His first book, *Youth and Life*, was published in 1913. He graduated the same year with high honors, and received the Gilder Traveling Scholarship, which enabled him to spend the next fourteen or fifteen months in Europe. He was in England, Paris, Rome, Berlin, and Copenhagen. From 1914 to 1917 he was contributing editor of *The New Republic*. His book on the Gary Schools appeared in 1917. During that year he contributed to *The Seven Arts*; *Education and Living* was published in the spring, and in the fall he became an editor of *The Dial*, *sub* Martin Johnson. At the time Scofield Thayer and J. Sibley Watson set out to purchase *The Dial*, they intended making Bourne political editor of the reconstructed journal; and editorial meetings were under way when Bourne sickened.

Untimely Papers, a collection of Bourne's political articles, was published with an introduction by James Oppenheim in 1919. *The History of a Literary Radical* was published with an introduction by Van Wyck Brooks in 1920.

Alfred Stieglitz

Alfred Stieglitz was born on January 1, 1864, in Hoboken, N. J., near "The Elysian Fields." Edward Stieglitz and Hedwig Werner,

Port of New York

his father and mother, were born in Germany of Jewish parents; the former having come to America from Hanover-Münden in 1850. When Stieglitz was seven years old the family moved to New York. From 1871 to 1877 Stieglitz was a pupil at Charlier Institute. From 1877 to 1879 he attended Grammar School No. 55, and from 1879 to 1881 went to the College of the City of New York. In 1881 he was taken to Germany, and spent a year as guest at the Karlsruhe Realgymnasium. Next year he went to Berlin and began studying mechanical engineering in the Berlin Polytechnic under Professor Reuleaux. He took a course in photo-chemistry under Prof. H. W. Vogel, and gradually dropped work in engineering. He utilized the laboratory of the Polytechnic for his photographic experiments, becoming his own teacher. Simultaneously he took courses in chemistry in the University under various professors; always with photography in view. In 1886 Stieglitz sent work to England for competition for a prize offered by *The Amateur Photographer*. He received an honorable mention. Next year he made an Italian trip accompanied, as was usual on all his spring and autumn trips, by the large camera; worked passionately; and sent twelve pictures to *The Amateur Photographer* in competition for the amateur studentship competition. He received first prize, a gold medal, and $300. The prize was awarded by Dr. P. H. Emerson. In the winter of 1887-88, Stieglitz visited America for a few months, and then returned to Germany, to spend the next three years in more intensive experimentation. He sent prints to competitions and to exhibitions all over the world, and began his fight for the recognition of photography as an additional means of expression.

He returned to New York in 1890; and for the next five years was engaged in the photo-engraving and printing business in New York. He was one of the first to do color prints by the three-color process, and did original work in this line. He also became editor of the *American Amateur Photographer*, continuing his fight for photography, and never really interested himself in business as a commercial af-

Appendix

fair. In 1895 he withdrew from business, and began devoting all his time to developing his vocation and bringing into the world what is historically known as "American" photography. He developed the Camera Club of New York, and in 1897 founded *Camera Notes*, which he edited until 1902. He was vice-president of the Camera Club. In 1902 he resigned from *Camera Notes* and founded *Camera Work*; also the *Photo-Secession*. He still sent photographs to exhibitions the world over, receiving one hundred and fifty medals from London, Paris, Brussels, Turin, Hamburg, Berlin, New York, Boston, Philadelphia, Munich, Toronto, etc., etc., etc. He was an active member of the Linked Ring of London; generally considered the international leader, and was made honorable member of innumerable European societies; honorary member of the Royal Photographic Society in 1907. In 1905 he opened the Photo-Secession Gallery which eventually became the pioneer gallery, 291 Fifth Avenue. His photographs were purchased by the art galleries in Dresden, Brussels, Boston, Berlin, Buffalo, and for several private collections. His expulsion from the Camera Club of New York occurred in 1908. *291* was published from March, 1915, to January, 1916. In 1917 "291" was closed. In February, 1921, Stieglitz showed his life work at the Anderson Galleries. A show of more recent work still was held in the same rooms in April, 1923. In 1924 the Royal Photographic Society conferred upon him its Progress Medal in recognition of his services in founding and fostering Pictorial Photography in America, and particularly in initiating and publishing *Camera Work*, the most artistic record of photography ever attempted."

Stieglitz is the author of innumerable technical articles published in magazines. "One Hour's Sleep—Three Dreams," was first published in *291*, No. 1. It was reprinted in *Manuscripts*, No. 2, with two hitherto unpublished poems by Stieglitz.

THE END

311